Reading Shakespeare
on Stage

Reading Shakespeare
on Stage

H. R. Coursen

DELAWARE

Newark: University of Delaware Press
London: Associated University Presses

Associated University Presses
440 Forsgate Drive
Cranbury, NJ 08512

Associated University Presses
25 Sicilian Avenue
London WC1A 2QH, England

Associated University Presses
P.O. Box 338, Port Credit
Mississauga, Ontario
Canada L5G 4L8

The paper used in this publication meets the requirements
of the American National Standard for Permanence of Paper
for Printed Library Materials Z39.48-1984.

Library of Congress Cataloging-in-Publication Data

Coursen, Herbert R.
　Reading Shakespeare on stage / H.R. Coursen.
　　p.　cm.
　Includes bibliographical references (p.) and index.
　ISBN 0-87413-538-9 (alk. paper)
　1. Shakespeare, William, 1564–1616—Dramatic production.
2. Shakespeare, William, 1564–1616—Stage history.　3. Theater—
Production and direction.　4. Theater audiences.　5. Acting.
I. Title.
PR3091.C67　1995
792.9'5—dc20
　　　　　　　　　　　　　　　　　　　　　　　　　　　　94-39270
　　　　　　　　　　　　　　　　　　　　　　　　　　　　CIP

This book
is for my friend
and fellow observer of the stage,
Sam Crowl.

Contents

List of Abbreviations	9
Acknowledgments	13
Introduction	17
1. Television and Live Performance	29
2. The Concept of Script	37
3. 1987 and the Question of Space	67
4. Directors' Decisions: 1989	88
5. The Summer of *King Lear*	134
6. Winter of the Scottish Play	155
7. *Measure for Measure* at Stratford, Canada, 1992	173
8. The Good, the Horrid, and the In-Between	184
9. The Directors and the Critics: Stratford-on-Avon, 1992	211
10. *Richard III:* Large and Small	232
11. London: February 1993	247
Postscript	261
Appendix	266
Works Cited	275
Index	289

Abbreviations

For convenience, I have included in parentheses some abbreviations of the names of newspapers and journals in which reviews of productions appeared, as follows:

A	*Atlantic Monthly.*
AT	*American Theatre.*
BHC	*Beverly Hills Courier.*
BM	*Burton Mail* (G.B.).
BP	*Birmingham Post* (G.B.).
BPP	*Brighton-Pittsford Post* (Canada).
CC	*Canadian Champion* (Ontario).
CE	*Cahiers Elisabethains.*
CET	*Coventry Evening Telegram.*
CL	*City Lights* (London).
CoL	*College Literature.*
CS	*Critical Survey.*
C'sC	*Critic's Choice* (London).
CSM	*Christian Science Monitor.*
CS-T	*Chicago Sun-Times.*
DB	*Daily Breeze* (Los Angeles).
DE	*Daily Express* (London).
DeN	*Detroit News.*
DFP	*Detroit Free Press.*
DM	*Daily Mail* (London).
D-L	*Drama-Logue* (California).
DN	*Downtown News* (Los Angeles).
DT	*Daily Telegraph* (London).
DV	*Daily Variety.*
EM	*Evening Mail* (London).
ES	*Evening Standard* (London).
FT	*Financial Times* (London).
G	*Guardian* (London).
G&M	*Globe and Mail* (Ontario).
GPN	*Grosse Pointe News.*
HD	*Hamilton Daily* (Canada).

HLQ	Huntington Library Quarterly.
HR	Hudson Review.
HRep	Hollywood Reporter.
I	Independent (London).
IHT	International Herald Tribune.
IonS	Independent on Sunday (London).
IT	Ingersoll Times (Canada).
JAE	Journal of Aesthetic Education.
JC	Jewish Chronicle (London).
KE&S	Kiddermaster Express and Star (G.B.).
KR	Kenyon Review.
KWR	Kitchner-Waterloo Record (Ontario).
L	Listener (London).
LAT	Los Angeles Times.
LB	Listowe Banner (Canada).
LFP	London Free Press (Ontario).
LFQ	Literature Film Quarterly.
LTN	London Theatre News.
MonS	Mail on Sunday (London).
MSAN	Marlowe Society of America Newsletter.
MST	Maine Sunday Telegram.
NYer	New Yorker.
NYR	New York Review of Books.
NYT	New York Times.
O	Observer (London).
Ob	Observer (Ontario).
OCR	Orange County Register (California).
OonS	Observer on Sunday (London).
PA	Performing Arts (Los Angeles).
P&P	Plays and Players (London).
PI	Plays International (London).
R T-D	Richmond Times-Dispatch.
Q	Quarto.
SB	Shakespeare Bulletin.
SDU-T	San Diego Union-Tribune.
SEL	Studies in English Literature.
SFNL	Shakespeare Film Newsletter.
SfS	Stratford for Students (Ontario).
SH	Stratford Herald (G.B.).
ShS	Shakespeare Survey.
ShSt	Shakespeare Studies.
SLP-D	St. Louis Post-Dispatch.
SM	Sun Mercury (G.B.).

SO	*Stratford Observer* (G.B.).
SQ	*Shakespeare Quarterly.*
SR	*Simcoe Reformer* (Ontario).
ST	*Sunday Times* (London).
STel	*Sunday Telegraph* (London).
T	*Times* (London).
TBC	*Thunder Bay Chronicle* (Canada).
The	*Theatre* (London).
TLS	*Times Literary Supplement* (London).
TN	*Theatre Notebook.*
TO	*Time Out* (London).
TS	*Toronto Star.*
TSR	*Times Saturday Review* (London).
UC	*Upstart Crow.*
UTC	*University of Toronto Quarterly.*
VV	*Village Voice.*
WO	*What's On* (London).
WP	*Washington Post.*
WS	*Windsor Star* (Canada).
WT	*Washington Times.*

Acknowledgments

Credits: Much of this material appeared originally in *Shakespeare Bulletin* and *The Marlowe Society Newsletter,* whose editors, Bruce Brandt, Jim Lusardi, and June Schlueter, I thank. The Theatre in England program, conducted by Homer and Laura Swander, has given me a chance to meet actors, directors, and theater critics and serves as a direct inspiration for this book. Thanks also to Dan and Karen Kirk, Bob Schlosser, and the many participants in Theatre in England who have helped me formulate the criteria described in these pages. People who have been particularly helpful in my getting to see many of the plays I treat herein are Candi Adams, Lisa Brudy, Cameron Duncan, Amanda Glanville, Mary Kelsey, Chris Millard, and Pat Quigley. Thanks also to Jim Andreas, Pamela Mount, Sam Wanamaker, Bill Watterson and Anita Gaffney of the Stratford, Ontario Festival, and Helen Cross and Ian Rowley of the Royal Shakespeare Company, Stratford.

Photo and diagram credits: Amherst College *Hamlet:* Amherst College. Amherst College *Julius Caesar:* Folger Shakespeare Library. Arts Centre, Coventry: Amanda Glanville. Barbican Theatre, Stratford-on-Avon Main Stage, Swan Theatre, and Royal Shakespeare Company's productions: Cameron Duncan and Zoe Mylchreest, and *The Architects' Journal: City Lights,* photos by Mark Douet (Noble *Hamlet*), Ivan Kynel *(The Taming of the Shrew),* Richard Mildenhall (Daniels *Hamlet,* Hytner *King Lear* and Warner *Titus Andronicus*), and Richard le Poer Trench (Mendes *Richard III*). Blackstone Theatre, Chicago (now The Merle Reskin Theatre), and Branagh *King Lear:* Mary Kelsey, Alisa E. Regas, David Parfitt, photo by Robert Barber. Bob Jones University *As You Like It* and Rodeheaver Auditorium: Bob Jones, Dwight Gustafson, and Bill Pinkston, photo of *As You Like It* by Unusual Photos. English Shakespeare Company's *Macbeth:* photo by Laurence Burns. Mark Taper Forum and *Richard II:* Robert Schlosser, photo of *Richard III* by Jay Thompson. McDonogh *A Midsummer Night's Dream:* John Van Meter, photo by Susan Fagan. Outdoor Theatre, Regent's Park, and Breeslaw as Malvolio: Shelia Benjamin and Ian Talbot, photo of theater by Alistair Muir. Peter Hall *Merchant of Venice:* Sir Peter Hall. Royal National Theatre (Olivier and Lyttelton) and its productions: Stephen Wood, drawing by David Eaton, photos by John Haynes (Eyre *Richard III* and Hall *Antony and Cleopatra*), Neil Libbert (Warner *King Lear*). Schiller Theater *Macbeth:* Katharina Thalbach and the Schiller Theater Werkstatt, photo by Mark Borkowski. Shakespeare Theatre: Candi Adams, photo of theater by Katherine Lambert, of Tom Hulce by Joan Marcus, and of Gary Sloan by Rhonda Miller. Stratford Festival (Ontario) and *Measure for Measure:* Lisa Brudy, Anita Gaffney and Pat Quigley, photo of *Measure for Measure* by Cylla von Tiedemann. The author has made every effort to establish credit for photographs used. Please call his attention to any oversights in this list of credits.

Reading Shakespeare
on Stage

Introduction

Peter Brook states: "If the play does not make us lose our balance, the evening has been unbalanced" (*Shifting Point*, 54). Within this book I will try to articulate the balance within the imbalance, to encourage informed response to production, and to suggest how an individual's reaction to a production can find a voice. I will uncover "the moment" of a given production by looking at what reviewers have discovered in each production as it appeared. The moment itself will be seen to have been full of conflict, as brief chronicles disagree about the nature and effect of a production.

The reviewers' criteria for judging a play go well beyond the questions below. "The plays," says Irving Wardle, "are out in the world leading a life of their own" (*Theatre Criticism*, 66), and that life communicates different things to different people within the emotional and imaginative transaction on which live performance of Shakespeare's plays insists. Wardle says that "the idea of a codified set of standards is a myth" (37) and that "any reviewer would be asking for trouble if he started laying down the laws of theatrical literacy" (95). Still, some categories—as opposed to "laws"—can be helpful in framing a response to a given production. They are not "the closed system [of semiotics] that seems to have been devised with the express purpose of discouraging intruders" (57). Instead, they are questions that those who attend a Shakespearean production can ask. The answers will help a spectator to articulate a response to and an evaluation of a given production.

Is the "story" told clearly and effectively?
How does the "space"—the size of the auditorium and playing area—affect the delivery of the script?
Was the pace of the production rapid, with effective variations in rhythm?
What is the "degree of difficulty" for this script in this space?
Were the words audible, understandable, and did they contribute to character and action, as opposed to being just "speeches" or background noise?

17

What of production values—set, costumes, lighting, "style"—
and their contribution to the production?
What was the genre of this production?

Obviously, these questions, which are the criteria this author
applies to production, reveal biases in the asker. In addition, they
raise many more questions. The basic question is: Who is
responding?

The criteria should not dictate a response but provide the language for one. Much more is involved than some bodiless, bloodless, "objective" reaction. What Gary Jay Williams says of the critic
is also true of the informed spectator: "It is not only the production, but the critical self that is the subject of the [critique]. Those
who cry for 'objective' theater criticism do so in frustration with
a given critic's entire sensibility" (SQ [1985]: 600).

The criteria are not meant as "a convenient way of dodging the
historical differences that may separate early modern spectators
from postmodern spectators" (Bruce Smith, 429–30). We can assume the rapidity of transition from scene to scene on Shakespeare's stage by considering the linkages that such seamlessness
enforces—Sebastian stepping into Malvolio's "dream" after the
Madhouse Scene in *Twelfth Night*, Macbeth already in view as
Duncan says "absolute trust." Pauses between scenes are the sign
of amateur direction, even if the director is getting well paid for
his work. Clarity and pace are hallmarks of Granville-Barker, Peter Hall, Peter Brook, and Deborah Warner, for example, directors
who span the intersection of the modern with the postmodern.
That directors like Bogdanov and Lepage do not observe such
criteria may make them trendily "postmodern," but that label
does not necessarily make their productions good.

The director is a "storyteller" only insofar as he uses the techniques of theater to drive the script toward and past the audience.
He does so by using his space effectively. That seems a simplistic
statement, but all spaces present challenges, as do all scripts.
Julius Caesar, for example, has "big" scenes that may seem
cramped and compromised in small theaters. At the same time,
it also has intimate scenes between Portia and Brutus, Calpurnia
and Caesar, and Cassius and Brutus that can lose their tonalities
when thundered out into a vast amphitheater.

Clearly, Shakespeare's stage could accommodate both the public and the private. Indeed, it employed such contrast for structural and thematic purposes, as shown in the first act of *Richard
II*, which alternates between formality and intimacy. Although

technical ability has developed remarkably since Shakespeare's time, when sunlight, props, traps, and the occasional "quaint device" had to suffice, the modern stage has often become less flexible and our imaginative abilities as an audience have diminished for that reason.

Chapter Three will deal with the concept of space at length, as will discussions of many of the productions. For now though, I'll provide a brief example. The McDonogh Players (Maryland) have a long, narrow stage that has no depth, and, therefore, no opportunity for entrances from upstage. A shrewd director would make a strength of such a feature which might otherwise be considered a weakness. In *A Midsummer Night's Dream* (May 1993), John Van Meter created panorama. In the final scene, Oberon, Titania, and their now combined retinues gathered above the grotto, stage right, which had been Titania's bower, and observed "Pyramus and Thisbe." The Court looked on from stage left. The presence of the fairies reinforced the play-within-the-play concept, reminding the audience of the now resolved confusion in the woods being parodied by the fatal mistakes of Pyramus and Thisbe. The fairies anticipated coming down from their observation post and "bless[ing] this house" and emphasized the "interactivity" of the worlds of the play. Two "audiences" responded to the inner play from the two "sides" of the script.

Van Meter was "visualizing" the script for us and reminding us that Puck shows his knowledge of theater in his response to Quince's rehearsal. We could smile with superior knowledge at Theseus's skeptical "'Tis almost fairy time." Not almost—it *is* fairy time. The fairies had only to move down to center stage to confirm and complete the play's action. Van Meter's use of the long, narrow stage suggested that harmony and cooperation ruled at the end. This effect was largely the result of an intelligent use of the inherited space. If the director's original intention was to achieve such an effect, it would have had to be produced in other ways in other spaces.

A Shakespearean production should move with such speed that we must be constantly "catching up," so that the play is like our "experience," even if the production is creating an imaginative and psychic construct that is not that of that "unlike thing"— ourself. The spectator should not be permitted to fall back to the merely personal. That lapse breaks the metaphor that production and spectator are creating. Pauses within scenes—for Cleopatra's "O," or before Laertes's "What—'out of this,' my lord?"—are there for directors and actors to make. And they pull us forward.

Rhythm can occur within pacing and provide the effect of spontaneity. Good actors make us believe that all of this is happening for the first time.

"Degree of difficulty" is a very subjective criterion. The Arena Theater in Washington produced an excellent *Cymbeline* in the 1982–83 season. It was directed by David Chambers, with Peter Francis James as Posthumus. The critics, who panned the production, did not account for the challenge the script presents or for the way the Arena company translated the play to the "theater in the round" format. One major change, dictated by the space, was that "Nature" was not a power descending from above but a quality that comes up from below—from the earth and the deeply interfused healing forces therein. The critics simply would not accept the production on its own terms, which insisted, as good productions of Shakespeare must, on a reinterpretation of the words as encountered by those actors and in that space. It was, then, the critics who failed, not David Chambers and the actors.

Another of the late plays, *A Winter's Tale,* can be difficult in any space. It is not just Leontes's seemingly out-of-nowhere fit of jealousy or the Statue Scene that make the play difficult. The sheep-shearing festivities can get so out of hand that this long scene becomes its own play, scripted by Autolycus, and obscuring any contact we have with the larger play surrounding it.

Jazz musicians say: "All he can do is play the notes." Similarly, Peter Hall once complained that actors speak the words but not the lines. The line, whether of a play or of music, carries something in addition to the word *or* the note—phrasing. Phrasing contextualizes the word *or* the note. In turn, the line exists for what Peter Hall calls "the secret play." It awakens "the sleeping dragon" within the inherited script (as Michael Elliott says), the elusive whatever that is the "heart of the mystery" (to paraphrase Hamlet), aware of such a quality even if incapable of expressing it. That quality, often referred to as "subtext" (cf. Halio, *Plays in Performance,* 39–49), is that which the verse-speaking, the acting, and the other attributes of the production serve. It varies with *Zeitgeist,* culture, director, and lead actor, and these inevitable variables explain why productions of the same script can be so radically different. In addition, the script itself is endlessly accommodating.

Production values should be at the service of the actors. Take, for example, the set—the space where the actors work. If the set dazzles the audience but inhibits the actors, it is a bad set. Costumes, on the other hand, should represent the characters and/

or their status in the play—unless, of course, the director is making some point "against the script." The script usually presents a hierarchy of position or wealth, which is sometimes a source of conflict, as when Tranio becomes the master, or Malvolio hopes to become "Count Malvolio," or when great men like Lear and Gloucester and Richard II are toppled from their secure posts. In most cases, however, as in *Middlemarch*, even the dogs know their place.

Eclectic costumes or the drab sameness typical of some recent British productions can make it difficult for an audience to learn who the characters are and what their relationships to each other are. The eclectic approach can work well, however, as demonstrated through the "rehearsal clothes" that John Gielgud used for his 1964 version of *Hamlet*. Hume Cronyn, as Polonius, showed up elegantly attired in an expensive cravat. This actor had never quite made it, but dressed to suggest that he had. His elegance proclaimed the shabby truth. The production's "subtext" was developed by contextualizing the play's theatrical metaphors within a 1964 "rehearsal" that gradually became "real," as the "fiction" took hold of us. The production looks dated thirty years later in the filmed version of the stage play, but the concept is not dated because the concept and the power of theater are deeply imbedded in the script.

Lighting should reinforce emotional tonality, usually unobtrusively, except perhaps to emphasize extremes. For example: the stark shadows used for the storm in Deborah Warner's *King Lear*; a harsh, blinding light into which Ian McKellen's Macbeth strode on "young in deed" in the Nunn production; and perhaps the super-romantic moonlight that bathes Jessica and Lorenzo in Act Five of *The Merchant of Venice*. But lighting is an evocator of mood, time, and place within the script and is, for Shakespeare, often supererogatory. Directors should try to remember, if not recreate, the conditions that Alan Dessen describes for The King's Men: "The actors provided the signals and then the audience co-operated in supplying the darkness. For us, one figure fails to see another *because* the stage is dark; for them, one figure failed to see another and therefore the stage was *assumed* to be dark . . . modern lighting or other supposed 'improvements' . . . impose an anachronistic logic upon a distinctive Shakespearean effect" (*ShS* 36, 62–63; his emphasis). If everything is done for us, we are unlikely to become involved, too likely to retain our workaday "balance."

Lois Potter suggests how modern techniques can interfere with

the effects imparted to "the Globe . . . audience. . . . The characters might be in physical or moral darkness, but the spectators
were never in doubt as to how they themselves were to respond
to events. The peculiar horror of *Othello*, often blunted in productions with overatmospheric lighting effects, is that [the spectators]
are forced to watch in helpless clarity as the hero walks blindly,
in his private darkness, over a precipice" ("Realism vs. Nightmare," 187).

Some productions ask us to cooperate with them, as Dessen
suggests the Jacobean spectator was asked. The script can become
clearer for us—in fact, we can help clarify it for ourselves—if it
is set in a particular period and not just in a universal time frame
that blurs distinctions. Conversely, though, distinctions can also
be blurred, when the production is heavily entrenched in a period, as in the much-celebrated *Much Ado* of the late A. J. Antoon.
The Spanish-American War motif left nothing to imagination and
was, like a Norman Rockwell painting, the perfection of the cliché. Shakespeare's play remained buried somewhere under the
totalizing surface.

The stage itself imposes a "style," of course. The fourth wall
tends to prohibit the speaking of a soliloquy or an aside to an
audience. Our space in the fourth wall convention is inviolate, as
it is when we watch a soap opera on television. Entire scripts
can be ignored because of convention, as was that of *Antony and
Cleopatra*, which presented the "problem of alternating scenes between Egypt and Rome on older proscenium stages, [but] has
been given full scope on the bare stages of the modern theatre"
(Price, 182a).

"Style" must accommodate the contrasts built into any Shakespearean script—between court and tavern, that is, between
"high seriousness" and the mocking of politics; between the
styles of plots and subplots—the silly romance of Hero and Claudio (though not without his hardheaded sense of where Leonato's
money is going) versus the wit and bite of the "round characters,"
Beatrice and Benedick; the plotting of Antonio and Sebastian versus that of Stephano and Caliban, each conspiracy very serious
but in different ways; and, of course, between places like court
and forest, Scotland and England or Rome and Egypt. If the style
of a production does not serve all elements of the script, it follows
that the script has been badly served. The director's "concept"
should, as Wardle says, "energize . . . the actors, not burden"
them (*Theatre Criticism*, 115). When directors dominate the pro-

cess as they tend to do, the actors often struggle but seldom complain. They must eat.

Directors seem to strive for "relevance." Thus, they often hit us over the head with analogies to our times, as they see them. Often these are the most shallow, trivial aspects of our times, for which theater might serve as a compensatory activity, not just a reinforcing reminder. Directors often rob us of our ability to perceive analogies, to make connections in our way, to feel the impact of recognition that good theater engenders. Furthermore, "relevance" is likely to be "irrelevance," as Cary Mazer's "Mazer's law" suggests: "that those aspects of the theatre that writers of a particular time and place assume to be the most universal and timeless are likely to be the ones that are most peculiar to that time and place" (SQ [1985]: 658). Today's fad is "relevance" (as opposed to "timelessness"), the fallacy kept alive by a wash of phrases like "how modern Shakespeare is!" or "how *post*-modern," if one is being chic or cheeky. John Barton's production of *Richard II* in the early seventies occurring simultaneously with Watergate was an accident that in no way enhanced that ponderous and gimmicky production. Terry Hands's mid-seventies *Henry V* found all kinds of resonance with Great Britain and even the Royal Shakespeare Company. This was to some extent a function of "theme," even of "synchronicity," a series of echos from and back to a superb production.

A production invariably picks up its *Zeitgeist* and shows us, as Mazer says, that: "Theatrical conventions and tastes change with the passage of time" (SQ, 658). One of the best measures of the ways in which time changes and informs is the contemporary review because, as Mazer says, "even the worst theatre review speaks with the voice of its own time" (SQ, 658). In such reviews we find what we know of our own time (we tend to take that for granted) and what we tend to forget of times past—that conflict and not unanimity is the rule, and even about what makes a good play and certainly about what makes a good production.

This book speaks to those who attend Shakespearean productions—and possibly to fellow Shakespeareans—and promises that those who have seen some of the productions discussed here will find their evaluations of a particular production represented.

Shakespeare is, of course, "our contemporary," but that does not mean that productions must, perforce, modernize their values to fit a perception of "what an audience wants." That process is the province of admen and politicians. An audience may *not* want, for example, a blatant reminder of the latest disasters. Shakespeare is our contemporary because of what we as spectators bring to the productions. If, as new historicists argue, the Elizabethan age was struggling with the concept of "interiority," then that experience is central to the experience of several of Shakespeare's major characters. Since we, too, are struggling with our inner selves (that struggle is one of the great mythologies of the twentieth century) it follows that the struggle as depicted by an actor playing Hamlet, Othello, Macbeth, or Lear will engage us centrally. The issue of "interiority" may be "there," however, because it is so centrally "here." The search for evidence by the new historicists tends to confirm what we already know about many of the issues of the plays. It is a commonplace that Shakespeare reflects, in criticism and in production, the issues of the *Zeitgeist* of those presumably looking at Shakespeare but actually demonstrating a version of "the indeterminancy principle." As in psychology, the subject and the object of the inquiry are interchangeable, even as the terms of the inquiry shift. Irving Wardle suggests that "as the ghost of Betterton was displaced by his early eighteenth-century successors . . . [r]ealization dawned that Shakespeare was not an ever-receding Platonic ideal, but a store of energy that could be released into hitherto unsuspected forms. The same play, the same part, could render up different meanings depending on who was performing it. . . . So, as acting emerged as the dominating factor, it subverted the Aristotelian primacy of plot . . . paving the way for Hazlitt's view (which would have seemed raving lunacy in Dryden's time) that Shakespeare's best commentators were his actors. This also marked a victory for Hazlitt and his colleagues, for, as acting undercut the authority of scholarship, reviewers recognized this as a *fait accompli* and gained journalistic power by renouncing the claims of academic pendantry" (22–23). "The Romantics embraced [Shakespeare] as a fellow alien, sensitive to their lonely, nightingale stage," says Robert Willson. "For the Victorians he was their moral and educational guide, leading them steadily through the rubble of materialism and social decay" (210). As for reinventing Shakespeare today and tomorrow, we can agree with Charles Frey: "Since Shakespeare holds the mirror up to each succeeding age, one delineation of his intent will always be the response that wins the most sustained, coherent, and vigorous dialogue from each generation" (221). One delineation of his intent that even he would recognize is the continued performance of his plays. Performance—a dynamic that moves with and into history—continues to draw sustained, usually coherent, and certainly vigorous responses.

Production values should support our ability to hear the lines and to understand them. Directors would do well to recall the relative illiteracy of the original audiences and the relative emptiness of Shakespeare's stage. As Bert O. States suggests, "The very thickness of Shakespeare's world is derived from the way in which poetry triumphs over neutral space" (56) *and* over the limitations of an audience most of whom would have been defeated by the words on a page. The plays in performance must also triumph over the "neutrality" of a spectator who, today, is possibly anticipating the inert mode of an auditor of television. Language itself has changed, of course, since 1600, even in *intent*, if George T. Wright is correct about the poetry of Shakespeare's plays. The language of a Shakespearean play, he says, served "the function of fixing the culture's important knowledge more firmly in the cultural memory [and served] as a secular instrument of sacralization" (165–66). A modern production should remind us that Shakespeare's "art worked mainly from the stage and that the language we find in the plays, though he *wrote* it and though . . . his actors learned their lines largely from written scripts, had its primary reality for actors and audiences as sounded words" (Wright, 161). Shakespeare's plays came before audiences trailing clouds of sympathetic magic, where human activity still had efficacy with the gods. His plays should still come to us with the effect of our *hearing* the play, not just seeing it. Furthermore, a production can re-educate us to a worldview very different than ours, so that we can understand what happens when, for example, Macbeth and Lady Macbeth make decisions in the world they are in, and know themselves to be in. Modern directors seem not to make the effort to create a version of "Elizabethan World Picture," as the chapter on "The Scottish Play" will suggest, but rather seek modern equivalents or simply ignore material in the script which conflicts with a director's "concept."

Genre means, very simply, what it was that produced our response. Do we laugh because important people have been placed in ludricrous postions—the Bishop must hide in a closet while his trousers dry after the teapot has been upset—as in a farce? Do we smile because characters we have come to love learn who they are—as in comedy, or because they have been reunited with people they thought dead—as can happen in comedy and does happen in romance? Are we shocked when, as Bergson would say, a sequence is interrupted, as when Malvolio seems to accept that the joke has been on him, then suddenly turns to the chuckling tricksters and says that he "will be revenged?" That moment can challenge comedy, as Malvolio must do, to a great or small degree. Do we experience the simultaneous kinship and distance that tragedy induces, a profound glimpse of our greatness and our frailty? Is that response still possible in the age of Willy Loman? Are we faced with the ambiguity of "the problem play"— the issue of Isabella's response to the Duke at the end, or the series of "ifs" at the end of *All's Well*? Are we asked to sort out the incomplete theories represented by characters in "history plays," where every "solution" brings new problems?

How has a production dealt with the genre within it? Polonius's eavesdropping behind a curtain is a standard farcical situation. Indeed, Hamlet treats it that way: "Thou findst to be too busy is some danger," and perhaps increases our horror at what he has done. We may also share with Hamlet some sense of wild joy within the obligatory words of his repentance. Our sense of how the play was interpreted helps us understand how our response was evoked and why it was enthusiastic or not. We are told that, in Shakespeare's time, Shylock was a "stock villain in a red beard" and therefore a character in melodrama. If so, we encounter one problem in historicism. Antony Sher was that stock character in Alexander's RSC version, and Sher's tendency to overact was not curbed. Dustin Hoffman was more "rounded" in the 1989 Hall production. The characters were products of different genres— melodrama and problem play—and that fact may help explain why some of Shylock's co-religionists were offended by the former production, but not, at least not as much, by the latter. The approach to production through genre is not necessarily outmoded because out of fashion. Genre is tricky to define but useful in moving from the pre-critical to the critical phase (cf. Northrop Frye). Consideration of genre helps us to move from the event to the evaluation of it, to understand and thus to regain our imaginative and emotional experience as we explore it with language.

Ironically, as productions of Shakespeare's plays increase and spaces for production improve, Shakespearean scholarship has been conquered by atheatrical and anti-theatrical forces. One result is that little relationship exists between the productions available and the "literacy" of the audience. In fact, many members of the audience enter the theater without the basic vocabulary necessary to discuss their experience. Old-fashioned "reading" may help in learning a version of the "story," but most of the newer critical modes are unhelpful in dealing with the plays in the only place they can exist—the theater. Against the invasion of the new historicism, a countervailing force of scholars—J. R. Brown, John Styan, Bernard Beckerman, Marvin Rosenberg, Philip McGuire, Alan Dessen, Cary Mazer, Michael Goldman, Stanley Wells, Jay Halio, Peter Reynolds, William Worthen, Anthony Dawson, Thomas Clayton, James Bulman, and others—suggests that Shakespeare-in-performance, even as that concept itself is debated, will prevail against more transitory trends in criticism. The reason is simple. Even if the language becomes more difficult with time, and even if some scholars ignore Shakespeare on stage in their quest for "intertextuality," good productions continue to emerge and continue to be attended. Productions can be ignored by the scholars—to the impoverishment of productions that once were informed by scholarship (not always effectively, one must admit). They are not being ignored by their audiences: thus, the effort to address the issue again, as do Jay Halio and Peter Reynolds in recent books. This book is indebted to their books and the many others cited on the following pages. More than usual in a critical work, this one is also indebted to the critics who write against deadlines to "find . . . words," as Wardle says, "to fix the image that has disclosed the hidden life of the text" that a given production has revealed (*Theatre Criticism*, 80). This finding of the words is a more intrinsic part of the process of live theater than is the criticism of something that is merely words on a page. The words on the page of a Shakespearean text are a potentiality that is completed by response to production. The process is a "reading of Shakespeare" as it is meant to be read, at a particular moment and in response to a specific production. It is a matter, as Blake would say, of "catching a joy as it flies." We, the audience, are Aristotle's "final cause" of art, that towards which the material (words), efficient (playwright), and formal (plays) causes are directed. Our response, then, is part of the art itself, when the art form is theater.

Peter Brook says that "A strong presence of actors and a strong presence of spectators can produce a circle of unique intensity in which barriers can be broken and the invisible becomes real. Then the public truth and the private truth become inseparable parts of the same essential experience" (*Shifting Point*, 41). We do share an essential—communal—experience when theater is working well. We will differ, however, about the nature of that experience. It becomes existential as it contacts our individuality. Like the spectator, the "reviewer," as Ralph Berry says, "is not a camera" (*SQ* [1985]: 597). What follows will not a slavish pursuit and application of announced criteria. The guidelines remain implicit and sometimes become very explicit within an existential treatise that may help others befriend and energize their experience as they read Shakespeare on stage.

This book begins with a discussion of how television affects our ability to be spectators at live Shakespeare performances. Next, an exploration of the concept of "script" should give the reader a sense of the complicated process and transaction that a script entails and of the spectator's central role in the activity that a script demands. The book then looks at three seasons in Stratford-on-Avon and London: 1987, 1989, and 1992, all of them examined on the basis of space, director, and critical response—but with additional criteria applied to each production. The book examines several productions of the same scripts—those of *King Lear, Richard III,* and *Macbeth* and rates different productions of *Richard II, As You Like It, Hamlet,* and *A Midsummer Night's Dream* on the basis of the author's criteria for evaluating Shakespeare on stage. The book also looks at several major productions—the 1992 Stratford, Canada *Measure for Measure,* the 1993 Adrian Noble version of *Hamlet* with Kenneth Branagh, and the 1993 Royal Court *King Lear.* The author hopes that readers will have seen one or more of these productions and will use the criteria outlined herein to enhance their sense of how Shakespeare works and does not work on stage. The process should result in useful disagreement.

Since I have written this book, Dennis Kennedy's superb *Looking at Shakespeare: A Visual History of Twentieth-Century Performance* (Cambridge: Cambridge University Press, 1993) has appeared. While the nature of Kennedy's book is captured in his title and is therefore very different in scope and intention than mine, Kennedy contextualizes many of the issues with which I deal, particularly style and playing space. I can only say that I wish that I had had his book in my hands as I worked on my own.

1

Television and Live Performance

FIGHTING against the effort to restore the Shakespearean script to a space where it can work to its fullest potential, is television. The medium imposes habits of viewing upon its audience that contradict the attitudes and expectations a spectator should develop in the face of the thrust stages that seem to be the best zone for live performance of Shakespeare's plays.

Television blocks our ability to respond to live Shakespeare on a thrust stage in many ways, of course, but this chapter will deal with only four. First, television tends to induce passivity as opposed to pulling its audience into the continuum that good live theater encourages. Second, television tends to reduce the emotional and thematic scale of many scripts as it inevitably reduces the size of the image. Third, television tends to equate to "realism," even if, as Raymond Williams argues, "television only employs certain aspects of naturalism" (*Television*, 56). That means that our ability to suspend our disbelief as we encounter an acted work of fiction has been eroded. That erosion may also be a function of the decline of literacy itself. We seem no longer able to put ourselves within imaginative constructs that depend even upon a "once upon a time" distancing-and-involvement. Fourth, the techniques of television are "invisible" and unreadable, the three-camera format being so inculcated into studio practice and our expectations that we do not notice it. We will probably notice the difference in film between deep-focus camera work, where many characters can inhabit the same frame (a technique that television cannot employ) and montage, where, for example, the same event is reflected at us from several different points of view. This is a technique that television can employ by using close-ups but which is usually incorporated within the restricted rhythms of the three-camera format.

What television cannot achieve is a sense of "metadrama," that is, the invitation from the world of the play to enter it and participate in the creation of illusions that become powerfully real in the emotional and imaginative sense.

If television wishes to suspend our disbelief, it does so through cartoons or by having an announcer say, "Ladies and gentlemen, the President of the United States." In most cases, however, we look at a fourth wall, what used to be called "a window on the world." In the naive cartoons of the 1950s, this wall was easily broken by a baseball that landed in a pile of broken glass on the living room floor. But those cartoons misinterpreted the energy flow, which is *toward* the set, however unconsciously projected, and however mild. In theater, on a stage that acknowledges its audience, either explicitly as the actor looks at the audience during an aside or a soliloquy, or implicitly as the playing area and auditorium connect without a proscenium barrier, the actors and the spectators create a continuum of energy that can build powerfully over the course of a performance. It is in that "half perception, half creation" that the "reality" of the experience develops—not on some detailed set for Chekhov, Ibsen, or O'Neill, but in a collaborative process that completes the script during its performance. The process insists that each spectator make choices, however unconsciously, in response to the choices being made by the actors. The script then is, as Gary Waller says, "a mode of producing, not merely *reproducing* meanings . . . as it is loosed into the world, as production, within changing signifying systems and historical formulations" (*SQ* [Spring 1992]: 103; his emphasis).

One might add that a production is aimed at an audience made up of unique "receivers," even if the audience is homogeneous from a socioeconomic standpoint. The script, Waller says, is *not* "an apparently fixed textual meaning waiting to be read atemporally from the text by the attentive critic armed with appropriate . . . terminology" (102). Shakespeare is a canonical author, no doubt, particularly to those who wish to rid the curriculum of that and other names. As a playwright, however, Shakespeare contributes continuing excitement to new audiences and ensures his future even as the trendy authors of today fade quickly into "non-canonicity." The experience in the theater is dynamic, psychologically interactive, and partaking of a *Zeitgeist* that is sometimes dropped on our heads by meddling directors. The experience is not "televisual"—a static non-transaction that "kills time" and in which yesterday's issues are today's laugh lines (cf. Marc). Theater is, as Northrop Frye suggests, a "precritical experience": "As long as we are reading a novel or listening to a play on the stage, we are following a movement in time and our mental attitude is a participating one" (8). And that is true even if we know the end of "the story" as we watch a Shakespearean play and want to see "how it happens," or, in that variant, *Measure for Measure*, what *does* happen at the end. That script may have even more "*intrinsic* radical openness" (Dunbar, 1; my emphasis) than others. They all share that radicalism, no matter how conservative the texts may seem to be in their apparent support for heterosexual marriage and political stability. Attendance at a different version of the same script is always a new experience, while reading a mystery story again or watching a recorded version of a Shakespearean script cannot be, even if we learn something new in the process.

The scale of television is limited. A correlation exists between the size of the screen and the "depth" of what can be presented on it. Given good acting in the inevitable close-ups—Elizabeth Garvie reacting to the announcement of Mr. Darcy's arrival in the BBC production of "Pride and Prejudice" or Charles Gray responding to Carlisle's indictment of Bolingbroke in the BBC's *Richard II*—television can transmit emotional power. But such transmission seldom becomes the cumulative effect of a production, which is not even granted the moment the lights go on in a movie house but has been absorbed by the lamps and tables that have been present during the television show. It follows that a television version of *Othello* will not be concerned "with the fall of the great but with the disintegration of the ordinary" (Jonathan Miller, quoted in Willems, 98). The medium seems to demand a "naturalism" which, in turn, tends to domesticate the issues of tragedy. Those issues invariably involve an exploration of borderlands and cannot always be served by their moving inside, into rooms that reflect our own living space (which is appropriately reflected in the set when it is turned off). Furthermore, as Willems argues, the televisual approach to Shakespeare's scripts does "away with that unique combination of detachment and involvement which causes dramatic emotion, as well as passing off the poetical density of the blank verse as everyday informational prose" (98). Lack of depth necessitates shots that do not invite emotional participation, as Stanley Wells suggests in describing the ending of the BBC *Winter's Tale*: "The focus on individuals denies us the sense of simultaneous involvement, the thrill of ritual participation as the stone is made flesh. . . . the medium has reduced the message" ("Exit, Pursued," 197). "Farce may romp in a closet," Sheldon Zitner says, "but miracles can't be crowded" (8). Not only does television have built-in limitations relative to Shakespeare's "larger scenes," it also conditions us away from the experience of those scenes when we get to the theater. In the recent (1992) celebrated version of *Winter's Tale* at Stratford-on-Avon, we watched the reaction of Leontes and the others from behind the statue, so that we were blocked from participation in the "miracle." We were, one had to suppose, producing the miracle (although how or why no one could say), but the effect was like observing from behind a television set as other people watched television. Bad staging, obviously, can block us from "celebrating the script," as Peter Hall says. The RSC *Winter's Tale* imposed a point of view upon the final scene that, along with editing towards "concept," which eliminated lines about "fine chisel[s]" and "wrinkle[s]," insisted on a "televisual" response—meaning very little response at all.

The very existence of television has eroded our sense of theater as "an event," one that requires more than just the booking of tickets and getting there on time. Assuming that "theater occurs," it has probably become part of the blur that Raymond Williams describes: "It seems probable that in societies like Britain and the United States more drama is watched [on television] in a week or weekend . . . than would have been watched in a year or in some cases a lifetime in any previous historical period. . . . It is clearly one of the unique characteristics of advanced industrial societies that drama as an experience is now an intrinsic part of everyday life" (*Television,* 59). But Williams talks of *televised* drama—soap operas and sitcoms—which tend to disable us for the experience of plays that are being produced within the space that we also inhabit.

It may be that television's version of "naturalism" interferes with our ability to suspend disbelief when we go to the theater. Television depicts violence, but we don't believe that it is really happening. Thus, when we witnessed Vietnam on the news or were shown a picture of a child on the NBC evening news in November 1992, and told that she "was beaten to death and thrown in the garbage," the medium suddenly included those elements of naturalism that Williams suggests are not part of "normal programming."

In the theater, "shows of illusion demand that the acts remain illusory," as Bernard Beckerman says (59). That may sound simplistic, but Beckerman defines the fine line on which our participation balances. We want to enjoy the illusion even when we realize—as with a magician's trick—that it *is* a trick. We want to be surprised and delighted, as when in a production of *Macbeth*, Banquo suddenly appears behind Macbeth's sweeping gesture on "would he were here!" (Thalbach 1992). A carefully contrived staging, of course, but breathtaking. At the same time, as Beckerman suggests, the line between the "virtual" and the "actual" can be crossed. Things can get "too real," and the audience can find the action "painful and distasteful" (59). In Lepage's "Mud Dream" of 1992, which will be dealt with later, the young lovers gradually became naked and more and more muddy, so that they were no longer characters in a play but human beings suffering in the chill of the air conditioning of the National Theatre. This was an alienation beyond anything that Artaud or the "Theatre of Cruelty" ever intended. In Peter Hall's film version, the muddy lovers were amusingly besmirched. It may have been a rainy summer in Warwickshire, but the film, though non-illusory, made it clear to us that dishevelment and dirt were elements that the youngsters had run into willfully, however unintentionally. The film did not place us in the presence of suffering humanity. It was merely an "imitation of an action" (which any depiction of a Shakespearean script should be), and not the action itself (cf. Weil).

The distinctions between reality and illusion have become blurred, and again, one must place some of the blame on television. It has, quite simply, became the normative "window" through which we look at the world. On 15 November 1992, NBC's "Eyewitness Video" debated the use of a television simulation of a crime at a murder trial. The prosecution claimed that the simulation depicted a summary of its evidence. Why build it up witness by witness, detail by detail, when it can all be shown, like "The Murder of Gonzago"?

While one can understand the prosecution's enthusiasm for its new technology, one can perhaps also worry about the ability of the medium to express reality. Suppose, for example, the prosecution produces a tape in which a person of the defendant's height, weight, posture, and so on, "commits" the crime. Only the defendant's face is "sparkled out," for the sake of fairness, of course. The jury, quite naturally, looks at the defendant and fills in the face. The jury is also likely to believe, although it will not say so, that it "saw the defendant commit the crime." Here a "fiction," to use Hamlet's word, becomes a "reality," but the process diminishes our ability to respond to "illusion." That response is voluntary. It allows us to return to what was best about childhood—the sense of wonder that down-we-forgot as up-we-grew. Television, then, erases distinctions that we accept as part of the theatrical experience and makes it more difficult for us to engage in the negotiations necessary to being a successful member of a theater audience. Television makes for bad theater audiences that seem satisfied, too often, with bland, televisual stage productions, like the Jones-Plummer *Othello* or Alexander's *Twelfth Night*, each a proscenium production, scaled to the emotional level of television. The former was actually produced by CBS Television.

The seamless, three-camera format of television drama tends to erase the "theatrical metaphor" that Shakespeare is invariably making (Willems, 100). (That is, unless the metaphor is recreated for us, as in Jane Howell's splendid version of *II Henry VI*, for BBC.) Television, as Dessen argues, replaces the supernatural with the merely psychological (cf. Dessen, *SFNL*). We are conditioned away from many of the elements that make stage productions exciting.

On television, for example, a Ghost does not enter stage left (to the audience's right) and tend to inhabit an upstage left position. No stage exists, and spatial relationships are established by two-shot, close-up, and reaction shots. In the Kevin Kline television production of *Hamlet*, however, and in the closet scene in "Prince of Players" (a depiction of a late nineteenth-century *Hamlet*, with Richard Burton playing Edwin Booth), the Ghost does appear from stage left and maintains that position. Why is this important? Because theatrical practice, based on years of experience about what works in what space, suggests that up left is a place where ghosts appear, where the supernatural occurs, where isolation can be emphasized.

When Peter Hall placed Dustin Hoffman's Shylock downstage right in the 1989 *Merchant of Venice* at the Phoenix Theatre, Shylock occupied the most privileged position on the stage—a place of intimacy that invites our association with the character, and our sympathy. Down left, however, can be a place where schemes are hatched, where Iago might deliver his soliloquies, inviting us into uncomfortable association with him. Even in a three-sided stage like the Other Place in Stratford, England, Ian McKellen's Iago tended to let us in on his plotting, though he seldom looked directly at the audience. Television cannot use space this way, except in the instances where, as in the Nunn *Macbeth* and *Othello*, the production is based on a live studio production or in the case of a stage play actually directed for television. Television replaces the tonal qualities of each area of the stage with an indeterminancy that flattens response and erodes our ability to "read" other media, including the stage. We grow accustomed to vagueness and accept it, even if we are vaguely aware that it has not been a very satisfying experience. We are accustomed, one might say conditioned, to the "up center" tonality. That is where thrones are placed and where kings sit on stage, and it is where politicians speak at their conventions.

Shakespeare's stage had a built-in reference to the cosmos and the ultimate truth that frame was believed to hold. The heavens were above, so that when Hamlet points at "this brave o'erhanging firmament . . . this majestical roof fretted with golden fire," he indicates not only the roof above the stage, painted with the zodiac, but the larger powers held in the stars or by the real, but unseen spectator, God. And Hell lay below, so that even a play that questioned the inherited dispensation, like *King Lear*, occurred within a frame that depicted the truths being challenged. Shakespeare's stage had a balcony from which mayors of beseiged towns could confront enemy commanders, or kings their deposers, or Juliet her invading Romeo, and an inner stage, where a king might attempt to pray or a Caesar fall at the base of his predecessor's statue, giving the latter some marble satisfaction, and even, perhaps, as Evert Sprinchorn speculates (*TN* 46:2), a raised stage-level from which Gloucester could fall and be convinced his tumble had been from the Cliffs of Dover. Furthermore, the place on the stage from which certain tonal qualities and moods could be conveyed has probably not changed from then to now, regardless of the shape of the stage. The placement of the Ghost, for example, goes back at least as far as the illustration for Rowe's 1709 edition of Shakespeare, in which the Ghost is precisely mirrored by the portrait on the wall of Gertrude's sitting room. Stage left is the space of the supernatural—of isolation, despair, difficulty in communication, and one reason why Gertrude cannot see the Ghost (except when she can, as in John Barton's 1980 RSC production). Down center is the place of harshness, quarrels, strength, the zone from which Iago confronts us. Down left is where conspiracies are hatched. Up right where Juliet stands is soft and romantic.

Movement from space to space must be motivated. James Walker played Orsino for Steve McConnell in Merrimac's 1993 *Twelfth Night* (Lowell, Massachusetts). During much of the final scene, he stood upstage on a raised platform. When he realized that Cesario was actually a young woman, he came down to the level on which the other characters stood and closer to where we, the audience, sat. He then knelt to propose to Viola. The recognition of Viola, the movement downstage, the act of kneeling all helped humanize the Duke for us, as for the characters on stage, and made up, to some extent, for his earlier self-indulgence, imperception, and nastiness. Thus, the stage itself and its areas made their statement about how we were to respond to a character. A director ignores these areas at his peril, but he does so often enough these days that one was happy to see McConnell make them work.

And, of course, as television erases spatial distinctions, shallowness becomes the only dimension of a medium that occurs on a single physical plane close to the camera. Willems suggests that the "conventional play-within-the-play is a major hurdle for television" (99). Jonathan Miller, for example, simply eliminates the Sly Induction from the BBC *Taming of the Shrew*. On the other hand, Rodney Bennett's version of "Gonzago" in the BBC *Hamlet* does depict the scene effectively, by means of a perspectival stage, skillful editing of shots, and a willingness to stay with the inherited script. Indeed, Bennett suggests that Hamlet invades the Player's space. Bennett provides at least some depth within a physically shallow field. And Bennett's Hamlet, Derek Jacobi, does address us, but that only emphasizes his isolation within the play world. Anthony Quayle's Falstaff also speaks to us, in conspiratorial, radical closeups, to suggest that Falstaff is a breaker of conventions. He is an intruder from the fourth wall, however, and may make us uncomfortable by invading our space and thus interfering with our understanding of the play. Television tends to place emptiness between us and the screen, as opposed to the energy field that good live theater builds between actors and audience. The energy for television comes from the plug behind the set and the plugs within the illuminated rectangle.

What follows will suggest how the theater that is emerging for Shakespeare—the thrust stage that provides several acting levels—can be appreciated and evaluated. While space defines what can occur, the thrust stage does demand good acting and directing that permits good acting to emerge. As Nicholas Shrimpton says, in a response to Shakespeare productions of 1981–82, "fine Shakespearean productions are achieved by thinking outward from the text" (155). A very good space—the theater at Warwick University, for example—can be filled, literally, with junk, as in the Bogdanov *Macbeth*, and can lead to the cynical question of one fifteen-year-old schoolgirl to another after the show, "Well, are you suitably inspired?"

2

The Concept of Script

Recent critical trends denigrate previous critical trends. The current indictment is that former critics tended to see the Shakespearean play as if it had written itself. True, the play may have had sources—many in the case of *King Lear,* few if any in the case of *Love's Labour's Lost*—but Shakespeare's plays subsumed all prior manifestations of the narrative as if they had existed, unknowingly, merely to be amalgamated into a master narrative woven together by Shakespeare's genius. This approach ignores the Foucaultian notion of "cultural authorship" and suppresses the "intertextuality" within which all documents are equal manifestations of a culture, perhaps even of a dominant ideology.

A useful tenet of the new historicist canon "contextualizes" Shakespeare's plays by saying that they are creators of the values and attitudes implicit in a "culture," rather than merely reflectors of those values. I suggest that that is *still* true; that is, that Shakespeare's scripts in production still force us to confront issues as yet unresolved in our own theoretically evolved "culture." Some new historicists, of course, justify their conservatism by claiming that the plays of Shakespeare and his contemporaries were "subversive" (cf. Barroll, Wiggins). The older critics examined the plays as if they were unique and isolated entities—glimpses of "reality" for Bradley, who could ask where Hamlet was at the time of his father's death or "poems" for L.C. Knights, who sneered at Bradley while still committing some of the fallacies that deconstructionists and new historicists now indict. The new historicists suggest, as Stephen Greenblatt argues, that literary and non-literary texts "shared [a] code, a set of interlocking tropes and similitudes that function not only as the objects but as the *conditions* of representation" and that "texts serve [institutions]. For it is important to grasp that we are dealing not with the reflections of isolated individuals musing on current events but with expressions whose context is corporate and institutional" (147–48; my emphasis).

The concept of "script" (what some call "play-text") insists that we incorporate some of what the newer modes offer. Some would claim, in fact, that deconstruction is a process in which actors and directors have long engaged, without, admittedly, the weighty structures of theory and jargon that seem finally to produce "old readings." That the newer approaches say little to or about the plays themselves may mean that these critical techniques are simply not seeing the plays as plays, but rather as cultural documents implicated in another game, one that may have something to do with history but little to do with drama, except as the historicists link the concerns of the plays with an "early modernism" whose concerns and issues we share here in the "postmodern" world. The concept of script insists that we look again at *old* historicism and the New Criticism (as defined and debated in the thirties through the sixties) to discover what, if anything, these outworn creeds still may offer to the script. The process is called "recuperation." One tendency of the old historicism that does not merit recuperation is the following:

> Shakespeare and his contemporaries were not anthropologists and they were not concerned with questions of "race." The debate as to whether Shakespeare intended Othello to be a Berber or a Negro is beside the point. Shakespeare neither knew nor cared. . . . The unhappy times when men would read some suggestion of racial prejudice into every piece of literature concerned with alien characters lay some centuries ahead. (Louis Wright, xiii–xiv)

The new historicists have developed a dynamic in the past that helps performance critics to see productions as dynamic in the present. It is helpful, for example, that Karen Newman discerns a link between the African and excessive sexuality in Elizabethan times. Travelers to Africa reported black men "furnished with such members as are often a sort of burthen unto them," according to Hakluyt (Newman, 148). "Early cartographers ornamented maps with representations of black men bearing enormous sexual organs" (ibid.). It is helpful when Michael Neill suggests that "*Othello* is a play full of racial feeling, perhaps the first work in English to explore the roots of such feeling; and it can hardly be accidental that it belongs to the very period in English history in which something we can now identify as a racialist ideology was beginning to evolve under the pressures of nascent imperialism" (394). Such findings make the script a system in which the "discourse of race" is still being conducted and reveal Wright's statement quoted above as irrelevant, an effort to dismiss Shakespeare's contemporaneity at a time when Dwight Eisenhower was living in the White House a few miles away from where the passage was penned. The findings of the new historicists make Shakespeare our contemporary not by aligning his vision with that of Beckett, Brecht, or Sartre, but by showing that his scripts emerged from issues that still confront us. The historical moment or cultural context determines what is possible in a given work and what is understood by it, so that we do not have to claim Shakespeare's "transcendence" of his times in order to discern racism in *Othello*. The new historicists are helpful, then, in refuting statements like that of Jonathan Miller, who claims: "When a black actor [plays Othello], it offsets the play, puts it out of balance . . . makes it a play about blackness, which it is not. . . . The trouble is, the play has been hijacked for political purposes" (Barnet, 285). Miller hijacked the play for his own political purposes in casting Anthony Hopkins in the role for BBC, which meant that Bob Hoskins's Iago *had* to be a psychopath, as opposed to another jealous character within the script, one whose feelings could be "explained" by racism, even if Iago's rationalist orientation could not delve to the root of his motivation.

As with "poetry," it is often easier to say what a Shakespearean script is not than what it is. Philip McGuire suggests that *"The playtext . . . is not its enduring essence abstracted from the particularities that inhere in all performances. It is a verbal (rather than mathematical) construct that describes the ensemble of possibilities.* It establishes a range, a distribution of possible events during a performance, including acts of speaking. . . . Its statements do specify what *cannot* happen, and in doing so they permit whatever possibilities are not prohibited" (138–39; his emphasis). In other words, the script, or playtext, is not a fixed entity but rather words that offer a myriad of options for director and actor. It is, then, a set of choices waiting to be made. "More than our brother is our chastity," says Isabella, employing a curious plurality. Is the statement that of a woman displaying an excessive pride that will meet chastisement or is it that of a woman very insecure in her rationalization, and moving uncertainly into the friction of experience? Estelle Kohler read the line in the former mode in John Barton's 1970 Stratford, England, production. Cheryl Williams gave it the latter interpretation at the New Jersey Festival in 1990. While both interpretations made sense for the characterization and production, neither reading is "correct," nor do the two possibilities begin to exhaust the available options.

As McGuire implies, a script is a flexible system of signals, fixed neither in meaning nor in time. It is, as Irving Wardle says, "the blueprint from which other artists can create an event" (*Theatre Criticism*, 94), but since the lines are meant to be spoken, not merely reshaped in marble or steel, the script is even more dynamic than a blueprint. It is an energy system awaiting the kinesis of actors and musicians, and even the director, who brings to the script a sense of adventure as opposed to merely a concept. In fact, a production of a Shakespearean play is meant to create a disturbance, to shake us free from our preconceptions and biases, not to confirm our complacency. In that sense, Shakespeare is the most radical playwright who ever lived.

Ann Thompson suggests that "In some sense all future readings can be said to be already 'there' in the text, but we have to wait for the historical circumstances that will make them visible" (81). What we have to do is to await the production that will make them visible. Production becomes the discovery of things we did not think we knew. Thus a *Measure for Measure* that merely emphasizes sexual harassment is already dated. A *Richard II* that mirrors Watergate, as did the over-directed and over-praised Barton production of 1972, merely reconfirms what we already know and simply uses the energy of *Zeitgeist*, contributing nothing to it. "The dead man moves," says Peter Brook of Shakespeare, "we stay still" (*Shifting Point*, 55).

We must ask of any production whether the "other texts" or "historical circumstances" are merely being reflected by the production. Is the director merely leaning on current events or cultural trends to reinforce the preconceptions of his audience or to make a political point? Placing a script in a contemporary environment may be superficially arresting, but often calls attention merely to a director's "bright idea." As Wardle suggests: "The idea of staging *Romeo and Juliet* as a feud between Catholic and Protestant Irish blinds you to the fact that nothing much is going on inside the fancy new framework" (91).

What should be happening is an intervention into our time frame and emotional space, a disturbance during which something is going on within the theatrical frame and within its spectator-participants. The superficially arresting concept that Wardle describes will draw praise, perhaps, but will not serve the deeper goals that Barbara Hodgdon defines: "critical reading seeks to stabilize the text . . . performance acknowledges, in its every aspect, its ephemeral nature. Such an acknowledgement is truer to history—both critical history and performance history—than creating a text that will not be disturbed by time. For disturbance—one might also call it transformation—is just what Shakespeare's texts are about. . . . Perhaps Shakespeare's texts can even prompt the most radically subversive transformation of all: changing critics to directors or actors" ("Parallel Practices," 65). The problem is that directors are, with notable exceptions, a guild unto themselves. They admit few to their mysteries, and they tend to create productions like those that Emrys Jones describes: "The play Shakespeare wrote seems constantly to be intruding into [these productions] as if it didn't belong there, never quite fitting and sometimes getting in the way. . . . In big Shakespeare productions, the designs are much more vivid than the actors. It's as if the sets and the lighting, the music, even the costumes existed in their own imaginative right, taking some kind of priority over the actors and their words. Shakespeare is becoming Shafferized, drama demoted in favour of 'theatre'" (1159). And, too often, directors do what Alan Dessen describes: They "reshape . . . the evidence [like] a detective's rewriting of the clues to conform to his solution" (*ShS* 36, 61). In order to suggest that Shylock's revenge is motivated by Jessica's escape, for example, Jonathan Miller cut lines from his script that challenge that interpretation in his 1974 production with Laurence Olivier.

Halio's chapter on "Finding the Subtext" (*Understanding Shakespearean Plays*, 39–49) concentrates on how actors build character out of the subtexts they discern in the characterization and supply from themselves as actors and human beings. *Zeitgeist* is also the inevitable subtext of any production and is invariably transmitted from a production, even though the process may be undefined or unconscious. If we look at fifty- or hundred-year-old photographs of productions costumed in ostensibly authentic Elizabethan dress we can see that the productions actually reflect an "Elizabethan England" as glimpsed by 1943 or 1893 and not by some fixed and immutable historicism. *Zeitgeist* can be overexpressed in production, in which case the production shrivels to the dimensions of a moment perceived by the director. It can be ignored, in which case it emerges disturbingly from under the "museum piece" of the production. What a director must do is to negotiate skillfully between what the script provides and how a modern, or postmodern, audience may be sensitized to "current issues." The balance is between the "universal" as concept and "relevance." Neither will work by itself. The tension is between "how Shakespeare might have done it" and what works in today's theaters, with modern audiences, who often must be educated back to what theater does differently and/or better than other media. What gets communicated is a continuum of historical energy, from Shakespeare's day, and before (since he pulls "history" and myth forward with him), to today and into the future, where meanings as yet unperceived will be discovered when the historical circumstances open our eyes to them, as Ann Thompson suggests. This continuum is particularly powerful because it communicates through the exchange of chemistry and electricity, of emotion and imagination, in which actors and audiences engage during a live performance of one of the scripts. We can think about it later and make it good or bad or in-between, but it is not at the rational faculty that Shakespeare aims primarily. That is one huge fallacy that blocks our ability to respond to the plays in performance. But because language is rational and inevitably a rationalization, the "rational fallacy" can only be exposed through the use of rational arguments, with the occasional invective and ad hominem.

The scripts themselves contain their own undercutting commentary, or subversion, as "new critics" have often pointed out. We do not always glimpse the subversion until our own awarenesses as a culture catch up with elements already in the scripts. For example: while Shakespeare's Pistol can be seen as a commentary on Henry V, Pistol *per se* does not permit us to dismiss him as merely a debased and deservedly cudgell'd character or to mourn his departure as the exiting of our chance for amusement—attitudes we could assume only recently. We can no longer ignore Pistol as a product of war, a half-man who now must crouch for employment in the alleyways and backstreets of the city. He has been produced by the policies of a government that has accrued benefits as a result of war but that disowns the by-products of war.

Pistol has a line from an old play ready for almost any occasion, but he has not been formally educated. Noam Chomsky says that the formally educated "tend to be the privileged and they tend to have a stake in the indoctrinal system, so they naturally tend to internalize and believe it. As a result, not uncommonly and not only in the United States, you find a good deal more sophistication among people who learn about the world from their experience rather than those who learn about the world from the doctrinal framework that they are exposed to and that they are expected as part of their professional obligation to propogate"

(*NYR* 27 June 1986, 39). We find in the plays the very challenges to "the system" that the plays ostensibly uphold—in this case, in Pistol's farewell soliloquy:

> Does Fortune play the huswife with me now?
> News have I that my Nell is dead i' th' spital
> Of a malady of France;
> And there my rendevous is quite cut off.
> Old I do wax, and from my weary limbs
> Honour is cudgelled. Well, bawd I'll turn,
> And something lean to cutpurse of quick hand,
> To England will I steal, and there I'll steal.
> And patches will I get unto these cudgell'd scars,
> And swear I got them in the Gallia wars.

We cannot say, with Dr. Johnson, that even if Pistol is "beaten into obscurity . . . every reader regrets [his] departure" (Sherbo, 563). In a modern "contextualizing," Pistol comes at us because ideology is haunted by what it represses (cf. Goldberg), just as is the individual psyche. The Vietnam memorial is underground, invisible from the boulevard, but there. As Rabkin says of Pistol, "Our regret is for something more than the end of some high comedy: it is for the reality of the postwar world the play so powerfully conjures up—soldiers returned home to find their jobs gone, falling to a life of crime in a seamy and impoverished underworld that scarcely remembers the hopes that accompanied the beginnings of the adventure" (57). Pistol was criminal from the beginning, but in the great 1977 Terry Hands production at Stratford-on-Avon, Pistol (Jeffrey Dench) was momentarily inspired by Henry's speech and felt, for an instant, part of something greater than he or his company had been. That the feeling had been produced merely by rhetoric made his disillusionment no less. He claims, "these wounds I had on Crispin's day," but that fact only hollows-out Henry's great promise of a happy futurity and its display of painless Purple Hearts. The old "New Critics" showed by staying inside the play, without appeal to "historicity" or to Marx, that the plays have plenty of "resistance" within themselves (cf. Harold Goddard), even if the new historicist approach helps us to isolate them, perhaps to phrase them more accurately, and certainly to see them as a making of culture as opposed to just a reflection of it.

In a recent book on Shakespeare in performance, Sam Crowl examines newer critical approaches to production. Citing Ihab Hassan, Crowl isolates "Indeterminacy"—the poststructuralist rejection of determinate meanings of a text, "Fragmentation"—the rejection of notions of organization or synthesis, and "Decanonization"—the rejection of master codes and authorities (53). Deconstruction, says Joseph Litvak,

> unlike traditional humanistic criticism, which sees the work as a balance of conflicting forces or as the fulfillment of the author's intention . . . shows how the work undoes itself as a result of these conflicting forces, and denies that the author's intention can even account for the work's full complexity. . . . The whole repertoire of binary oppositions that pervades Western thought is nothing more than a set of fictions designed to confer symmetry and stability on a much messier state of affairs, where difference, not opposition, is the order of the day. (2, 9)

Deconstruction "is good at discovering the various ways Western culture succeeds in repeating the ritual of the scapegoat, finding different victims but adhering to the same time-honored strategies" (Litvak, 15). One strategy, of course, is to see a Pistol as merely a character in a play, as opposed to "contextualizing" Pistol as a person who is very much present in a society that believes that "The only history worth telling is the history of the ruling class [and] that philosophy is a way of making that class feel good about itself" (3).

Again citing Hassan, Crowl uses the term "Performance" as part of "the reconstructive agenda" (52). "The very nature of the postmodern ethos," Crowl says, "invites participation. Indeterminacy insists that the reader-auditor-critic (as the re-reader) is essential to the creation of the very text itself" (52). When the text is a dramatic text, or script, further creative steps are necessary. They involve the imagining, by a director, of the words as performed, the performing of the words by actors with other actors, and the completion of the process by an audience using its imagination, as Shakespeare suggests "to eke out our performance with your mind." The words on the page are to be explored as if they have become magically three-dimensional—because they are so on the stage—and we are children entering a wonderland where new meanings and combinations await our participation, because it is we who must complete the riddles, answer the questions, discover the options that the actors pose and have themselves discovered. "I will none of your money!" Williams insists in *Henry V.* But does he say this to Henry, bravely rejecting the King's bribe, to Fluellen, easily dismissing a pittance insultingly meant to go toward mending Williams's shoes, or to both? Does he then put his palm out to accept Fluellen's money, as in the BBC production, and permit the scene to end with a hearty laugh all around? The line calls for interpretation and allows for several.

Production, then, is at once a deconstructive and a reconstructive process. Even if it deals with kings, the script does not necessarily project the inscription of a king's will as its meaning. If anything, the script shows the limitations of a king's power, as history does, and the futility of even the most successful kings, like Henry V, whose time on earth was "small." The new historicists wedge open the time between us and the script to show us how dynamic it was in its time. Actors and directors "deconstruct" the inherited script in our times to show how dynamic it continues to be in its journey through the "performance present," as Barbara Hodgdon calls it (*Theatrical Dimension*, 29–49), of a given time and place.

A script involves a process and is not, like "literature," a finished product. As R. B. McKerrow says, a Shakespearean "manuscript . . . was not a literary document at all. It was merely the barebones of a performance on the stage, intended to be interpreted by actors skilled in their craft" (253–75)—and by an audience still becoming educated by the actors to possibilities within the scripts these four hundred years later. What was a given, however, now seems very much a minority view. The concept of script insists, however, as Cary Mazer says, that the plays themselves "are somehow incomplete, or unrealized until they exist in the act of performance" (*SQ* [1985]: 650).

William Worthen expands on Marvin and Ruth Thompson's catalogue of the activities of performance criticism in *Shakespeare and the Sense of Performance* (13–15). "What is 'preserved' in performance and in performance criticism," Worthen says, "is manifestly not the text—which *as* text is against performance of all kinds, in criticism as well as on the stage—but rather an interpretation, a reading. . . . To the degree that it claims for performance the authority of the text, performance criticism becomes blind to its own ideological redundancy, its unacknowledged captivity to preconceived notions of the text, notions usually derived from the textual or 'literary' study it repudiates" (*ShSt* 21, 301; his emphasis). The current study does not acknowledge captivity to the "text." The received text itself is edited to become a script, true, but the editing is part of the process of a production. Does Fortinbras—assuming he gets to say anything—say "Take up the body," or "Take up the bodies"? Does he mean that he is using Hamlet's body to make sure that now "the King is with the body" in a Kantorowiczian sense, or does he mean "clear the stage"? The text offers those options and is hardly a fixed entity. Conceptual spaces other than the stage—film, for example—call for a script only a fraction of which can be Shakespeare's "text," whatever that may be. Script is not an epiphenomenon of text. Rather, text is a codification of script. These plays were scripts originally, and remain so today. Performance, as Worthen says, is "a richly localized signifying practice, one bound and defined by its relation to other modes of signification, representation, and empowerment informing cultural life" (*ShSt* 21, 302). Or, to put it another way, script is a destabilization of text.

Shakespeare becomes our contemporary in that moment in which production brings him—or it, the energy system—alive again in our presence—the "sights and sounds, stillness and motion, noise and silence, relationships and responses," as John Styan says of performance (*Shakespeare and the Sense of Performance*, 199). "No author," according to Peter Donaldson, "can permanently fix his meanings against change, nor control the use his works will be put to by later readers, actors, critics" (6). Indeed, Shakespeare's scripts build into themselves precisely the options against fixity that allow them to be performed as more than "readings" or scenes viewed behind a velvet rope. We are driven by history to discover our history, and the new historicists create an imperative that assists in the process of finding current meanings as opposed to just those embedded in 1600. Those meanings are as varied and as subject to a variety of interpretations as are the issues that confuse us today. Production helps clarify that confusion by linking us into an energy that explores the human condition and forces us to confront our existential selves in the communal setting of theater. That "nowness" is an element that Shakespeare continues to create, along with the bombardment of other information, and it may counter or at least inform the partial theories of history that serve the agendas of an Adolf Hitler or a Ronald Reagan. Whether whatever "Shakespeare" may be has deeper social possibilities in a world of homelessness, famine, and terrorism is a question that goes beyond the scope of the present work, but it is one that we who have enjoyed careers within that field had better ask.

"There is no escape from contingency," Greenblatt says (3) and it is into contingency that production launches us. Paraphrasing Greenblatt, Steven Mullaney adds, "The aura of autonomous existence and transhistorical vitality we associate with major canonical authors [like Shakespeare] is generated not by an escape from contingency but by a full embracing of it" (495). That is uniquely so of Shakespeare because he wrote plays that continue to be full of options for interpretation, options that, in turn, come to light as *Zeitgeists* change. Some of the signals within the sign-system of the script will change as the times provide the means to decipher them. The meanings are there. The historical circumstances necessary to "read" them have not yet occurred. The scripts are an energy system that remains potential in many ways and variable in unpredictable ways. The new historicist debate helps create the spectrum of variability. Is drama, as Margaret de Gratzia argues, the terminus toward which all Renaissance culture flows? Is drama an intervention in history, as opposed to a system that stands outside history and feeds on it? Is drama a subversive intervention? Is drama apolitical in its effect upon perceived reality, as Paul Yachnin argues? (see Wiggins, 179–80, for his summary of this debate). The postmodern director probably does not care what the play was in 1600, but he or she must decide what it will be in the 1990s—a reflection of culture, a challenge to culture, or some neutral artifact that becomes an alternative to culture. The "neutral" stance is impossible, although the attempt can be made, as it was in the Coe *Othello*, with James Earl Jones and Christopher Plummer a decade ago. Moreover, no production can impose its meanings on *every* spectator, as the responses of reviewers prove in their range from praise to condemnation. The reviewers help "historicize" a given production by suggesting how it emerged into the culture and how the culture claimed it for its own or rejected it as somehow not fitting the needs, expectations, and artistic criteria of the moment at which the critics responded. Few critics, of course, are trying consciously to "historicize" a given production, but they do so nonetheless and their responses are almost invariably illuminating. The reviews culled from the vast flow of disposable newsprint and cited here are much more than abstracts and brief chronicles of the times. Our productions of Shakespeare and our response to those productions tell us what our times mean.

The "openness to interpretation" of Shakespeare's scripts is not a function of modern theory, although modern theory, both historicist and deconstructionist, does help open up the scripts. The meaning of a script is a temporal quality that shows how a script reflects, reinterprets, or reemphasizes the cultural and ideological assumptions of a particular moment in history. It has taken time to make that point to us, so that looking back at production history becomes an archeological expedition in which we uncover the assumptions and prejudices of an age in which the approach to Shakespeare tells us what the runes and the ruins mean. Just because production that does capture the ideology of a particular moment is timely does not necessarily mean that the production is good. An emphasis on "multiculturalism" or "harassment" may actually inhibit response to, for example, a racially mixed *Richard II* or a *Measure for Measure* suddenly found to reflect today's headlines. And just because a *Richard II* happened to pick up the historical accident of "Watergate," as did John Barton's early 1970s production, does not mean that the production could somehow transcend its assumption that Richard and Bolingbroke are interchangeable entities or its heavy-handed imposition of props and speeches from other plays upon a script that needs clarification, not idiosyncratic complication. Shakespeare should not be forced into the service of some momentary glimpse of current "meaning." Just as certainly, however, the force known as Shakespeare cannot be isolated from the culture that constantly reappropriates the scripts and creates new audiences for them. It does help us to know what they may have meant because that helps us to glimpse what they may mean as the scripts hurtle through time, like empty space ships awaiting crews to inhabit them and take them away somewhere.

Shakespeare translates to television, for example, because TV tends to be an auditory medium (derived from radio, not film) and because we are growing accustomed to a scale that suits the cassette and the shallow depth-field of television.* It may be that *Hamlet* must become "Chekhovian" because of the pressure that televisual expectations bring to bear on stage production. Shakespeare survives domestication, but in ways that demand investigation about why and how the scripts work on TV when the script charges the medium with more than its usual source of energy, and about how TV may be affecting other media, as it certainly is affecting film and the market forces that drive film production. Is the tendency toward the thrust stage that has only recently emerged from prosenium premises now beginning to back under the proscenium again, as in the new Shakespeare Theatre in Washington? If the answer is yes, then it may follow

---

*For this argument, see "A Space for Shakespeare," in my *Shakespearean Performance as Interpretation* (Newark: University of Delaware Press, 1992), and *Watching Shakespeare on Television* (Madison, N.J.: Fairleigh Dickinson University Press, 1993).

that TV has something to do with it. Our expectations condition what happens in the media.

All actors and some directors must concentrate on one of the most scorned of all critical categories—character. Character does not always "intertextualize." In today's critical climate, Pistol moves into oblivion as a character unless linked to an anecdote discovered by a new historicist in the archives of 1599, or placed within the Marxist cultural materialist agenda as a constant present, a reminder of our political system, not just Shakespeare's. But Cleopatra and Falstaff, to name two, will not abide our question. Even feminist critics, freer than others of the need to "contextualize" in historicist terms, struggle with Cleopatra's "surrender" to love at the end of the play, wishing that she had defeated Caesar more convincingly than she has. The important point, however, is that, however much these characters challenge the limits of critical modes, they must "contextualize" within a production, as actors undertake them in the company of other actors depicting the inhabitants of "the world of the play." Characterization, as Gary Taylor says, "enables Shakespeare to multiply and intensify the amount of felt life he can squeeze into a few hours of playing time" (406). One of the few current approaches that permits a discussion of character *per se* is feminism, which tends to allegorize, but which also focuses on the ways in which attitudes within the "world of the play" impose allegories on other characters, thus marginalizing them. As in modern times, the resistance of these characters to the powers that diminish them usually destroys them.

Theme (the concept that organizes a specific production), imagery (the visual qualities of a production), and character are what the making of productions are all about and thus, inevitably, what the reception of productions is also all about. Do these terms impose a closed circle around the energy system known as Shakespeare and a straitjacket limitation on the system as it pokes into and creates shockwaves with the future? They would be some danger were these categories really value-laden, as their critics contend they are. They can be, of course, trailing clouds of Matthew Arnold and Dover Wilson in their wake. Shakespeare can, of course, be appropriated by the dominant ideology, as Terry Hawkes argues and as Frank Rich has recently complained of Branagh's "Prince Charles" version of Hamlet. But perceptions of Shakespeare's relationship to a given culture are not necessarily accurate descriptions of "the truth." Instead, they are efforts to suggest "a truth" caught as the insight itself fades into mere language.

Characters, says Goldman, "negotiate between their self-conceptions and their conception of the world, altering both as they respond to new experiences of world and self" (66). In the process their imitation of an action alters us, as our own inner crystals shift in imitation of techtonic plates as we sit quietly, but not passively, in a theater. The ideological emphasis that sees the plays appropriated for the sake of authority is itself constantly shifting to show how themes, images, and conceptions of character reflect or refute the biases and often unexamined or intentionally masked preconceptions of a given *Zeitgeist*. A production reintegrates the fragments that have been discovered, analyzed, and categorized like shards in an archeological expedition in the critical process that precedes and is subordinate to the approach to production. The process uncovers the "stage realities present in the text," as Hodgdon calls them ("Dramatic Present," 29), realities which must be there, since this is a dramatic text designed for production—that is, a script. Production itself is not "fixed," but develops over the course of its run, often squeezing running time from its length as it tightens and coheres within the space that includes a live audience. The cultural materialist argument that authority encourages simultaneous subversion and containment describes a process, not a binary opposition. Is that what Shakespeare's plays are? Or are they used to create a seeming subversion only to recapture and control it? Or are they radical documents awaiting the director willing to demonstrate that the issues a play raises challenge and defeat any sense of successful closure? The concept of script incorporates the process of reinforcement or refutation. The spectator must determine what stance a particular production has taken. Shakespeare, the writer of plays, was neither reactionary nor revolutionary. He created scripts that demanded interpretation and still do. "Let Time's news be known / When 'tis brought forth."

The Shakespeare Theatre (D.C.). Set for *Much Ado About Nothing*. Seats 450.

A proscenium production of 1951, F. Curtis Canfield's *Hamlet* for the Amherst College Masquers. Notice the precision of the "stage picture." Ray MacDonnell, Hamlet, Russ Moro, Claudius, Scottie Monteith, Laertes, Nick Evans, Horatio. The author stands, stage left, stunned because he had yet to read Act Five.

John Van Meter's *A Midsummer Night's Dream,* The McDonogh Players. Photo by Susan Fagan.

The Rodeheaver Auditorium. Seats 2611.

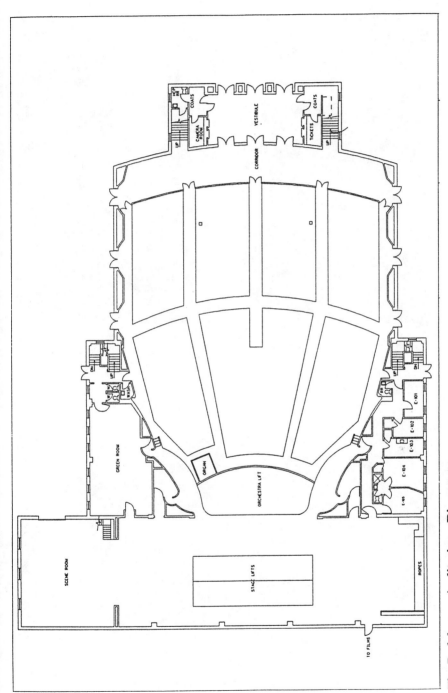

The Rodeheaver Auditorium. Diagram.

The Open Air Theatre, Regent's Park. Photo by Alastair Muir.

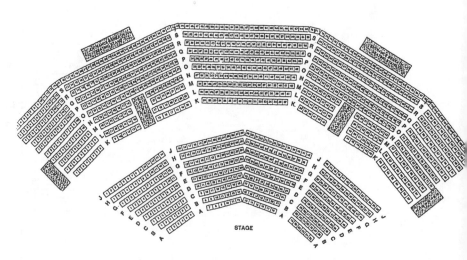

The Open Air Theatre, Regent's Park. Diagram.

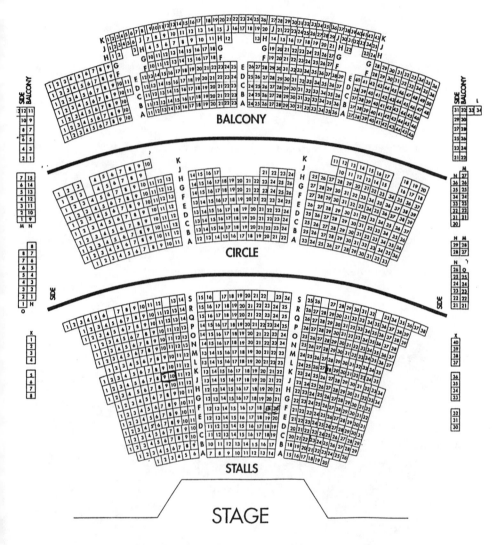

The Stratford-on-Avon Main Stage. Diagram.

The Stratford-on-Avon Main Stage. Seats 1500.

The Swan, Stratford-on-Avon.

The auditorium of the Swan, Stratford-on-Avon, as viewed from the platform stage left. Note the height of the balconies and the length of the playing area (right foreground) and the extent of its thrust into the auditorium.

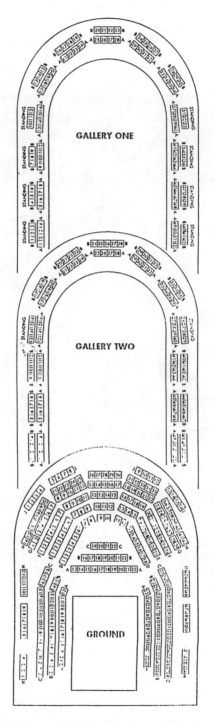

The Swan, Stratford-on-Avon. Diagram.

STAGE
LOWER LEVEL

C B A ... A B C

[Two rows of balcony seats extend above the seats to the right and left.]

Numbered seats are reserved

The Other Place, Stratford-on-Avon. Diagram.

The Barbican. Notice no aisles. Entrances exist for each row along ramps down each side of the auditorium. Seats 1166.

The Barbican in action.

The Barbican. Diagram.

The Lyttelton at the Royal National Theatre. Seats 890.

The Olivier at the Royal National Theatre. Seats 1215.

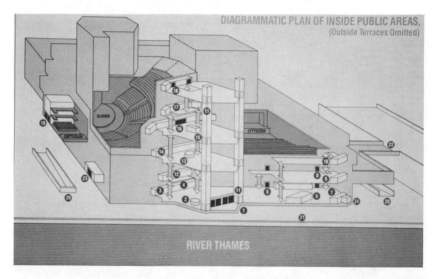

The Royal National Theatre. Drawing by David Eaton.

The Arts Centre. University of Warwick, Coventry.

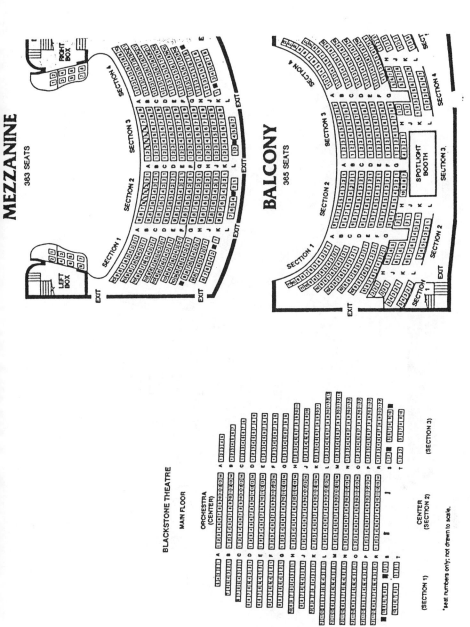

The Blackstone Theatre. Diagram. Seats 1458.

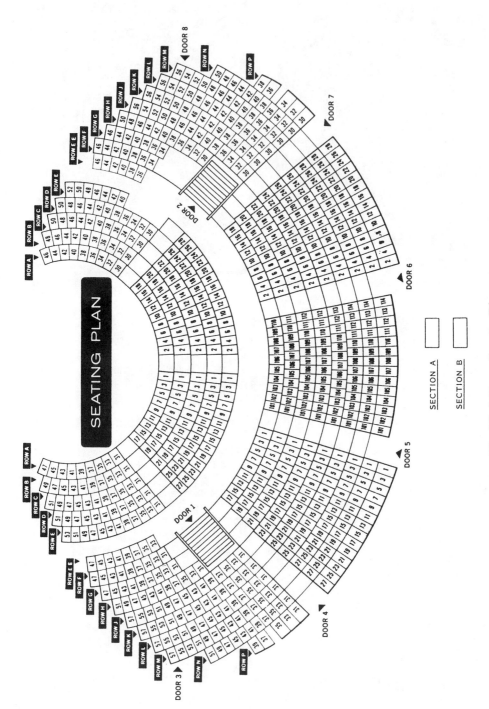

The Mark Taper Forum. Diagram.

The Festival Thrust Stage, Stratford, Ontario.

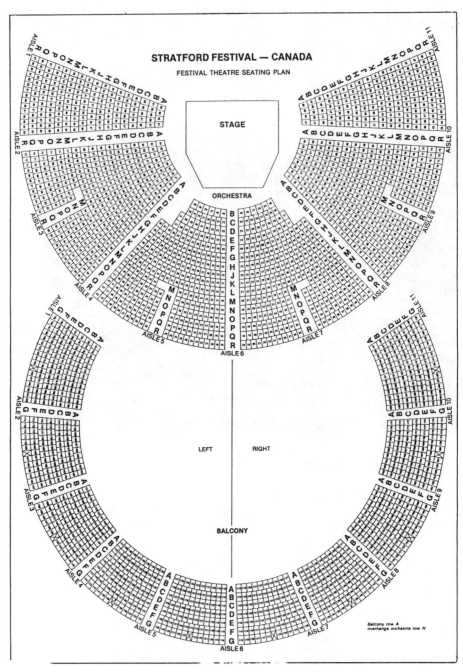

The Festival Thrust Stage, Stratford, Ontario. Diagram.

3

1987 and the Question of Space

SPACE was a major issue in the summer of 1987. The newest of Stratford-on-Avon's theaters, the Swan, featured a powerful *Titus Andronicus*, directed by Deborah Warner. The shape of the stage and its effect on the actor/spectator relationship helped the production: in fact, they were responsible for what happened within the space. In comparison, the Stratford main stage, suffering from the proscenium format imposed upon it in 1932 when it was built, continued to provide productions that seemed dated and were unexciting. In addition, the Olivier Theatre at the National Theatre in London is a difficult space, one that seems to daunt directors and to distance spectators. Stanley Wells says that he "never see[s] a performance in the Olivier Theatre without being made conscious of the demands made by the building. . . . It is not easy to create a sense of communication between the stage and the nether reaches of the auditorium" (*ShS* 41, 176). Two productions there in 1987 proved that "the space is not necessarily the message." One was very good, the other was very bad.

With the years, Peter Hall's *Antony and Cleopatra* has grown past the size of dreaming in the imaginations of those who have seen it, and was very good. The vastness of the script places *Antony and Cleopatra* near the top of the list of difficult plays to produce, but the great cross-cultural leaps and the soaring verse found a home on the Olivier stage. One of the few objectors to the set was Irving Wardle, who suggested that "The text seems to demand the strongly contrasted world[s] of Rome and Egypt. Hall and his designer Allison Chitty have replaced this with an environment drawn from Renaissance painting. The effect is to create an idealized environment. . . . However . . . there are powerful effects to be gained through exposing fallible human behaviour in a super-human setting" (*T* 11 April 1987, 14).

Judi Dench brought absolute energy to her role, at one point dashing downstage to tell us that Antony "shall have every day a several greeting"—as if we were her kingdom and had no choice but to agree to her use of messenger-power. Later, she swallowed "Pity me, Charmian, / But do not speak to me," a very funny line that assigns both inner response and external behavior from Cleopatra's concept of power, unshaken and merely readjusting to the news of Antony's marriage. Had Sir Peter been sitting in the auditorium, he might have made a note to suggest that Cleopatra is really asserting command over a new situation and not bathing in self-pity. Dench was exciting, even thrilling at moments, "very much the Cleopatra who hopped forty paces through the street," as J. P. says (*CE*, 104). However, some who saw Janet Suzman's version in the early 1970s—an elegant woman smoldering with a volcanic sensuality filtered through the cool assessment of observing eyes—might have preferred Suzman. Another noteworthy variation was Katherine Hepburn's haughty, amusing, stately queen of act five, at Stratford, Connecticut, some thirty years ago, breathing a great sigh of relief and saying, "Ah— the stage is mine at last!" as Robert Ryan's six-gun Antony was toted off some two hours too late.

Dench's entrance to act five was inhibited by directorial choices. The production set a rapid pace, as Hall's productions always do. The auditorium resounded with drums and trumpets. Entrances and exits were conducted up and down the aisles of the vast ampitheater. The production had space, then, for modulation, for a pause for Antony's return "from / The world's great snare uncaught," when he and Cleopatra achieve for an instant the relationship that has thus far been figured only in words. It is more than Cleopatra's birthday. It is the birth of concept into being. But Hall, it seems, felt that with an uncut text and a running time of three hours and forty-five minutes, he could not pause for emphasis during his scenes.

The monument scene, which proves Antony's love for Cleopatra beyond all game-playing, was unfortunate. One could see it as an effort to use the great heights above the stage, just as Hall had employed the rest of the Olivier space so completely. Cleopatra and her ladies perched on a narrow shelf. Antony was raised to Cleopatra in a giant fishnet —"Ah ha, you're caught!"—a process awkward, slow, and seemingly dangerous. Antony increased the crowd on the shelf and seemed about to topple off until Charmian tucked one of his legs behind a fragment of wall.

The staging called attention to itself and away from an exchange that is at once consummation and parting. Hall robbed us of the scene and took from Dench the chance to launch into her own play against Caesar on the basis of a sense of that Antony who was and is "past the size of dreaming."

Tim Piggot-Smith played an Octavius who loved his sister (some thought incestuously), if not against the script, certainly against the icy Corin Redgrave interpretation for Trevor Nunn.* According to Piggot-Smith, who spoke to Homer Swander's Theatre in England group in August 1987, not only is the confrontation between Antony and Caesar in 2.2. *not* a trap constructed by Caesar for Antony but the Seleucus scene (5.2) is *not* a trap contrived by Cleopatra and her Treasurer.

The Antony-Caesar meeting was played straight. Agrippa did not confer with Caesar before popping up with his scheme for the disposition of a sister for whom this Caesar really cared. Caesar was already onstage when he said, "I do not know, Maecenas, ask Agrippa," a line Piggot-Smith attributed to Caesar's anger at Antony's line about setting off "to Parthia." It may be that Antony does not tumble over-confidently into a trap here, but Hall's very literal reading made this scene wooden and undramatic.

The premises of the Seleucus scene are also debatable, but it can be carried off as an amusing gulling of Caesar rather than a betrayal of Cleopatra. If the scene is about Caesar's solicitude rather than Cleopatra's skills as impresario of an impromtu playlet, then the big line is "feed and sleep." This production made the scene a parallel to the first messenger scene (2.5) rather than to the one in which Caesar traps Antony (2.2), which did not really occur here, as explained earlier. What are we to make of Cleopatra's "He words me, girls, he words me," just after Caesar exits if the Seleucus scene has not been arranged to reassure Caesar that Cleopatra intends to stay alive? Again, Hall's literal interpretation erased the depth the scene might convey and our enjoyment at sharing Cleopatra's strategy. Dench's energetic Cleopatra deserved a chance to carry off this *tour de force*. A sympathetic Caesar should not prevent her worming her way to victory over him. Let Caesar have his world. Our imaginations might be

---

*The "character's impassive drive towards Empire is here supplemented by a neurotic fear of contact and a near-incestuous feeling for his sister" (Everett, 439): "a compelling performance of restless energy and suppressed power" (J. P., 104): "His love for Octavia was intense and possibly more than brotherly . . . this Octavius emerged as a figure . . . more complex than Antony" (Warren, *SQ* [1987]: 364). It was "a brilliant study in graceless tension" (Wardle, *Times*, 11 April 1987, 14): "a credible wielder of power, as well as a porcelain, humourless puritan" (Hiley, *Listener* 23 April, 1987, 35). See Dessen's detailed analysis of Piggot-Smith's complex characterization (*SQ* [1988]: 221–22).

allowed to swing back to Cydnus with Cleopatra and her first meeting with Marc Antony.

Critical response suggested that this production had been the exploration of the script that we expect of Peter Hall, an experience of a play we do not understand until we see it performed, an experience that proved that we understand the play only through performance.

Dench's Cleopatra drew the most enthusiasm: "She extended herself into every aspect of the role, from the sordid to the sublime, while never losing the sense of a unifying self that could encompass Cleopatra's 'infinite variety,'" said Wells. The "comedy of the role was realized with perfect timing and brilliant transitions" (*ShS* 41, 177). Wells pointed at the dimension of the role, which has a range challenged in the canon perhaps only by the Falstaff of the histories, and by Hamlet. She "spoke 'I dreamt there was an Emperor Antony. . . .' with rapt, hushed lyricism," said Wells, "to a Dolabella who stood in the auditorium aisle with his back to us, so that she was addressing us as well as him. At moments such as these an audience, even in the Olivier auditorium, can be united in a single emotion" (178). The speech, said Alan Dessen, "was directed through [Dollabella] at us (as potential doubters or liars)" (*SQ* [1988]: 222). This configuration forced us to believe that Cleopatra, at least, believed in this Antony, and insisted on her vision "up to the hearing of the gods," which meant up to the ears of those sitting at the furtherest reaches of the ampitheater. We were silent before her power, harboring what private doubts we dared. It was, said Irving Wardle, "a performance of fearless self-exposure, going to the brink of farce even in the death scene." She was "a creature moving too fast ever to be pinned down. Her restless prowling and incessant jerks of the head reflect her inner caprice, instantly cancelled orders, and emotional somersaults that ensure that she always has the whip hand. Then, just when such a thing seems impossible, she melts into submissiveness and the true voice of feeling" (*T* 11 April 1987, 14). She became, in death, said Barbara Everett, "an icon ablaze with gold" (439).

Gerald Berkowitz looked not at individual performance but into what he believed to be the perceptual core of the relationship between the two lovers: "Anthony Hopkins and Judi Dench played middle-aged lovers past their most passionate years but bound together by their memories. Dench in particular captured a woman who *had been* beautiful and sensual, and who was not afraid to show the unattractive and even comic sides of such a person, letting those flaws enrich the image of what had been. So if this Cleopatra was an aging flirt for whom flightiness and whimsicality had become exasperating habits, without the girlishness or sexuality that would have made them enticing, Dench still showed the faint ghost of that sexuality, so that we understood that Antony was still seeing and responding to the memory. . . . Because she was incapable of censoring her emotions, we believed that she was incapable of feigning them; her love for Antony was absolute, despite the sometimes trivial manner in which it was expressed" (SQ 38, 496; his emphasis).

James Fisher suggested that Cleopatra "is not even sure she cares anymore. Only jealousy periodically revives her full power" (37). The subtextual playing from "what had been" lent pathos to the lovers' efforts to regain that past, but the moment when the past does return—Antony's emergence from "the world's great snare, uncaught" and Cleopatra's rebirth—needed a clearer zone for its emphasis.

Hopkins's Antony was only briefly mentioned by the critics: "slow . . . in establishing the center of his Antony," said Berkowitz. He "remained a fairly simple bluff soldier until Actium. It was then, when his deep shame and despair at his disgrace were cut short by one kiss from Cleopatra, that we saw him realize she meant more to him than honor. . . . he had chosen this path, and . . . it was worth it" (SQ 38, 496). Wells said that Hopkins "was more convincingly the 'old ruffian' than the noble warrior" (ShS 41, 176), and Dessen established a consensus by saying "for me, as for others I talked with, this Antony was not the strong point of the rendition" ("Exploring the Script," 220). Roger Warren suggested that "Hopkins charted Antony's decline precisely but rather monotonously; so the production sagged somewhat in the middle" (SQ [1987]: 364). Hopkins's Antony, said Jim Hiley, "is a wry, bluff, almost passive but not malevolent man. . . . The Act Three scenes with Cleopatra have . . . a monotonously regretful, downbeat tone. Weirdest of all, his reaction to the news of Cleopatra's false death is hardly more animated than at Fulvia's demise" (L 23 April 1987, 35).

While Cleopatra's role has more range than Antony's and is challenging for that reason, Antony's part demands that the actor reflect a former greatness through his tarnished armor, actually reachieve it for an instant, and be, if not an objective correlative for Cleopatra's arias in act five, at least plausible enough to elicit such grand imagery.

Richard Johnson's Antony opposite Suzman's Cleopatra in the

early 1970s combined a gravelly overconfidence with eyes that couldn't quite figure Cleopatra out, so that we got a sense of his playing politics only half-heartedly—his full heart remaining entangled with Cleopatra. Antony's nonchalance in the Nunn production made it easy for precise Octavius to move his pawns across the world's board and checkmate an Antony who felt that that world was well lost. As Robert Speaight said of Johnson's Antony, he "had a careless grandeur and irresistible largesse; you realized that he was beaten by Octavius because Octavius was a political animal and Antony was not—or was not any longer. There was no trace of the diplomacy which had carried him to victory in the Forum, and one liked him the better for it" (*SQ* 13, 386).

Granville-Barker says of this script (and by inference of all of Shakespeare's scripts), "We are to keep Shakespeare's stage well in mind if we are to realise the dramatic value to the spectator of the quick shift from singing and dancing and the confusing of tipsy embracings to the strict military march that brings Ventidius 'as in triumph' upon the stage, There is no pause" (121–22). Other directors keep forgetting the "no pause" rule, but in the Hall production, as Dessen said, "One of the stongest features of this very strong show was the Elizabethan flow of the scenes, whereby entering figures appeared and began to speak while exiting figures were still in view. As a result, scene beginnings often commented meaningfully (or ironically) upon scene endings so as to produce a larger counterpoint than I have ever before seen realized so effectively onstage" ("Exploring the Script," 220). Shakespeare, it seems, kept the seams in view as he wrote, and good modern directors do the same. As Dessen said, the "comings and goings of various generals in the short segments that make up the battles of Acts III and IV may seem confusing or superfluous to the reader, but the point that came across in performance was not the importance of each of these figures . . . but rather a sense of shifting allegiances . . . of the numbers swelling . . . on Caesar's side and diminishing on Antony's" (221).

Thus does simple stagecraft make a point about the action imitated. One of the few weak aspects of the staging was the opening. Philo and Demetrius came through the great double doors. Philo closed them carefully, then began "Nay, but this dotage of our general's. . . ." We were to infer that Philo had put his fingers to his lips and said, "Let's go where we can talk." This approach robbed us of a coming in in the middle of a conversation—Shakespeare's adaptation of the *in media res* tradition. A play was beginning, as well as a great sequence continuing, the sequel to that rabble-rousing *Julius Caesar* we had seen seven years before. But from this undramatic opening the play did flow, for an arresting three hours and forty-five minutes.

This fluidity was served, as it had to be, by the design. As Wells suggested:

> Alison Chitty designed a great, bronzed, crescent-shape structure that could define a manageable acting area, but was capable also of rearranging itself to suggest changes of location, and of retreating altogether when the full stage area was needed. It was tall enough to occupy some of the void over the stage and to provide an upper level for Cleopatra's monument, and it incorporated a massive, central doorway. . . . The event was theatrical in the grand style that the auditorium demands . . . but was humanized by a mode of production that gave the actors every opportunity to exploit to the full that interest in the idiosyncrasies, the rich irrationality of human behavior that Shakespeare indulges in his late Plutarchan plays. (*ShS* 41, 176)

Wardle's wish for contrast had to be fulfilled here, as on Shakespeare's stage, by the actors who inhabited a specific zone at any given moment as two very different worlds tugged against each other for possession of Antony.

Enobarbus is one of the great secondary roles in the canon. In the Nunn production, Patrick Stewart played disapproval against his loyalty to Antony, until the former won and the latter retaliated, with fatal effect. Stewart's was a typically intelligent charting of the role. Michael Bryant's version for Hall tended to support the play's vision of Cleopatra as memory and thus to buttress Dench's sense of her character. The staff officers gather once the "photo opportunity" is over to trade stories. Enobarbus begins, as Berkowitz said, "with the half-seriousness of [a] soldier . . . telling [a] tale, but moved into a reverent, elegiac tone that showed that, perhaps without realizing it, he was describing the one transcendent experience of his life" (*SQ* [1987]: 497). We expect this of Bryant—the ability to describe something while at the same time furthering the dimensions of the character he is playing.

One of the few who questioned Hall's production was Barbara Everett. She suggested that some who had seen both the Nunn production of the early 1970s and the Hall version preferred the former: "Hopkins's Antony has a grizzled charm and mildness which make his farewell to his servants extremely touching; he communicates less, however, of the world-leader's range and generosity, his courage and lechery, above all of his dangerous edge, the power to alarm. . . . Dench . . . never quite . . . gets what is terrible and beautiful in Cleopatra: the repose of her effortless sense of power. . . . Something vital to Shakespeare has got lost. . . . Peter Hall has given us a major rendering of something curiously like Dryden's Restoration *All for Love*" (439). Hiley was correct to assert that the production was "hardly as total an achievement as has been suggested" (*L* 23 April 1987, 35).

But Hall's production must be seen in context. None of Hall's care or intelligence was evident in David Hare's *King Lear*, produced in the same space during the same season and with some of the same actors. Hare's instructions to his actors must have been: "Stand stiffly, do not look at the other actors, and pretend that every speech is a soliloquy to be mumbled to yourself." As Edmund was introduced to Kent and said, "My services to your lordship," Edmund stood still, twenty feet from Kent. He did not even incline his head. Since that is an action which even an amateur actor would make, one has to assume that Edmund had been commanded to "be a post." As France exited on "Come, my fair Cordelia," he strode past her, arms stiff, eyes front. His "fair" was merely politically correct, like Lysander's "fair Helena." Word and action were divorced from each other and the huge space of the Olivier was thrown in our faces like an alien and alienating zone. That was Hare's point, of course, emphasized by hunks of slaughtered beef, later by hunks of slaughtered soldiers that hung down from the vast reaches above the stage, along with a bizarre figure on a trapeze, a pagan goddess at which we were forced to share in stupified avoidance of what was not happening on the stage. "The play itself was dwarfed," as Dessen said ("Exploring the Script," 220).

Berkowitz was kind to say that the production "came close in its worse moments to being below the minimal standard for a company of the NT's stature" (*SQ* 38, 496). Hare, Berkowitz said, "left his actors to fend for themselves while he created stage pictures that were illogical, inconsistent, and ineffective. . . . Lear carried [the dead Cordelia] to a sort of picnic table downstage and sat himself comfortably on the bench behind it as if awaiting a hotdog rather than his death. Even the most intimate scenes were played from opposite ends of the large Olivier stage, the Fool in particular rushing as far as he could from everyone else to bawl his lines back at them. And there was a distressing amount of three-quarter-front shout-at-the-back-wall acting far more appropriate to high school drama clubs than to the National Theatre. . . . [Hopkins's Lear] fell apart completely in the second

half of the play, Hopkins finding no way to integrate Lear's madness and return to sanity with the earlier scenes" (495–96).

When one is faced with disaster that seems to have been
planned in advance—as opposed to the hubris that rushed the
Titanic toward consummation with that sinister mate—it may be
wise to seek intention rather than just shake one's head. Were the
appointments of Meese, Bennett, Pierce, Watt, Burford, et. al.,
just a series of grisly miscalculations? Hare's "concept" was, one
supposes, "Brechtian." In such an interpretation, dramatic sequences would be broken up by title cards, as in *Galileo*, where a
life was interrupted and dictated by the imposition of external
criteria that could only interrupt a "natural" movement toward
truths that the Catholic Church could not tolerate. Some of that
kind of blockage does occur in *King Lear*, as the King bangs his
agenda down on his court, will-you or nill-you, at the outset.

Peter Brook understood the "absurdist" element in the script
and captures it profoundly in his harsh, jagged, intentionally
awkward film version, even at the cost of some of the more hu-
manizing elements of the conflated script: the sudden kindling
of a qualitative value system in France and the "kindness" of
Cornwall's servants. Film can approximate the intentional discon-
nectedness of modern drama, which has been influenced by
filmic techniques, and can create that quality even with old
scripts. Film is another "space for Shakespeare." But Shakespeare's stage looks at "humanity," as Sheldon Zitner says, "in
the open middle distance of social relation. Shakespeare's stage
is a relational not an essentializing or ideologizing stage: not [a]
stage preempted by convictions that must focus on one causal
chain, psychological or sociological, but a stage closer to the tenor
of encountered experience in which causes and motives of all
sorts jostle. It offers whole human figures disposed in patterns
that exhibit what is primarliy a social (often familial) meaning" (9).

Hare's production emphasized the truth of Zitner's statement.
The only moments that worked in this *Lear* were those in which
the actors created a fleeting sense of relationship—the Fool and
Lear playing together against Goneril as she complains about
Lear's knights; Lear stumbling between Goneril and Regan as the
former shows up at Gloucester's place. Those moments showed
that the play is about relationship and its destruction, that is, that
there has be "something" before the concept of "nothing" has
meaning, that "sometime" makes "never" powerful, particularly
if delivered with five trochees. It is surprising, in retrospect, that
Hare permitted the few instances of relationship to occur, as his

concept was, from first to last, that the play depicts a disintegration that has already occurred or a world that has never embodied
a sense of family and "bonds," marriage, fatherhood, brother-
hood, sisterhood, or love. A reading of the script will suggest that
while such a concept can work in a heavily edited, minimalist
film (and the Shakespeare script must always be heavily edited
for film), it cannot work on the stage that Zitner describes, whose
every cubit cries out that relationship must be.

In other words, Hare must be given credit for an approach that
was murderously applied to the script, as if it had been directed
by Himmler. Hopkins, for example, somehow recognized his
"child, Cordelia" from twenty feet away, in a reconciliation scene
that erased Cordelia's love and Lear's rebirth even more completely than did Brook's film. Hopkins's kneeling was not to Cordelia, but seemed to be an allusion to Nebuchadnezzar. However,
Lear had been through the Nebuchadnezzar experience by this
time. Lear's final words were "look there—her lips," a new reading that defeated those of us who were looking for an interpretation other than Bradley's. But it did not matter, because Hopkins
had slumped virtually out of sight by this point. The response to
this finale could be no more than that Roger Warren attributed
to himself—"an outside observer is a hospital ward intruding
upon a private bereavement, sympathetic but not involved" (SQ
[1987]: 364).

At the very end, the plastic map that Lear had shattered at the
outset had been reconstituted with Elmer's Glue. Edgar gave one
of his strange flicking motions over the map. All was well in Al-
bion again or, perhaps, nothing significant had happened. Humpty Dumpty could be put together again, or perhaps was still on
his wall, just as meaningless and empty-headed as he had been
before his great fall.

Hare's Lear was a radical misreading of Shakespeare, particularly of a script that lacks the "essentialism" of a Macbeth, but
that does demand that the characters make the discoveries about
themselves and others that are the "essence" of existentialism.
The script can begin in the apparent security of rigid patriarchy,
shatter off into a Reaganesque or Thatcherite rhythm of greed
and competitiveness, and then end in reconcilations and annihila-
tions, but it has to go somewhere. Hare, it seems, did not permit
his actors to establish relationships with each other onstage; since
these included some good actors, one is forced to assume that
they were following his directions. They could not, then, establish
any relationship with the audience, except one of anger, even

rage. Hare did read his space correctly. The dark, wide Olivier auditorium and stage took this empty production and miniaturized it.

To be fair, however, one must quote Warren's statement that, "Several reviewers felt that David Hare's production of *King Lear* at the National Theatre was the best since Peter Brook's RSC one in 1962" (*SQ* [1987]: 363). Wardle said, for example, "Hopkins's Lear is stupendous" *(Times)* and according to the *Daily Express*, "Hopkins's triumph as Lear makes 'theatre history'" (both quoted in Pierre Virey, 80). Jim Hiley said that this production "oozes belief in the play and its modernity. Seldom has the Olivier arena come closer to the mix of epic sweep and intimate sweep its designers dreamed of. Hopkins is as good as everyone hoped he'd be; and Hare, uncompromisingly spare but incisive, leaps to the front rank of classical directors" (*L* 1 January 1987, 29). Richard Hornby said: "Anthony Hopkins was a fine King Lear, ably supported by a strong cast [but] the production was hamstrung by David Hare's inept direction. . . . the big stage was kept bare and unarticulated, with actors floating about or taking meaningless positions. One example out of very many of the wretched blocking occurred when Lear brought in Cordelia's body. Hare had Hopkins place her on a table, and then sit down behind it for his final speech, effectively disappearing from half the audience" (*HR* [Winter 1988]: 644).

The same space could produce very different results. A very different space could produce excellent results, as in Deborah Warner's *Titus Andronicus*, at the Swan, Stratford-on-Avon, in its second season in 1987. The critics were very positive, able to overlook some weak casting. Wells suggested that Warner's *Titus* "offered no theatrical glamour, none of the allurements of pageantry or of sumptuous costumes with which directors have sometimes sugared what they have obviously regarded as a bitter pill of a play. [Warner's] staging, which seemed based on the most austere interpretation of Elizabethan methods, could have been transferred with little difficulty into a reconstruction of the Globe" (*ShS* 41, 178). The production had "pagentry," at least a kind of processional elegance that, like Nazi ceremonials, formalized brutality. Otherwise, Wells was right to suggest that a very different space can serve a script superbly. The Swan has a long apron that extends some three-quarters of the way into the auditorium. The auditorium itself towers above the stage, which has a high upstage area—a space for balcony scenes, spiral ladders, and all kinds of effects of height, the more effective because the height is real. The comparison between Hall's *Antony and Cleopatra* and Warner's *Titus Andronicus* was according to Wells, a matter of playing the script "exceptionally 'straight' [so that] the director did not appear . . . to be inviting us to see modern parallels in the action, or . . . probing a subtext for psychological resonances" (*ShS* 41, 178–79). Warner stayed with the script and found in it elements that still work for modern audiences. "Warner's approach," Wells said, "revealed the hand of an immensely skillful, even cunning, director. The rhetoric was plumbed for its deep sources, which were then brought to the surface so that even the most artificial verbal structures become expressive of emotion. [Donald Sumpter's speech as Marcus after the rape of Lavinia] represented an articulation, necessarily extended in expression, of a sequence of thoughts and emotions that might have taken no more than a second or two to flash through the character's mind, like a bad dream" (*ShS* 41, 178–79). In other words, Warner worked with the actors to discover the emotional equivalent, or "intention" behind the rhetoric. Dessen provided another clue about how such a speech can work onstage, by asking, "What if that sense of Lavinia as a fountain spouting blood is not what we see but is a product of Marcus's poetic image in conjunction with the imagination of the audience?" (*SQ* [1988]: 223).

In other words, what if we, the audience, have been invited to help make or complete the metaphors in the play's language or in a character's imagination? Shakespeare does that constantly simply by insisting that, for example, "The deep of night has crept upon our talk," when it is still broad daylight, even if the sun has shifted across the Globe stage to slide new shadows across Brutus and Cassius. Warner, like Shakespeare, respects her audience enough to invite them into the participatory mode. Marcus's imagery, as Dessen said, "*can* be theatrically potent if his words do more than merely convey to the audience's ear what their eyes have already seen" (*SQ* [1988]: 223).

Behind the production was its rehearsal period, which was described by Estelle Kohler as a cooperative, exploratory process, as opposed to the rigid, "here is the concept and here is the design" approach that destroys so many scripts before our very eyes, the approach that may, in fairness, be dictated by playing spaces less flexible than the Swan. But Warner's approach emerged from the script, which she trusted to be completed by an audience, which she also trusted.

Breathtaking entrances charged down the long platform atop the last syllable of the previous scene. Kohler's Tamora asserted a convincing sexuality that this role demands (as do other Shakespearean roles that don't get that prone and speechless dialect and that thus fail to convince us that the others onstage are convinced). Her Tamora, said Irving Wardle, was "a sexually invincible monster . . . whose smiling rectangular mouth snaps shut like a rattrap with every fresh stratagem" (*T* 13 May 1987, 21). Thus, Kohler explicated Tamora's rise from chains to throne. Brian Cox's Titus wandered convincingly through a bad dream from which he knew he could not awaken. The production was played at top pitch throughout, even in the "revenge" scene, which is playable as a kind of farce that moderates the tone of a play that is very heavy when played straight. Dessen, however, found that "By allowing or calling forth laughter early in the play, Cox . . . made possible a wide range of effects or reactions later on. The mixture of tones . . . could then be especially telling. . . . shock, irony, and laughter were so intermingled that no 'normal' reactions were possible. The effect was stunning" (*SQ* [1988]: 224–25). H. R. Woudhuysen suggested that "The audience . . . is made to feel that laughter need neither be innocent nor happy" (551). As Warner dealt with it, Wells said, the play "is profoundly concerned with both the personal and the social consequences of violence rather than one that cheaply exploits their theatrical effectiveness" (181). The production should have been televised—as redesigned by a good television director—to be compared and contrasted with Jane Howell's gripping version for BBC. We need two versions of plays like *Titus Andronicus* and *Measure for Measure*, but no one is listening to that request.

A point that can be taken for granted except when one sees inept actors at work was nicely made by Luc Borot, F. Laroque, and J. M. Maguin: "The production makes the most of the sports and physical attainment clues found in the text. . . . The actors make a good job of handling bows and the arrows realistically shot backstage on to the upper level convey Titus's messages to the Goths" (99). This is the kind of realization that only production can bring about. Otherwise the "physical attainment clues" remain stage directions on the page.

Wardle objected to Warner's approach to the audience. He did not agree with her "decision to capitalize on the Swan's design and treat the audience as assembled Romans. . . . When Titus makes his triumphant first entrance he looks decidedly put out when the house fails to rise to its feet in his honour. I think this is a mistake, as it implies a weight of civic maturity which the play does not carry. . . . Set aside the republican framework, and the production makes better sense; as it recognizes that 'character' in the full Shakespearean sense does not exist in this play" (*T* 24 October 1988, 21). The latter statement is true of this script, but it is not certain that the production was trying to create a "republican" rapport with its audience. If anything, the contact between stage and spectator heightened our sense of being helpless within a nightmare, as Cox's Titus was.

The Swan does call attention to relationships between actor and spectator that are unavailable in other spaces, to what Peter Holland calls "the visual consequence for Shakespeare production of theatre architecture" (*TLS* 7 May 1993, 3). The consequences are more than visual. As Holland says: The Swan's "visual dynamic is less the work of the set-designer than of a redefinition of actor-audience relationships outside the established traditions of British theatre. The activity of looking at Shakespeare in the Swan is radically unlike that in any other major theatre in its sense of audience communality, in the possibilities of spectacle and in its closeness of contact between actors and playgoers" (*TLS* 7 May 1993, 3–4). That overstates the case, but it is probably true that the Swan's apron does open up possibilities for actors and directors that they do not believe available in other theaters. Both the Other Place in Stratford-on-Avon and the Donmar Warehouse in London offer some of the advantages of the Swan, though admittedly, those small theaters do not afford the opportunity for spectacle so vividly exploited in performances of *Titus, King John, Dr. Faustus, The Jew of Malta,* and *Tamberlaine,* for example.

Wells commented: "It seemed perverse to give the role of Aaron to an actor who looks Greek instead of the raven-black Moor of the text" (*ShS* 41, 180–81), and this piece of casting represented a major problem. The RSC had good black actors in 1987, as Hakeem KaēKazim demonstrated with his somewhat overacted, and therefore badly directed Morocco in *Merchant*. Woudhuysen said, "What this [*Titus*] most disappointingly lacks is an Aaron who can convey the theatrical glamour of evil, [who can] enjoy the wickedness he should revel in" (551). Kohler agreed, even citing the Peacham illustration of *Titus*, which shows a really black Aaron. We needed that dark, threatening, outlaw energy here—to make an implicit statement about race itself and to give Kohler something to respond to. Even she could not convince us that she was mildly interested in this pale imitation speaking such menacing poems. A play is made up of each moment of its existence on stage, and this production did not exist when Aaron was the focal point.

Stratford's main stage is a difficult space for Shakespeare. Certainly the summer of 1987 seemed to make that point. Still, Terry Hands's 1977 *Henry V*, with Alan Howard, played in that space and that is one of the great productions of our times. Was it the exception? Ten years later the flat, proscenium stage erased the qualities that *Julius Caesar, Twelfth Night,* and *The Merchant of Venice* can offer a director, actors, and audience. The directors and their designers apparently believe that they must design productions for that stage in which actors are mere pawns within a rigidly defined format.

Julius Caesar can work in a small auditorium, as Earl McCarroll demonstrated many years ago at Monmouth, where the orations were to the spectators. The Roman crowd/mob moved from the back of the auditorium during Antony's speech to circle Caesar's corpse and then offstage to do their pillaging and to draw our own aroused energy with it. Cinna followed as a scapegoat to further absorb a response that had resulted from the invasion of our space. It was a remarkable and daring expansion and reintegration of the playing area. People were still very excited by it during the interval, which followed the mob's decision that bad poetry is a capital offense.

The Terry Hands version at Stratford-on-Avon in August 1987 moved rapidly and without interval. It used the entire space of the huge main stage. Hands's emphasis on Caesar made some points, reiterated by a statue of Caesar, which, as Wells said, "dominated the opening scenes" (*ShS* 41, 171), the statue's shadow later, and "the presence of Caesar's reanimated corpse stalking the field of battle" (171–72). Joseph O'Conor's Caesar summoned Cassius from the group of sheeted nobles, delivered the lines about "such men as he" directly to Cassius, and forced Cassius to kneel with an imperious finger. As the conspirators began to exit after a stylized assassination that tried to be ritual as Brutus wishes it to be, they turned to stare at dead Caesar, perhaps feeling his power, as opposed to just his supposed tyranny, for the first time. "What have we done?" The deed would be chronicled in a book Antony would write, not Brutus. Roger Allam, who played Brutus, said that he employed as his subtext for the killing of Caesar a dream he had of killing his father with a knife in an empty swimming pool. It was a fierce motivation that became suspect as soon as it was fulfilled.

The production moved powerfully toward emptiness. The spare

stage did not create, as Wells noted, "a sense of Rome—of a densely populated city whose inhabitants form an important section of the community of characters" (*ShS* 41, 173), those witty plebians of the opening who become the mob that Antony forges. The play does not exist, as *Richard II* tends to, along the single plane of the aristocracy. Hands's production self-destructed at precisely the point where we needed the sense of mob that McCarroll had forced upon us so potently at Monmouth. Both Brutus and Antony delivered their orations down front. The mob's reactions were rendered through loudspeakers at the sides of the auditorium, perhaps an effort to simulate the orchestration of the Nuremberg Party Conference of 1934, right after the "Night of the Long Knives." The curious result of Hands's approach was that Brutus's speech, rhetorical and mechanical, was enhanced by a sound track. He needed no "None, Brutus, none!" (although some people, gnawed by a sense of the script, must have been tempted to provide one).

Unlike Brutus's, Antony's oration asks for and needs the response of flesh and blood, of individual mind becoming mob will. In the National Theatre production of some years ago, which featured Ronald Pickup's splendid Cassius and Gielgud's dominating hook-nosed fellow, the plebians were grouped down left and right below the edge of the stage, so that the audience became the larger group for whom they were a synecdoche. That was a good way to employ the Olivier space, though hardly as powerful as what McCarroll achieved in a space about twenty percent the size of the Olivier. In Hands's 1987 version, Antony's strategically contrived and tactically dictated speech fell flat. It could only be insulted by artificial noise. The unfortunate effect merely emphasized the superiority of Roger Allam as an actor over Nicholas Farrell, who was a weak Antony—"a whining fop" (*CE*, 113), "too drippy even to convince as an innocent in public life" (Hiley *L* 16 April 1987, 47). Mark McManus had also been weak in the National Theatre production in a role that seems to call for power, both physical and vocal, and not much else in Shakespeare's early manifestation of this character. McManus, however, had had a crowd to work with. Farrell did not, and this was not his fault. Hands did not give us a Rome and, clearly, did not intend to. Just as a promising production needed to swell toward its full political dimensions, it shrunk to something like television—"sound of crowd becoming angry in background." The RSC space itself became diminished, shrunk to this little measure. As Dominique Goy-Blanquet said, "The point made . . . by recorded sounds of

cheering and applause . . . that crowds are infinitely gullible, ignores the more disturbing one that something is wrong in the
State which puts such crucial issues to the judgment of the mob.
This treatment reduces the plot to the interplay of the main characters" (414).

It may be that "a set" is demanded by that stage. If so, Bill
Alexander provided one for his *Twelfth Night*. Wells called it "a
jumble of archways, alleys, stairways, windows, and benches, all
glittering white against a permanently blue sky [which] allowed
scenes to flow into one another with easy continuity" (*ShS* 41,
166). The set, however, "sacrificed the sense of two distinct households" (166), which the BBC production achieved so well. Olivia's
was a Tudor manor house—ample, dark, drafty, tapestried, with
Holbeined ancestors hanging in the halls—old money. Orsino's
palace was sheer wealth and the indulgence attendant thereunto,
including a mixed consort providing constant background music
for Orsino's silly fantasies. That production made its point about
distinctions between the upper classes tellingly and thus helped
us place characters like Toby and Malvolio. This is a script, after
all, that poises the status quo against upward mobility. It is as
English a script as *The Merry Wives of Windsor*. Jeremy Kingston
praised the RSC set: "Houses huddle around the corner of a small
town square beneath a sky of cloudless blue. . . . Within each
scene, the white walls take on the appearance of inner courtyard
as readily as street, public place as well as private. . . . This
fixedly urban setting inevitably does away with the distinctions
between Orsino's court [and] Olivia's house" (*T* 8 July 1987, 18).

In contrast to the convincing background of the televised version of the play, Alexander's huge blob of a set, in its need to be
Yugoslavia, introduced a host of extraneous issues that called for
a guidebook rather than a program. Even Wells admitted that
Alexander's "use of the set was over-confining." The eavesdroppers on the Malvolio letter scene were placed "in windows where
they had little freedom of movement. [This placement] upset the
balance of the scene, throwing too much emphasis on Malvolio's
fantasies, too little on the tricksters who had stimulated them"
(*ShS* 41, 166).

Yes, the scene is interactive, and verges on the possibility that
the eavesdroppers will reveal themselves to Malvolio. Furthermore, the fascinating scene between Feste-Tophas and Malvolio
(4.2) was upstaged by Maria and Toby in one of those windows,
playing at foreplay. Apparently, Alexander could make nothing of
the scene as written so he made sure that we couldn't either. Feste

was lost in this haphazard production, having been told, it seems, to stay out of the way of the actors. But if Feste "must observe their mood on whom he jests" and if he is telling us what the likes of Orsino, Olivia, and Toby are ignoring, his function was lost here. He can find no sense of humor in Malvolio in a scene that depicts the limits of "fooling"—as do *Love's Labour's Lost*, and, profoundly, the play which finds Feste lost in a storm, *King Lear*. This production lost any sense of the issue that Wells describes epigramatically: "Feste's wisdom lies in his admission of folly. Malvolio's folly lies in his belief in his own wisdom" (168). A production of this play should make that distinction for the audience.

Instead, the audience was asked to explore the problems of a young, gifted, and unfortunately alcoholic Sir Toby, a late Elizabethan counterpart of F. Scott Fitzgerald. Toby had nothing to do but to bilk David Bradley's wonderfully woebegone Andrew. But this "core concept" could not carry the play. Nor could the Orsino plot, since the casting possibilities had been exhausted by the time Alexander got to Orsino. Donald Sumpter had been a fine Marcus in Warner's *Titus*, indeed had shown us how important the role is when underplayed against the tumult of that script, but one had to wonder in *Twelfth Night* (as too often in productions of this script!) what Viola could see in him. This wizened, senescent character looked like a trader trying to sell a few pieces of pottery on the streets of Dubrovnik. Casting alone made a vacuum of what can be a moving love story. The play, as Wells says, "will not fulfill its true potential unless the balance is right" (165). That means that Malvolio doesn't go mad, as he did here, because "If Malvolio has a tragedy it is not that he goes mad, but that he remains irremediably sane" (Wells, *ShS* 41, 168).

The major problem here, however, was pace. To call the movement Chekhovian is to insult Chekhov. This production dragged its lugubrious length along for three hours. Moments where some relaxation of rhythm might occur were just swallowed up in this giant digestive tract of a set. "I left no ring with her. What means this lady? . . ." is a speech that can get some laughter if an actress like Eileen Atkins (in an Old Vic production of the mid-1970s) shares her awakening to Olivia's infatuation with an audience that knows of it already. We laugh with each other. But not here. Without pace, a production cannot have rhythm. The production seemed intent upon cueing us to its meaning. Sher's Malvolio was badly overplayed. This Malvolio was, according to Jim Hiley, one "of stage-hogging, barn-storming vulgarity, distinguished mainly by its irrelevance to everything his colleagues do" (*L* 16 July 1987, 30). "The effort to be funny was all-too-apparent" (Wells, *ShS* 41, 167), and thus was a paradigm of an uncontrolled production. After Malvolio exited, pumped up by Maria's letter, the conspirators staggered in with mimed laughter that lasted, literally, for minutes. "Stage time" is much shorter than "real time," but here, time itself yawned.

Either the Malvolio bit is funny or it is not. It is not when we get the "actor rather than the revelation of a deeply imagined character" (Wells, *ShS* 41, 167), nor does a silent-film invitation to laughter compensate for what has not worked onstage. The Alexander *Twelfth Night* lacked pace. This production "educated" its audience away from the values and complexities of the script. Alexander provided a built-in laugh track. This production suggested that theater is no longer an alternative to television. It is just more expensive.

In Alexander's *Merchant of Venice*, Sher's Shylock was a Turkish Jew, squatting in front of a tent as camels munched on their dates just out of sight and the "Rugs for Sale: Cheap!" sign hung in the alley. Shylock was not just an alien in Venice. He was alien to the script. Something might have come of this had it not been for Alexander's penchant for introducing action that undercut the lines. Young Gobbo wasn't up to his soliloquy, but the words were erased by the slow, cane-tapping entrance of Daddy Gobbo. As Portia announced her plan to disguise herself—a significant speech in that it reveals her real attitude toward men and may be read as initiating the ring sequence—we watched her servants, down center, packing up the caskets for their trip to the mint. Since they had emerged by means of a quaint device, they could have disappeared with equal facility. Urchins sat on the bridge that sighed irrelevantly above the Trial Scene, one swinging pudgy legs throughout. The scene itself was awful, rising to decibels of frenzy as a knife-whetting Sher engaged in a pagan ritual. "The sheer physicality of Sher's performance is a joy," said Hiley. "But though mimetically and rhetorically effective, it is never for a moment moving" (*L* 14 May 1987, 41). J. Fuzier and J. M. Maguin said that "Sher's performance . . . was very enjoyable, though perhaps lacking somewhat in coherence, wavering between cowardice and cruelty without one being totally sure that this reflected his understanding of the part" (106).

Neither Portia nor Nerissa knew which casket held "fair Portia's counterfeit." Her "Therefore, for fear of the worst, set a deep glass of Rhenish wine on the contrary casket" was just a little joke, not a hint that she would interfere with her father's will. While Deborah Findlay (Portia) explained that her ignorance heightened her own suspense, her tension would be greater were she to watch each suitor pause to consider lead, knowing that it is not the contrary casket. Of course, the problem gradually resolves itself so that by the time Bassanio arrives, Portia knows which is which if she's been paying attention. Findlay's Portia was young, schoolgirlish, convincing neither as lawyer nor as manipulative wife, and real only in her racism. John Carlisle's Antonio was convincing only in his homosexual desire for Nicholas Farrell's Bassanio. This Antonio "continued to offer his body to the knife even after Shylock's defeat" (Wells, *ShS* 41, 165), preferring self-imposed execution to the loss of Bassanio.

Alexander showed us a violent and excessive world peopled by characters who had no wish to explore the issues that drove them to a consistent frenzy. But to show that violence without exploring its causes, as Alexander did, was not to "achieve . . . contemporary relevance" (Wells, *ShS* 41, 162). It was to be contemporary and irrelevant.

An escape from the murky values of weak productions to London's Regent's Park is a movement back in time, to the daylight in which Shakespeare's plays were performed. Here, the acting space merges with real trees, with real birds flicking across the stage, an occasional neighborhood hound poking out from the bushes, real rain at times, and jumbo jets grinding through the sky to Heathrow (something Shakespeare did not have to cope with). The Outdoor Theatre at Regent's Park attracts children to its audiences, a fact that makes the plays even more enjoyable for adults, who can enjoy their own responses and those of the younger people around them. That represents another movement back in time. The space is communal, particularly in the afternoon under the natural lighting, and includes the generations within its community.

Simon Higlett's set for Caroline Smith's 1987 *A Midsummer Night's Dream* permitted entrances and exits from the sides of the stage and from several levels. The effect was not so much simultaniety but a weaving together of the multiple strands of this brief but complex script that provided remarkable visual and thematic cohesion. The play made sense in inverse proportion to the confusion of its characters. The clarity was at least partly a function of pace. The play explained itself as it went along and before we had a chance to withdraw our own involvement in the production.

Smith had the ducal audience assemble on the ramp behind the stalls and in front of the second deck of the ampitheater. Those within the stalls became part of an audience and could turn and smile at their Duke and his Amazon as all watched the splendid ineptitude of Quince & Company. Watching an audience watch a play is basic to "Gonzago" in *Hamlet*. Seeing a portion of an audience defeat and be defeated by a play is part of our enjoyment of *Love's Labour's Lost*. The metatheatrics can be difficult in *Dream*, however, particularly since the ducal audience verges on insensitivity. Here, we were given a license to enjoy "Pyramus and Thisbe," and, if our mocking came home to us, it was because we had chosen to attend a play in which our Duke had chosen to "hear" a play and become an actor too. Here, the Duke had come out to include us within his space. Space itself spread down to the stage and upward and outward, as it had for Shakespeare's audience. The outdoor setting kept us constantly aware of the "sympathetic magic" that was one of the sources of ancient drama and of plays that, even today, can call gods down from the sky to entertain us and then take their bows.

4

Directors' Decisions: 1989

THE 1989 season in Great Britain proved that the director, in conjunction with the designer, can control what occurs within the inherited acting space, whether the latter is a fixed or a flexible zone. The summer of 1989 featured two superb productions—Travor Nunn's *Othello*, with which I have dealt in *Performance as Interpretation* and *Watching Shakespeare on Television*, and Ron Daniels's *Hamlet*, with Mark Rylance. Although each production appeared in a different space—*Hamlet* on the Stratford main stage and *Othello* as the final production of the "old" Other Place—each was marked by the director's decision to make it possible for good actors to *act*. The same could be said of the other big production of that remarkable summer, Peter Hall's *The Merchant of Venice*, with Dustin Hoffman as Shylock. That this chapter concentrates on acting is a tribute to the directors who, with their designers, created areas where the actors could develop their roles and relationships with the support of concept and not in spite of it. Other directors tended to impose their concepts upon the scripts and thus to smother the efforts of their actors. One ironic exception to any generalization was John Caird's *A Midsummer Night's Dream*, in which the actors prowled and howled, free of any directorial leash.

Adrian Noble's *The Plantagenets* at the Barbican picked up one of the mannerisms of the season and produced enough smoke to make one wish that Justice Holmes had not prohibited the shouting of "Fire!" in a crowded theater. It was, according to the blurbs, "One of the finest things the RSC has done in years" (*Guardian*). "The RSC has once again shaken hands with greatness" (*Sunday Times*). If so, greatness was saying goodbye. The effort to fuse four episodic plays into three coherent sequences—*Henry VI*, *Edward IV*, and *Richard III*—remains worthwhile. The failure of this effort could not be attributed to the space, nor to the imposition of "concept" upon the production. According to Robert Smallwood,

"The long rehearsal created the possibility, almost unknown in Stratford's main house, for designs to evolve through rehearsals rather than to have been decided and modeled before the first read-through" (*SQ* [40]: 89). In the early seventies, Noble "sought an arena [for these plays] rather than a theatre, and designed three leather-bound, overlapping angular stages; an angry, epic space—thrilling to look at, impossible to act upon. . . . though the great public scenes might relish such a space, the narrative proceeds through very precise and delicate political maneuvers, not at all suited to such Wagnerian proportions" (*Plantagenets*, vii).

The problem lay not in the space but in the telling of the story. The production gutted what Noble calls "the best of the three" *Henry* plays (xii), Part Two. The RSC blurb told us that "each play tells a story that can be enjoyed on its own." That is true, but what were we to make of the Margaret-Suffolk story? Neither Penny Downie nor Oliver Cotton had the conviction that Helen Mirren and Peter McEnery brought to the roles in the memorable Terry Hands revival of the *First Henriad* in 1977 or that Paul Chapman and Julia Foster provided in Jane Howell's superb television version. But Cotton was robbed of the wonderful scene (4.1) in which Suffolk dies by "Walter". Noble's introduction claims that "the play was extended to include the banishment and death of Suffolk in order to provide a more 'resolved' sensation" (xiv), but the scene with Suffolk's death, if ever included, had been dropped by the time the sequence reached London. Downie was left to blunder into Beaufort's bedroom with a bloody head under her arm. As Alan Dessen said, "the playgoer has no clue as to how [Suffolk] died" (*SQ* [41]: 363)—that is, except for the inaccurate program note that claims he is "murdered aboard ship as he leaves England." The next play in this sequence was *Edward IV*, in which Henry's line to Margaret, "still lamenting Suffolk's death" appeared, although the head by this time had disappeared. Margaret might as well have been grieving over Golden Grove's unleaving. The actors were denied crucial portions of the story they were trying to tell. As Dessen remarked, "the script often short-circuited the characters, and some of the actors were not strong enough to overcome such hurdles, so that I was left with the impression of many dead spots and an inconsistent overall effect that was less than the sum of its parts" (*SQ* [41]: 365).

What was the editing principle here? The "haughty French lady versus the jealous English lady" story is harmed if the "Fan Episode" (*2 Henry VI*, 1.3.136–45) is cut, as it was here. The seemingly endless pattern of deception and its discovery is reinforced by the splendid Horner-Thump trial-by-combat scene, which was cut here. Lord Say's eloquent defense and the kissing of the severed heads of Say and Cromer were gone, as was Somerset's death—although the prophecy was there, as was the one regarding Suffolk. What were we to make of the web of predictions—one of the structuring principles of these plays if the results of the prophecies were cut? Lines like "set the murderous Machiavel to school," "I am too childish-foolish for this world," and "Yet touch this sparingly, as 'twere far off, / Because, my lord, you know my mother lives," were gone. Yet the entire mawkish sequence as King Henry mourns on a molehill and watches, and moralizes the tedious allegory of civil war was retained.

Noble's filleting was simply butchery that destroyed the rhythms surfacing and submerging and surfacing again in this sequence. La Pucelle was permitted to be a witch here, and the Jourdain-Bolingbroke scene was retained. But all references to Jane Shore were cut; thus, an emphasis on witchcraft that Richard Gloucester craftily exploits was gone. Having established a unifying concept, Noble dropped it just when it might have begun to pay off. He punished those who tried to make sense of the mangled script he delivered. It was not "a vivid, enthralling story of the brutal struggle for the English crown" (*Plantagenets* jacket) but an incoherent sequence of episodes that could work for an uninitiated spectator only as an image, as opposed to an allegory, of the modern political "process." But Shakespeare is superfluous to that purpose. "What emerges," said Jim Hiley, "is an extravagant, almost camp epic" (*L* 3 November 1988, 38–39. But see his more positive reaction to the production in London (13 April 1989, 37). The "impression," said Wardle, is "of rootless flux" (*T* 24 October 1988, 21), while Jeremy Kingston said that "the themes remain absorbing for the duration of only about a play and a half [and] the dynamism . . . of the production as a whole [has] spent [itself] by the end of the middle play, making *Richard III* a curious anti-climax" (*T* 3 April 1989, 15). Mere reiterated spectacle without human and thematic elements linking the big scenes together gets overpowering after awhile. Mere drums, flags, and smoke get dull. As Dessen suggested, one reason these productions failed to provide an effective rhythm was that Noble's "compression [meant] that a high percentage of the violence in Shakespeare's Parts Two and Three is concentrated in the ninety-minute segment that begins play two" (*SQ* [41]: 364). The production reinforced the myth of the apprentice playwright learning his craft. Shakespeare as delivered by Noble showed little promise for any further career in the theater.

Many who saw Anton Lesser in Terry Hands's production of *Henry VI* in 1977 felt that Lesser had a long way to go before he could take on Richard III. His Gloucester of the late 1970s was bustling, ironic, and self-amused, and his Richard twelve years later was little more. He did well, however, in mocking a scarce-awake Anne, telling her that he "must be married to Edward's daughter, Elizabeth, / Else my kingdom stands on brittle glass." He delivered the opening lines of his "winter of our discontent" soliloquy while standing on Edward's throne, much of the speech to his Yorkist audience, but some of it—the reiterated emphasis on his deformity—delivered in chilling asides to us. He lifted the lid on the platter that held Hasting's head to terrify the Lord Mayor in 3.7. The naked threat powerfully refuted the "official" piety and patriotism of Richard's words. These effective moments aside, Lesser lacked the substance the role demands. He was, as Wardle said, "still the homicidally joking boy" and failed "to make the transition to kingship" (*T* 25 November 1989, 41). He was, however, subject to the story, at once rushed and abbreviated, that Noble was telling.

The good moments in this production (others are detailed in Smallwood's extensive review) were not enough to keep it from being a gawdy extravaganza hiding its little force behind a smoke screen. Hands's production of 1977 had its mannerisms, as well as a use of spotlights that made it often seem like an inverted air raid, but it had Mirren, McEnery, Alan Howard, Emrys James, et al., and the energy Hands brought to his productions in the 1970s. Those plays also had the inestimable advantage of being the first experience of these scripts in production that many of the audience had had, if we exclude John Barton's fascinating exercise in televised Shakespeare in his "Wars of the Roses."

Ralph Fiennes pressed a sensitive Henry VI through the general uproar, "the first I have seen," said Wardle, "who communicates the sense of a real moral alternative to his faction-riven court without sacrificing the character's gentleness. He has moments of spectacular strength and his political irrelevance and unresisting death are not those of an ineffectual weakling" (*T* 25 November 1989, 41). He "alone sees that all must be losers in this wasteful war," said Dominique Goy-Blanquet (*CE*, 98).

Most of the actors in Noble's productions were shrouded under flashy flags or the absolute billow of clouds, and the productions achieved the rare feat of punishing those who know the scripts and bewildering those who do not. As Smallwood said, "the effect . . . is to give a sense of helter-skelter scurrying from battle to battle, of derision at the hasty fallings-out and side-changings, of wonder at the futility, the brutality, and absurdity of all the war-making" (*SQ* [40]: 92). Smallwood missed the "grandly elegiac quality" that these plays provide "in moments of eloquently wrought theatre" (*SQ* [40]: 92)—that is the "changes of pace" that Shakespeare, even in his so-called apprenticeship, works into the drive of his plays. We got drive all right, but these productions often drove right past the "story" being told. It remained latent, imbedded in the script, awaiting another production. When will a director do just *The Second Part of Henry VI*, and let that wonderful play stand on its own?

As Goy-Blanquet said, "no significant sequence emerges from the pathos and savagery of each individual scene [of *The Plantagenets*]. After the excitement of the early stages, the pace slackens, the invention flags, and the cycle ends with a rather conventional *Richard III*, which gains little from what took place before. . . . where Shakespeare gave form and meaning to fairly shapeless stuff, the method applied here takes us one step back towards loose chronicle form . . . most of the emblematic scenes have gone, and much of the history of a nation with them" (*CE*, 95–96).

John Caird's *A Midsummer Night's Dream* was Stratford's big hit in 1987. According to *The Daily Express*, it "deserves to win every major drama award in sight" (RSC Poster). Smallwood said, "it was, certainly, a brilliant piece of theatre, exuberant, exhilarating. . . . A reviewer who failed to respond to that joy must be out of step with theatre audiences, a curmudgeon who ought to give up the trade" (*SQ* [41]: 108). Perhaps, but is a reviewer's job to be "in step" with theater audiences? It is, of course, possible to claim, while marching along, that one is the only one in step.

Jim Hiley mentioned the "*Cats*-style banalities" of this production, and suggested that "the aim seems to be 'accessibility,' but the effect on audiences could well be off-putting" (*L* 27 April 1989, 31). Dominique Goy-Blanquet claimed that "the brilliant central idea of John Caird's production is to create unity from a mixture of styles" (*TLS* April 1989, 424). Perhaps, but the contrast of styles that the play creates will work only if each style works within itself, so that Bottom's and Quince's misunderstanding of what drama is reflects back on what drama has been until the burlesque of "Pyramus and Thisbe." Smallwood, for example, suggested that the young lovers invited us "to watch a display of palpably pretended emotions, of funny acting, to perceive the gap between player and role as clearly as we perceive it in . . . 'Pyramus and Thisbe'" (*SQ* [41]: 108). P. J. S. said that "the four lovers are more at home in the pages of children's adventure literature than in the emotional and sexual confusions of Shakespeare's play. . . . Their elopement from the threat of paternal rage and their nightmarish argument and mutual discord are occluded by a ready and easy comedy. . . . [Some of it] seems calculated only to get laughs" (*CE*, 109–10). Smallwood suggests that the overall play "explores . . . our theatrical self-consciousness . . . in different ratios, not in one homogenized lump" (*SQ* [41]: 108). The young lovers "are much funnier," he argues, "if *they* don't know they're funny" [his emphasis]. Otherwise, "the laughter is cheapened and something of the heart goes out of the play" (*SQ* [41]: 109). The young lovers were *unfunny* precisely because of their conscious effort to be comedians. This was particularly true of the Helena, surely one of the great feminine roles in the canon. Stanley Wells suggested the options the young lovers presented to the audience: they were "constantly subjected to parody and caricature in a manner that you find hilariously funny if you regarded them as no more than puppets, or wearisomely effortful if you thought of them as human beings" (*ShS* 43, 201). What is funny about them in the script is that they try to behave "normally," finding reasons for actions ("She hath urged her height") within a context controlled by external agency. They are responding as characters, not stereotypes, within farce. If they are merely controlled by the director, as here, and not allowed to work within the area between what they think they know and "the truth," then they are, indeed, "wearisomely effortful." Wells came down on the positive side, calling the production "brilliantly clever" (*ShS* 43, 200). P. J. S. said, however, that "Theseus had taken 'Pyramus and Thisbe' with the same amount of seriousness as that with which John Caird had taken the *Dream* itself" (*CE*, 111).

The actors were not crushed by the director's overreaching here, as in so many concept productions. Instead, Caird let the actors do their thing, often more than once, so that we, the tourists, did not miss anything. Consequently, this short script yawned on for over three hours. By the time Thisbe said, "She stabs herself," speaking cues and all, the play-within had become interminable. Every sight gag had been twice done and then done double. The playlet alone could have been cut by fifteen minutes. The *Financial Times* critic was left hugging himself with pleasure (13 April 1989, 29). As P. J. S. said, "Popularising Shakespeare doesn't have to mean vulgarizing the plays . . . but this *Dream* is in real danger of losing sight of the complexities of this sublime script and patronising its audience. It refuses, point blank, to stretch its audience and gives them instead a 'simplified' . . . version of the play" (*CE*, 109).

The RSC *Dream* was hailed as "a glorious, warm-hearted, intelligent and unforgettable production" (*ST* 16 April 1989, C-9), and was compared with Peter Brook's famous version of 1970 (Smallwood, *SQ* [41]: 108). However, it was not as good as the Regent's Park version, which, in turn, was not nearly as good as other productions of *Dream* there, in what seems that script's natural habitat. Guy Slater put the Regent's Park play in the 1960s, as if Nixon and Johnson, tear gas and jungle, were easily erased with a little help from our friends. But for all of that, the production moved. Space was reserved for the actors, not for the collection of gears, cellos, and old bicycles that Sue Blane had piled on top of the RSC set for what one assumed was the fairy junkyard. The RSC's Theseus (John Carlisle) and Hippolyta (Claire Higgins) were angry at each other at the outset, in what we inferred was residual enmity after their war. At Regent's Park, Brigitte Kahn got mad when David Henry sentenced Hermia. While Higgins's Hippolyta mitigated Hermia's sentence and forced Theseus to overrule Egeus in 4.1, it was hard to tell whether any reconciliation actually occurred between them. Kahn and Henry established a clearer line, perhaps because they did not have to double as Queen and King of Fairies, as in Brook and Caird. That made a point in Caird, when Bottom seemed to recognize Hippolyta at the end, but the non-doubling of roles at Regent's Park permitted Sally Dexter's Titania to be herself, and not someone's "dream person" or unconscious. This autonomous Titania was very menacing. Her quarrel with Oberon in 2.1 seemed to have the cosmic resonance she claimed for it. One looked briefly, but apprehensively, at the skies above the Park.

Each production had a superb Puck. RSC's Bill McCabe moved with antic energy and trembled with malice. As Smallwood said, he captured "the frightening emotional emptiness of his lost boy's world" (*SQ* [41]: 109). But he made the rest of the production look like the slow-motion it was. Regent Park's Trevor Laird was a young Jack Johnson—coal-black, superior, and mocking. A creature of the shadows, this Puck was deathly afraid of light. He told us something of the dark incoherency back there in Fairy Land or, like Ariel, of a freedom from our "natural laws" that we mortals will never grasp. The characterization alone said that "something" was out there, just behind the illuminated space within which Puck spoke words that we could understand, some place where words that *we* use would be just unintelligible sound. Paul Fisher attributed Puck's response to his being "scared of his dealer's power to summon 'damned spirits'" (G 1 June 1989, 24). The program quoted Timothy Leary on our willingness in the 1960s "to make asses of ourselves," so the dealer analogy was there, but to see only the analogy is to be simplistic—to give an answer to a question that the production was still asking regardless of the "translation" that the sixties provided. Fisher was right, then, to suggest that the production "underlies a standard view of the sixties which has it that a price was paid for the good times, that what seemed insights then are vapid now" (G 1 June 1989, 24). The production did not stop short of the easy answers that the sixties seemed to provide, but rather used the script to qualify and challenge the times in which the script was set. And, the production moved. Regent Park's "Pyramus and Thisbe" engaged in a lot of business, but it consumed about a third of the running time of the RSC version, which was tedious precisely because it was not brief.

Cymbeline has to be one of Shakespeare's most difficult scripts, although Bill Alexander did it wonderfully at The Other Place in 1987 and the Arena's production in Washington years ago was excellent—regardless of what the reviewers said about it. In that production, the god did not descend from above. Rather, nature bubbled up from below—as Cordelia suggests in that other play where the King does not achieve his insights *as* king—to touch all valid human activity with an aura of benediction. Alexander's effort to translate the script to Stratford's main stage failed with remarkable utterness. Musical interludes covered the set changes, so that dramatic continuity was lost. A slouching David O'Hara played Posthumus with an incomprehensible Scots accent, either making a political statement that the play will not support or engaging in a piece of self-indulgence that the director did not correct. Shakespeare makes distinctions between regional dialects in *Henry V* and *The Merry Wives of Windsor*, and between class accents, as when Tranio is permitted to move upstairs in *The Taming of the Shrew*, but O'Hara not only ruined the evening, he sabotaged Naomi Wirthner's Imogen. She was fine as Fidele, when Paul Webster's Belarius gave her something to work with, but O'Hara's Posthumus gave her nothing. That Posthumus is characterized as very self-indulgent does not excuse the actor playing the role. O'Hara seemed, said Wells, "reluctant to adapt [his 'highly idiosyncratic stage presence'] to the role: he tends to stare fixedly at the person he is addressing; he slouches in a somewhat simian stance; he wears his own hair, and his long dark locks fall over his face, so that he constantly has to shake them back" (ShS 43, 190). Those who do not know the argument may well have been rooting for David Troughton's amusing clod of a Cloten, "deeply stupid," as Smallwood suggested, "yet faintly aware of it, which gave him just a touch of pathos" (SQ [41:1]: 104). This "Posthumus," said Wells, "had less charm even than David Troughton's portrayal of his brutal alter ego" (ShS 43, 190). While Posthumus is not one of the charmers in the canon, he is not usually lower on the charm scale than Cloten. The values of the production were strangely skewed by this inversion of "normal" responses to a comic hero who must grow up and a character beneath the reach of any positive process.

Alexander squandered the vastness of his stage. "If a sense of greater grandeur [than in his Other Place production] was the aim, the half-cylindrical metallic walls, enclosing a prison-like space with a well to fall down near its center . . . was distinctly claustrophobic" (Smallwood, SQ [41:1]: 103). The "misjudgment of scale," Wells suggested, "was reflected in the acting, in which very different styles co-existed uneasily together" (ShS 43, 190). But, with all the corkscrewing from the cellarage, Jupiter should have been worth waiting for. The visitation of the greatest of the gods would finally fill that space! Instead, Alexander had two shadowy figures come in and drop something on Posthumus's chest. He woke up and read whatever it was. What he spoke was Greek to the audience, which could not even say, "Nay, this was but his dream!" We could only be "baffled at the provenance of the prophetic disc left on the sleeping body of Posthumus" (Smallwood, SQ [41:1]: 104). We could not tell that a god had communicated with him—and with us. It should be our dream, too, one that presages peace and reconciliation, one that the final scene makes available to the other characters, as Cymbeline is free to be a Lear who has learned his lesson and still be king. That final scene, which we see too seldom, should fuse "emotional extremes" and evoke "visionary exaltation," as Wells says (ShS 43, 191), but could not work here. Most productions teach us something about the script. Alexander and O'Hara conspired to rob us of the play itself.

Alan Dessen asked why the great god Jupiter had been exiled from the skies of this Cymbeline. It seems that "Alexander started with a full script that, as it turned out, ran excessively long (one estimate given me was five hours). . . . Finally, during the previews, *all* of the lines in the sequence were eliminated. The father and mother of Posthumus were still included (and are credited in the program) but now had no lines, so all they did was enter, deposit the tablet on their son's chest, and depart. Like many last-minute compromises, the director's decision satisfied no one [but rather] mystified many playgoers, especially given the murky rendition of the subsequent wake-up speech by [O'Hara] (one waggish reviewer referred to the couple as two well-dressed prison visitors)" (*SQ* [Fall 1990]: 353). And, as Dressen points out, "the daunting final scene of this romance cannot be fully realized without this vision" (*SQ* [Fall 1990]: 353). Had Alexander not directed the play previously in an admittedly very different space, his problems with the script might have been partially excusable. As it is, anyone going to the production would have been convinced that *Cymbeline* is a lousy play, or one that "doesn't work" on stage, or both. Having seen a splendid version of the script years ago at the Arena in Washington, I know that the play is eminently playable. But for those who saw Alexander's main stage effort at Stratford-on-Avon, *Cymbeline* becomes just another play to cross off your list.

In John Dodber's Hull Truck *Twelfth Night* at the Donmar Warehouse, Malvolio recovered from Sher's madness to become, in William Ikley's interpretation, "a faceless, middle-management bureaucrat [not] particularly excessive in either prudery or folly" (Berkowitz, *SB* 35). But Berkowitz goes on, "the more complex characterizations were almost worth the loss" (*SB* 35). The "normalization" of Malvolio meant that the script could be updated to a time when the term "upward mobility" would not be grotesque but a widely accepted part of the term "yuppie." The more human aspirations of Olivia and Viola became more attractive against this conception of Malvolio. The setting was the courtyard of a university—a place for casual meetings, the wasting of time, eavesdropping, and "learning." The contemporary placement meant that Meriel Scholfield's Viola could emerge boyishly from a unisex catalog, yet, always verging on her wish to be a woman outright. She was at once winsome and poignant. Martin Ronan, on the other hand, was a melancholy Sir Andrew, forever looking back to the one time he had been "ador'd." And Paul Rider's Feste could sing! Why do directors not recognize that Feste's songs can lend richness to the play's dramatic texture?—perhaps because most lyrics these days are just part of the general cacophony.

Bernard Breeslaw's Malvolio, in Ian Talbot's *Twelfth Night* at Regent's Park, enlisted the audience in his upward mobility and thus created pressure against his enemies within the script. He smiled and shook his head at us when he refused to "Revolve." Since Breeslaw must be six-and-a-half-feet tall, his humiliation was potent. He was kept at the bottom of a well and emerged so muddy and bent that the audience gasped. In the recent Prospect Theatre production, Richard Briers was, literally, entombed. He emerged broken, and howled (like Olivier's Shylock) at the end. Although his vow to exact revenge was empty, his destruction certainly challenged the festive ending. Breeslaw had not been broken. His vow was to be taken seriously. Both Briers and Breeslaw shadowed the reunion and marriages. Sher did not, having become the madman the madhouse had made him, as, in another way, Alec McCowen did not in the BBC version. He had learned nothing and was still cocksure and angry, one of the self-excluded characters Shakespeare uses as a "control" within his comic world.

Our sense of *genre* hinges on what a director makes of Malvolio. Breeslaw believed his dream and forced us, the Nick Carraways, to believe it, too. However meretricious, it was huge. Part of us exited with Breeslaw's Malvolio as the others retreated behind their wealth. This Malvolio did not make the play unbalanced, as Sher had done, but he did make *Twelfth Night* a different play than it is when we are asked to associate with the aristocrats. One of the splendid touches Breeslaw gave his performance was that Malvolio studied the speech of his betters and mimicked it convincingly. But when he got excited, his words swung toward their Bow Bells origins. Robert O'Brien said that "a certain campness in the voice . . . prevented him from being a more dignified and forbidding figure" (*P&P*, 31), but it was because the voice was an "imitation" that we could feel the pathos beneath the reach for dignity.

A more recent *Twelfth Night*, Steve McConnell's for the Merrimack Repertory Theatre in Lowell, Massachusetts, had Will LeBow's fine Malvolio laughing with the others at the end and pointing at the letter which had suddenly translated into a final and ultimate humiliation. Warren Mitchell used the same approach during his "Hath not a Jew eyes?" speech in the BBC version of *The Merchant of Venice*. Having lulled the others—and possibly the audience—into the notion that he shared the joke,

LeBow suddenly shouted "I'll be revenged on the whole pack of you!" All chuckles stopped together, and the sky darkened. Was the coming rain a footnote to Malvolio's rage or just that it "raineth every day," as Feste soon tells us? Malvolio exited upstage center—the place where power comes from. Was history backstage grooming its Cromwell? No, but this Malvolio had been punished beyond his desserts. We were at least ashamed of what those Republicans had done to him. LeBow had not turned *Twelfth Night* into a tragedy but he had, literally, dampened the comedy.

How one responds to *The Merchant of Venice* indicates how one might respond to anti-semitism. This theme may be a more powerful force in the script if, instead of being tossed at the audience like a grenade, as in the Alexander-Sher version, it is underplayed, as in the Hall production. "Hall," as Jim Hiley said, "seems content to let the [play's] anti-semitism speak for itself." (*L* 15 June 1989, 34). "This production," said Irene Dash, "stressing individual characterization and avoiding shortcuts—the heavy beard, the strong accent, the hooked nose . . . revitalizes the text" (*SB*, 11).

In his role as Shylock at the Phoenix Theatre—an elegant old West End house—Dustin Hoffman did Shakespeare for the first time at 51. This says something very bad about the training and background of American actors, but something very good about Hoffman. At this point in his career, he did not have to be going through the grind of eight live performances a week.

This was a well-balanced production—the same set, columns, and archways were changed only by lighting. The set, Stanley Wells suggested, "had something in common with the Victorian pictorial tradition" (*ShS* 43, 186). The use of the same set suggested that Venice and Belmont both center around money and its attainment. In Venice, money is made in commerce. In Belmont, money is to be made by understanding clichés, as in "Wheel of Fortune." Belmont is an Elizabethan version of the game show.

Jim Hiley did not accept the metaphor the set was making by itself and said that "Hall takes no perceptible line on the reiterated theme of money" and that "Shakespeare's critique of [the character's] confusion of love with riches [is] obscure" (*L* 15 June 1989, 34). Hall played up the casket sequences, giving Morocco, Arragon, and Bassanio the entrances of princes—Magi coming to worship at the Shrine of the Golden Fleece, with music, attendants, and gifts. Clearly, Bassanio had bought his status by blowing his entire loan. "All Portia's suitors," Martin Dodsworth said, "are accompanied by masked servitors: their masks stand for what the characters cannot reveal of themselves" (*TLS* June 1989, 666). Jeffrey Kisson's Morocco was a brother to, not a parody of, Othello, and impressed Geraldine James's powerful, Pre-Raphaelite Portia. Alexander's Morocco, Hakeem Kae-Kazin, had been "grossly sent up," as Hiley said, "complete with martial arts gesticulations and staring eyes" (*L* 14 May 1987, 41), in a caricature typical of that production. Here, "complexion" meant temperament, and her "gentle riddance" resulted from his idealization of her. She wants to get *off* that damned pedestal! (James apparently does see "complexion" as meaning skin pigmentation, so she is credited here with an extremely subtle performance: cf. *NYT* 2 Jan. 1990, C13 and C17). The lights dropped as the first two suitors made the wrong choices, and they slunk out, in contrast to their bombastic entrances. Veiled women, strange Belmont votresses, replaced the caskets. The veils came off when Bassanio chose aright, his choice having freed Belmont from its chaste spell, as in the tales from which the Belmont story emerges. Having surrendered to Bassanio, this Portia determined at once to deploy the potency so long entombed in lead and to get the power back that she had ceded in matrimony.

Nathaniel Parker's callow Bassanio was no match for James's Portia. Her move from imprisoned princess to militant feminist was precisely charted and chilling. This approach was in marked contrast to Deborah Findlay's Portia in the Alexander version, a more obvious racist who "cuffs her negro servant with a relish which looks customary . . . keeps a polite but distinguishing distance from Lorenzo's new bride [is] all . . . elegant curls, flounced dresses and milky looks [who] never really wanted to be out of [her] bodice . . . at all" (Pitcher, 518). In other words, she *was* the cliché the men make of her. And it is not a "wrong" interpretation to make Bassanio and Portia, finally, just empty jet-setters, but it is not as interesting as having Portia "a country heiress with wits [who] recognizes a threat when she sees one . . . What she lacks," said Wardle, "is the slightest trace of humor; so that the ring episode changes from a mischievous game into a test of marital status, conducted in arrogant discourtesy to the embarrassed Antonio" (*T* 2 June 1989, 14). Sir Peter would claim that it is hard to read the script otherwise. This Portia "embarrasses . . . Antonio [and] brings home to Bassanio the meaning of his changed status as married man. Portia can honestly forgive Antonio because she knows he has understood where, in relation to her, he must in future stand" (Dodsworth, *TLS* June 1989, 666). And that is a lesson that the friends of men who get married must always learn, made "modern" here just by playing the script with that emphasis. "The future looks settled," said John Peter of this ending, "but not necessarily benign" (*ST* 4 June 1989, C-9). Says James of Portia, "She's a very spoiled rich girl who grows up in a world full of the most appalling prejudices . . . the people who talk most easily about mercy are the people who do not hand it out." Yet, she says, even though Portia is "infuriating . . . she's so honest. I think of integrity as one of her overwhelming characteristics" (*NYT* 2 Jan. 1990, C13). James's Portia was rigorously true to herself, a conception that sent some scary reverberations out from the limited but all-powerful frame of her intelligence.

In the fine RSC studio version of the late 1970s, with Patrick Stewart as Shylock, Antonio "placed" himself by becoming Bassanio's best man *and* Portia's "father," putting her hand in Bassanio's, ceding any "right" to him to Portia, but also establishing his new relationship to the newly married couple.

Hall's Belmont sequences were lavish, his Venetian scenes muted, so much so that William A. Henry could say that "Hall's . . . reading [of] the play is more comedy than tragedy and focuses more on Portia . . . than on Shylock" (*Time* 3 July 1989, 73), a point on which Michael Billington agreed (*G* 11 June 1989, 26). Hoffman's Shylock was quiet and misunderstood, and held his resentment in with a force we recognized only in the trial scene when "in a gesture which brilliantly cost him all of the audience sympathy, he spits . . . into the face of the kneeling Antonio" (P. J. S., *CE* 40, 94). "His Shylock is tough, shifty, and unpleasantly resilient: an unattractive operator . . . superbly contained . . . direct, circumspect, spare of gesture and relaxed; and we only realize how much effort this must have cost him when he almost leaps on Antonio in the trial scene and rips his shirt off" (Peter, *ST* 4 June 1989). The "message," said Clement Freud, "is that when people are treated badly, you cannot—when they have the upper hand—expect them to behave well . . . when [Hoffman's Shylock] loses he does so like one who is used to defeat" (14). A loving father to Jessica, even while aware of their mutual loneliness, a vulnerable man who could exploit others' vulnerabilities, this Shylock was human (unlike Sher's), yet did not necessarily ask that we sympathize with him. Hall gave Hoffman the privileged down-right position when Shylock considered the loss of the ring Leah had given him. "Much his most expressive scene," said Irving Wardle, "is with Leon Lissek's Tubal, where he lets the verse relax into down-to-earth conversational exchanges, very low key, and then performs the huge emotional reversals between despair and exultation with the deliberation and force of a giant pendulum" (*T* 2 June 1989, 14). Wells agreed: "He was at his best in the scene with Tubal, where his quick alternations of mood created a complex comedy" (*ShS* 43, 188). "Hath not a Jew eyes" was no liberal manifesto. It was a periodic buildup to "revenge," which Hoffman understood perfectly. Shylock's grief over the loss of jewels and ducats was a defense against the deeper loss of his daughter. An index of his isolation was that the Tubal he had embraced sorrowfully in 3.1 doubled as one of the judges who glared at him without pity in 4.1. Clement Freud suggested that "Hoffman . . . overwhelmed with his modesty. . . . The final curtain was an organizational triumph in which, by sleight of hand and visual trickery, Hoffman inveigled the audience into giving Geraldine James a louder ovation than he received" (14).

Shylock was an inadequate parent, but his affection for Jessica made her statements about life with Shylock a hyperbolic rationalization for running off with a fortune hunter. Lorenzo was a minor-league Bassanio whose "Beshrow me, but I love her heartily!" was delivered as he examined the treasure she had tossed from the window. If Jessica is this shallow, her speech in 3.2 ("I have heard him swear. . . .") may be an effort to ingratiate herself with her new set. Jonathan Miller cut the speech in his 1974 production to make her elopement the motive for Olivier's revenge. But the speech should say something about her and, possibly, about Shylock as well. Certainly it has to be interpreted in light of the relationship she and Shylock have established in the production. Here it was delivered "straight" apparently because it is in the script. Jessica and Lorenzo were quarreling in Act V of Hall's production. Was this Jessica, as in Miller's version, mourning her too-easily-discarded heritage? Had she begun to see through the "meretricious world to which she has fled so eagerly"?—as Kliman suggested (12). Is she perhaps the only character who "show[s] more than a passing concern with Shylock's fate"?—as Michael Ratcliffe suggested (*O* 4 June 1989, 44). The production did not explore her character so that we could understand it. Irene Dash saw her as a "'Jewish Princess' [who] has known neither Christian hardness nor discrimination but has lived in a protected world" (10). If that reading is correct, then Jessica is one with the rejected princes, another suitor to a world for which she cannot discover the magic words that open doors.

The critics made much of Hoffman's size. "He is notoriously not tall," as Dodsworth said, "a point of capital importance [when he is] seen alongside a boisterous Bassanio and a hulking Antonio" (*TLS* June 1989, 666). "The tiny frame of Dustin Hoffman is continually surrounded and jostled by thuggish Christians who pull off his hat and shove him from one to another" (P. J. S. *CE* 40, 93). After Portia's arrival at the trial, "we glimpse," said Hiley, "his little-man-on-the-skids persona. He blinks and shifts his weight uncertainly, angling his nose toward the heavens in a touching effort to maintain composure" (*L* 15 June 1989, 34). Frank Rich found in "Hoffman's stooped shoulders and shambling walk a pale ghost of Willy Loman" (*NYT* 21 June 1989, 15). "The effect of Mr. Hoffman's mild Shylock," Rich said, "is to shift the play's emphasis from the dark doings in Venice to the romantic couplings of Belmont" (15). Wells called Hoffman's performance "light-weight . . . stronger on irony than on passion" (*ShS* 43, 188). Ratcliffe, on the other hand, found this "a Shylock of striking physicality, unsentimental pride and sardonic power . . . he puts his case directly to the audience and moves us with the loss of Leah's jewel" (*O* 4 June 1989, 44).

But, said Billington, Hoffman lost "the tragic dimension . . . what Hazlitt, writing of Kean, called 'the hard, impenetrable, dark groundwork of the character of Shylock' . . . [A] performance full of buoyancy and elasticity of spirit [fails to provide] any strong sense of the character's inveterate malignity" (*G* 11 June 1989, 26). Hoffman, of course, was not trying to express that "inveterate malignity." Sher, at least, believes it *is* there and it follows that Billington did not find this "as challenging a production as the Alexander one which pinned down the timeless ugliness of racial hatred" (*G* 11 June 1989, 26). Ratcliffe suggested that the Hall is "a *Merchant* without context, in no way to be compared with the fierce and uncompromising [Alexander] version" (*O* 4 June 1989, 44). Frank Rich suggested that this "bland . . . Shylock . . . is overshadowed for many audiences by Antony Sher's highly impassioned interpretation" (*NYT* 21 June 1989, 15). Against those comparative judgments was Peter's statement: "I used to think that [the play] was simply full of disagreeable characters; Hall's production has made me realise that it is an essay in value judgments. The fact that you're persecuted doesn't make you nice. The fact that you persecute people doesn't make you a monster. You haven't begun to understand racism until you realise that it can be supported, even practised, by really quite agreeable people" (*ST* 4 June 1989, C-9),

Basic objections came from Richard Hornby, himself a director and actor. Hornby called the New York run "ill-conceived and ill-executed. The set, for instance, had a prettified design with Italian Renaissance arches and columns that was all wrong. Shakespeare's Venice is . . . a harsh commercial town of deals, ventures, debt, and scarcity. . . . Belmont . . . is exotic, romantic, and unbelievably wealthy" (*HR* [Winter 1990]: 632). That judgment contrasted strongly with the consensus of those who saw the London version, as did Hornby's statement that the New York "audience members unfamiliar with the play had trouble even figuring out where scenes were taking place much less having the proper emotional response to them" (632). "Furthermore," Hornby continued, "the blocking was overly busy. . . . Portia, for example, dashed around the trial scene like a dervish . . . . She is supposed to be the eye of the storm. . . . The understated 'Tarry a little' should be delivered in a still, small voice, which nonetheless stops Shylock, who is the busy one in the scene, in his tracks. Shylock was continually blocked surrounded by other actors, when he should instead be set apart from them, an alien presence. . . . Hoffman's version . . . became a B'nai B'rith anti-defamation homily . . . even managing to toss off lines like 'I hate him for he is a Christian' casually, as if explaining a distaste for artichokes" (632). "Shylock," said Hornby, "is a mixture of comic and tragic; the challenge is to play both" (632).

Again, we come down to the character of Shylock, the disagreement about it, and the inevitable debate that any production of this play will engender. Hornby directed the play in 1970, but his production was canceled by what have become known as "the events of May 1970." Clearly, he has definite ideas about the character and his placement and movement on the stage. While his response could be read as his effort to re-direct the play, his comments make one wish to return, with them in mind, to see this production. Nothing that has been said would have sent me back to the Alexander-Sher version, although Sher's more emphatic performance suggests why some very astute critics prefer it to the Hall-Hoffman-James interpretation. I made a plea in 1989 that the Hall production be produced for television. It may be that an archival version does exist, but the scale, attention to detail, and subtle acting of the production would have leant themselves well to an actual television production.

Director Ron Daniels placed the RSC *Hamlet* in two time frames that conflicted with each other. The interior of Elsinore existed in the 1930s (although critics did not agree about this placement[*]) before the full effects of the Crash had been felt and, in fact, were being ignored as Claudius ushered in a new era of peace and happy days. A huge window slanted down, as if looking out from the first class salon of the Lusitania, and a sea of troubles boiled beyond. Things were "disjoint and out of frame." The complacent interior chronology was challenged by another time of a Ghost ("convincingly a warrior" [Keyishians, 32]) and ultimately of a Fortinbras—the past threatening to invade the complacent court and finally succeeding. Prince Hamlet was the ambassador to the future. He failed, and Fortinbras stepped onto the battlefield that the court had become and became King. The specters of out-moded systems flooded over the battlements because no new value system had been introduced. As in modern politics, the old regime had a powerful and palpable representative much stronger than the Prince who would bring a new and humane order to the world. He was dead and defenseless against Fortinbras's order for a soldier's funeral. Hamlet became merely a political "body" that Fortinbras absorbed with ease and appropriated for his own reactionary purposes.

Ron Dungate found "Jarred Harris's quiet portrayal of majesty in Fortinbras . . . key. Hamlet's revelation that Fortinbras is 'a delicate and tender prince,' is, in this production, the beginning of his reassessment of himself, his image, his role—his start on the road to recovery" (P&P, 33). That may be, but only within the undertow of the ironies that a) the world of the play is bent on killing the recovering Hamlet, and b) Fortinbras, too late seen as "image of [Hamlet's] cause," is still Fortinbras, rather than an aspect of an individuated Hamlet. Here, Fortinbras was, in a sense, Hamlet's father without the advantage of the next genera-tion and what it has learned. Daniels reiterated his powerful 1984 ending, where, as François Maguin said, "Fortinbras . . . has been deliberately made to look like the ghost of the beginning. The stature, armour and chalk-white face make-up are visually com-mon denominators of supernatural and historical interference" (CE, 125). Here, the effect was just as powerful but more subtle.

---

[*]"Scandinavian, perhaps Bergmanesque. . . . One wouldn't be surprised if the conquering Norwegian turned out to be Ibsen" (Potter, TLS May 1989, 487). "Costumes were of the traditional nineteenth-century court style, perhaps remi-niscent of operetta, or the Senso style of dress, parodic in intention" (Luc Borot, 102). The "costumes [were] of indeterminate nineteenth- or early twentieth-century style, a time of the falling of monarchies" (Smallwood, SQ [41:1]: 105). It was "costumed to suggest imperial Europe in the 1920s" (Keyishians, 32).

The pace, wit, and intelligence of this production were irresistible. Claudius (Peter Wight) seemed to break his promise to let
Hamlet return to Wittenberg, the latter having made good on his
deal to attend the coronation as Crown Prince. His greatcoat on,
his bags packed, Hamlet was stunned at Claudius's sudden can-
cellation of his "intent." Patrick Godfrey's stiff Polonius was Claudius's man and the chief factor in the new King's ascent. Polonius
was so cold a father that the affections of his son and daughter
drifted toward incestuous sheets. Claire Higgins's Gertrude was
a foreign princess who had spent more time with the young Hamlet than with the old, again with tremors of incest apparent, but
not overtly.

The company proved Bernard McElroy's thesis that "a satisfying production of *Hamlet* depends on the subtle and difficult
business of realized character relationships even more than on
brilliant individual characterizations" (*SQ* [40]: 96). The Players
had been banished to the provinces, it seemed, for producing a
subversive play and would soon produce another one—without
their prior knowledge. The Players were angry at Hamlet's advice
to them, but had to accept it from their patron. Horatio and Player
King were angry at Hamlet's interruption of "Gonzago." As Mark
Rylance explained, "It is as if Ron Daniels had come down from
the stalls during a performance and told us what the play was
supposed to mean." And that is what Alan Dessen saw as the
culmination of a sequence in which Hamlet mentions the "dozen
or sixteen lines" to the Player, shows "frustration [in 3.2] at not
getting the desired results in the delivery of the new lines . . .
and [in] his subsequent interruption of Lucianus . . . the intervention of a high-handed director who feels he must take over from
an actor who is not doing his job" (*SQ* [1990]: 361; his emphasis).

While Hamlet could not sit still for his production, neither
could Claudius. At first offended for Gertrude's sake, Wight finally rushed toward the Player King, recoiled in horror, and fled
the room. Why? He had just encountered his dead brother. The
effect was achieved by the doubling of Ghost and Player (Russell
Enoch). "Gonzago" collapsed back into the outer fiction of *Hamlet*
with remarkable impact, partly because both Hamlet *and* Claudius
fell into the trap the former had set for the latter, and partly
because we shared the complex instant that captured Hamlet's
impatience with mimesis, Claudius's shock of recognition, and
the Player's annoyance at having *his* space so impertinently invaded by both King and Prince.

Robert Smallwood saw something else in this "Gonzago": Claudius "rises in panic, standing for several seconds mesmerized, like a terrified rabbit dazzled in the headlamps, before calling weakly for lights. There never was, surely, a more complete give-away" (*SQ* [41:1]: 107). Hamlet broke down as well.

One of the few versions that follows the script and shows that it is Hamlet, and not Claudius, who falls into the trap is the BBC version, with Derek Jacobi and Patrick Stewart. Here, Hamlet climbs up on stage with the Players and lets Claudius escape with dignity. Indeed, Stewart reverses Olivier's action in the 1949 film by holding a torch to Hamlet, as Olivier had to Claudius. As Robert Speaight says, "I am sure that it is wrong for Claudius to lose control at the climax. It is Hamlet, not he, who is excited. On the words 'you shall see anon how the murderer gets the love of Gonzago's wife' . . . the King rises, pale and speechless; and then, with a brusque 'Give me some lights—away' he strides—not rushes—from the room. What finishes him off is not Lucianus, but the glint in Hamlet's eyes" (*SQ* [21:4]: 442). The moment in the Daniels production combined the "conventional wisdom" that Claudius cracks with what the script as written demonstrates, and the results were spectacular. The instant linked Claudius and Hamlet, permitting Irving Wardle to discern "the heart of the performance [in] Claudius's . . . discovery of his deadly adversary, as Mark Rylance's Hamlet changes from a harmless idiot into a menace" (*T* 25 November 1989, 41). The resultant contest "is as though Tom and Jerry had been let loose in the tragedy. I have not been so held by it for years" (41).

Within this richly suggestive production, Hamlet was superb. As Smallwood said, "Rylance never seemed to utter a syllable to which he hadn't given deep thought. Added to this was an emotional integrity about the performance, a willingness to take risks, a brilliantly developed sense of the comedy of the part that made its inescapable tragic destiny all the more poignant. There was, too, a constant sense of openness to the audience that gave him a most touching vulnerability . . . that was the keynote of the performance" (*SQ* [41:1]: 104–5). Daniels kept this Hamlet from becoming a tour de force that would have erased frameworks of intentions that the script sketches in outlines that reach beyond the motivations of the title character. In the remake of the production for the American Repertory Theatre in 1991, Rylance was surrounded by a much weaker cast and thus emerged with a solo performance that even included an Elvis impersonation not in the 1989 Stratford version. Dorothy and Wayne Cook were correct in saying that "individual performances were mostly caricatures"

(39). Without the support of powerful surrounding performances, Rylance's was, then, "devoid of tragic dignity or meaning" (40), a fact that became obvious as the production, after the interval, was heard too clearly to "mock . . . the language and beauty of the play" (40). Clearly this script is much more than the interpretation of the leading role. In the RSC version, Hamlet was a young man in whom his father had been disappointed long *before* his death. Hamlet was, like Hoffman's Shylock, "surrounded," as Lois Potter said, "by men much bigger than he is, from his statuesque father to Fortinbras and his soldiers" (*TLS* May 1989, 487). The Ghost and Hamlet touched each other in 1.5, with Hamlet, in effect, promising to "make it up to Dad." Hamlet wore dirty striped pajamas throughout much of the production, beginning with "To be," which was given its early Q1 placement. This placement—or *dis*placement—was not positively greeted by those who noticed it. Smallwood assumed that "the decision [was based] on the belief that [the soliloquy] represents a regression to inertia after the determination of 'The play's the thing.' The notion that mental disturbance follows a regular graph of progression, rather than a jangled juxtaposition of moods, seems a little specious, however, and I am unwilling to accept that this team could not have made believable the order that Shakespeare and his company seem finally to have preferred" (*SQ* [41:1]: 105). Dessen said that the "soliloquy comes across . . . as an initial element in a long progression (especially as delivered by a Hamlet dressed in soiled striped pajamas). . . . Placement of such major elements *is* a significant part of theatrical meaning" (*SQ* [41:3]: 361).

This placement represented a "trade-off" for Dessen: "The nunnery scene did gain some force from being closer to Ophelia's report to her father in 2.1 but, in turn, lost a great deal without having as context Hamlet's interaction with Polonius, first in the fishmonger exchange, then at the appearance of the players (in this production, Hamlet and Polonius intensely disliked each other)" (*SQ* [41:3]: 361). What was gained was that the production got that dull, sententious, and out-of-context soliloquy out of the way early on, and in an interesting way, thanks to the pajamas. The soliloquy will still work if Hamlet enters reading Seneca and comments on the words. After talking about no traveler returning from the "undiscovered country," for example, Hamlet can look up from "puzzles the will" and nod at the audience, sharing an insight beyond "your philosophy," a discipline that seldom deals with ghosts. If the soliloquy and the nunnery scene are dealt with early, the production provides a rapid and unified sequence from the coming of players to the breakup of "Gonzago," as this production did. Our sense of climax was greatly enhanced here, as Dessen suggests above.

Denmark was a "prison"—an institution in which Hamlet could retain sanity only by being antic. To play Elsinore's game was to become *really* insane (cf. R. D. Laing and *One Flew Over the Cuckoo's Nest*). Michael Billington, the *Guardian* critic, found Rylance's Hamlet "unequivocally mad," and that this approach "animated long stretches of the play." The problem with the performance, Billington felt, was that Hamlet's soliloquies, in which he "reflects upon his moral dilemma, were inconsistent with his madness" (Remarks, August 1989).

The same Hamlet is different to different observers. "This," said Smallwood, "was a Hamlet who may only have been pretending to be mad—and to convince the sharply watchful mother and neurotically alert stepfather . . . as well as Denmark's very astute chief minister" (*SQ* [41:1]: 106–7). Smallwood saw this Hamlet as "deranged by the corruption he sees, yet, paradoxically, the only one sane enough to pretend that it isn't there, that everything's fine" (*SQ* [41:1]: 107). Hamlet seemed to adopt a conscious antic disposition—he knew who he saw even as he called Polonius fishmonger or Jephthah. Hamlet used his position as prince as protection for behavior he knew was outrageous. The soliloquies were an escape to a rational faculty he could not exercise in Elsinore. He began his first soliloquy with his back to the audience and maintained this position for eight lines, until "but two months dead!" He made us aware of his presence, pulled us in, and permitted us to become the listeners he could not find in the script. Director Rodney Bennett and Jacobi use the same technique in the BBC version. In the Daniels production, we, "but mutes or audience to this act," could do no more for Hamlet, up there on stage, than he could do in Elsinore. As Michael Pennington, who played Hamlet for John Barton in the 1980 RSC production, says, "Hamlet's purest and most distinctive encounters [are] those with his audience. These form the character's most confidential relationship; and in practice it meant preparing to meet the audience on terms as open and mutual as possible" (119).

Rylance found his inner friend not in Horatio, who was by turns puzzled and upset by Hamlet's bizarre behavior, but in Yorick. "Antic" also means death's-head (cf. *I Henry VI* 4.7.18). Yorick whispered the joke about "chop-fallen" to Hamlet, who repeated it with a chuckle. Hamlet carried the skull from graveyard to throne room, placed it on a shelf, and then went back to turn it so that it could watch the duel. The prop was brilliantly animated. Yorick became one of the script's few survivors, casting his bony gaze across the graveyard of Elsinore, as ghosts rose to claim it.

This Hamlet, then, fell back into what Smallwood called "the inbred, incestuous, inhibited, implosive court of Denmark" (*SQ* [41:1]: 105). Smallwood suggested that "Fortinbras, the prince from across the water" will sweep that corruption away (*SQ* [41:1]: 105). But to replace it with what?—the world of Hamlet's father, it seems, as if revenge means that the future must be canceled. That is what it meant to be this Hamlet. The inhabitants of Elsinore could wash themselves in the forgetfulness of the present. "What keeps a state from sinking," says Potter, "may well be the inability or unwillingness of its rulers to look into the abyss to which Hamlet is so hypnotically attracted" (*TLS* May 1989, 487). If so, that means that this Hamlet could never have led his kingdom into the future. But he was the only candidate available. He could only move, it seems, from unwilling jester to unwilling murderer. But the movement, as charted by Rylance, was compelling. Smallwood suggested that Hamlet's last request to Horatio shows "that death and 'felicity' are synonymous" (*SQ* [41:1]: 107). In other words, don't absent thee from *life* to tell my story, absent thee from easeful *death,* and *continue* to draw thy breath in pain in this harsh world.

"What makes this *Hamlet* interesting—if sometimes irritating," said Potter, "is its refusal to oversimplify" (*TLS* May 1989, 487). Smallwood added that the production explored "the central relationships (including that between Hamlet and the audience) with great honesty and seriousness, and offering a theatrical experience that was believable [and] often funny" (*SQ* [41:1]: 108). This production worked well partly because it didn't permit thinking to get in the way of imaginative response. Recollected in tranquility, the production got even better.

Derek Jacobi, one of the great Hamlets of recent decades, offers a key to what Rylance did, and to why actors playing the role can fail, as well as succeed: "the personality of the actor playing the role . . . is the determining factor. You don't actually have to play the character, you play the situation in which Hamlet finds himself and your own personality, your own outlook, takes over. That's why the part is played differently by so many different actors, all doing perfectly valid interpretations" (*CSM* 7 November 1980, 19). Jacobi adds that "the variety of Hamlets—political,

emotional, intellectual, spiritual, physical, [and] psychological
. . . can't all be done simultaneously. . . . An actor must choose
one area to emphasize" (19). Arthur Unger suggested that Jacobi
"made [Hamlet] a repressed, emotionally disturbed Hamlet, a
Hamlet who explodes into frenzy whenever his control slips a
bit" (19).

Rylance's version was mad in Elsinore and sane for his audience. Billington was convinced by what Rylance showed *inside*
the play and because it is society that defines madness and de-
cides what to do about it, Billington had a point. "Madness in
grea: ones must not unwatch'd go," says Claudius, right after he
has pronounced Hamlet sane.

Rylance captured the fancy of most critics. Ron Dungate said
that "this prince is not noble, not a genius, does not . . . leap
forth as First Renaissance Man, but he is one hundred fifty percent human . . . physically and vocally finely tuned and detailed,
while possessing a strong clear shape—which . . . establishes
the play's strong form on stage. . . . No matter how perverse he
becomes, no matter how violent, he never loses us for a second
of this production of three-and-a-half hours" (*P&P*, 33). The production, said Gordon Rogoff, allowed us "to see the play as the
remarkable document it is—always available to the pressure and
temper of another age. [Rylance is] just this side of a mocking
boyishness that threatens always to disturb the peace. [He] never
forces anything, and he speaks with a hushed persuasion that
never lapses into rant or aria. . . . Despite his cruelties . . . he's
the first Hamlet in memory who truly warrants Horatio's enco-
mium—the sweetest if most hair-raisingly complex prince I've
ever seen" (*VV*, 97). Stanley Wells found Rylance's Hamlet
"warmly human, often very funny, never heroic" and the production "a bold, original, internally consistent interpretation that engaged intimately with it its audience's attention, a reading that
had something to say about every detail of the text and was impossible to ignore, whether one liked it or not" (*ShS* 43, 200).

Of course, given such a non-traditional approach to this most
canonical of texts, some did remonstrate. John Gross, for example,
said that "The Royal Society for the Prevention of Cruelty to
Shakespeare has another case on its hands" (*STel* 30 April 1989)—
and characterizes Shakespeare as poor Black Beauty hauling a
cart full of beer barrels. "The only tragic aspect of the evening,"
added Peter Kemp, "is that this fiasco is the work of the RSC" (*I*
28 April 1989), and one has to admit that the production was not
reaching for elevated sonorities or statuesque effects. John Peter,

however, called it "a deeply shocking production in the most crucial sense," in that it achieved a "hard, brutal grandeur" (*ST* 30 April 1989), and Wardle observed that it was "a revival no spectator will forget" (*T* 28 April 1989). The images projected by this production retain their indelible imprint on the screen of a memory of many *Hamlet*s.

Anthony Sher as Shylock in Bill Alexander's *The Merchant of Venice,* **Royal Shakespeare Company.**

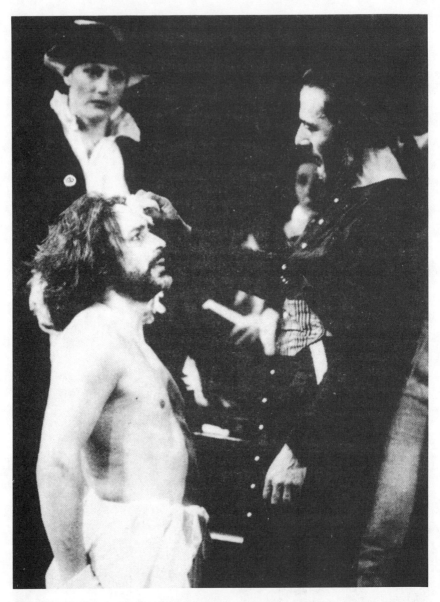

Geraldine James as Portia, Leigh Lawson as Antonio, and Dustin Hoffman as Shylock in Peter Hall's *The Merchant of Venice* **at the Phoenix Theatre, London.**

Judi Dench and Anthony Hopkins in Peter Hall's *Antony and Cleopatra* at the Olivier Theatre, Royal National Theatre. Photo by John Haynes.

Brian Cox as Titus, borne by Aaron (Peter Polycarpou), Chiron (Richard McCabe), Demetrius (Piers Ibottson), and Alarbus (Stephen Eliot). The other faces visible are those of Linus Roach (Martius) and Ian Bailey (Quintus). Photo by Richard Mildenhall.

Mark Rylance as Hamlet and Jimmy Gardner as Gravedigger in Ron Daniel's *Hamlet*, Main Stage, Stratford-on-Avon. Photo by Richard Mildenhall.

Mark Rylance as Hamlet in Ron Daniels's *Hamlet*, Royal Shakespeare Company. Photo by Richard Mildenhall.

Bernard Breeslaw as Malvolio at the Open Air Theatre, Regent's Park.

Richard Briers as King Lear and Emma Thompson as The Fool in Kenneth Branagh's Renaissance Theatre Production of *King Lear.* Photo by Robert Barber.

Kenneth Branagh as Edgar, Emma Thompson as the Fool, Jimmy Yuill as Kent, and Richard Briers as King Lear in the Renaissance Theatre Production of *King Lear.*

Linda Kerr Scott as the Fool, John Wood as King Lear, and Linus Roach as Edgar in Nicholas Hytner's *King Lear,* Royal Shakespeare Company. Photo by Richard Mildenhall.

Brian Cox as King Lear, Ian McKellen as Kent, and David Bradley as The Fool in Deborah Warner's *King Lear* at the Olivier Theatre, The Royal National Theatre. Photo by Neil Libbert.

Ian McKellen as Richard III in Richard Eyre's production at the Lyttelton Theatre, The Royal National Theatre. Photo by John Haynes.

Michael Pennington as Macbeth and Derek Smith as Duncan in Michael Bog-danov's *Macbeth*, English Shakespeare Company. Photo by Laurence Burns.

Guntbert Warns as Duncan and Peter Lohmeyer as the Bleeding Captain in Katharina Thalbach's *Macbeth* for the Schiller Theatre Werkstatt at the Mermaid Theatre. Photo by Mark Borkowski.

Kelsey Grammer as Richard, Robert Jason as Bolingbroke, and Carlos Carrasco as Northumberland in Robert Egan's *Richard II* at Mark Taper Forum. Photo by Jay Thompson.

A Multi-cultural *Richard II*, Directed by Robert Egan at the Mark Taper Forum. Front row, left to right: Barry Shabaka Henley, Nafsuko Ohama, Jelora Hardin, Jeanne Sakata, Armin Shimerman. Second row, left to right: Winston Jose Rocha-Castillo, Eugene Lee, Phillip Moon, Norman Snow, Tom Fitzpatrick, Ryan Cutrona. Back row, left to right: Luis Antonio Ramos, Carlos Carrasco, Robert Jason, Albert Owens, Kelsey Grammer, Michael Cerveris, John Vickery. Photo by Jay Thompson.

Simon Russell Beale as Richard III in the Sam Mendes production at the Other Place, Stratford-on-Avon. Photo by Michael Le Poer Trench.

Anton Lesser as Petruchio and Amanda Harris as Kate in Bill Alexander's *The Taming of the Shrew,* **The Royal Shakespeare Company.**

Ciaran Hinds as Richard III in Sam Mendes's production at The Donmar Warehouse. Hinds replaced an injured Simon Russell Beale.

Richard McCabe as Tranio, Trevor Martin as Baptista, Rebecca Saire as Bianca, and Paul Webster as Gremio in Bill Alexander's *The Taming of the Shrew*, Royal Shakespeare Company.

Brian Bedford as the Duke and Elizabeth Marvel as Isabella in Michael Langham's *Measure for Measure*, Stratford Festival, Ontario.

Gary Sloan, who alternated with Tom Hulce in Michael Kahn's *Hamlet* **at the Shakespeare Theatre. Photo by Rhonda Miller.**

Tom Hulce as Hamlet in Michael Kahn's production at the Shakespeare Theatre. Photo by Joan Marcus.

Kenneth Branagh in Adrian Noble's *Hamlet,* **Royal Shakespeare Company. Photo by Mark Douet.**

Jane Lapotaire as Gertrude, Kenneth Branagh as Hamlet, and John Shrapnel as Claudius in Adrian Noble's *Hamlet,* Royal Shakespeare Company. Photo by Mark Douet.

5

The Summer of *King Lear*

R.H. Foakes has argued recently that *King Lear* has replaced *Hamlet* as the most critically acclaimed of Shakespeare's major tragedies. Certainly *King Lear*'s holocaust vision accommodates the horrors of the twentieth century more adequately than does Hamlet's moody introspection, and perhaps the belated awakening of a social conscience in Lear rouses rationalizing energies in modern audiences. A play once considered too large for the stage seems to have confronted it successfully since the end of World War Two, a war which proved that history itself could reproduce, if not "the promis'd end," at least "image[s] of that horror." The stage itself has stepped out of its picture-frame premises and stretched, literally, to include more than fits decorously behind the fourth wall. The summer of 1990 saw three major productions of *King Lear*, none a triumph, each controversial, all helping us to understand the issues within the script and the problems in producing it. Each production had its champions and each its detractors. Certainly *Lear* is picking up some of the controversy that long surrounded *Hamlet*. In the case of *Lear*, the issues of power and patriarchy emerge more clearly than they used to do, thanks to modern cynicism about politics and the feminist focus on gender issues in the scripts.

Each of the productions set itself in a version of "timeliness"—"abstract modern limbo," as Frank Rich said (*NYT* 8 August 1990, C11) that, as Benedict Nightingale suggested, "tend[s] to look, often wryly, at larger issues" (*TSR*, 848). According to Nightingale, Adrian Noble, who directed the play in the mid-1980s, "now feels he could have concentrated less on the play's elemental grandeur, more on the psychology of parenthood" (*TSR*, 848). Jonathan Miller objects to "the cosmic . . . design": The play, he says, "is not metaphysical, not about man against the elements, not timeless, not Star Wars, but about human relationships and Jacobean ideas of sovereignty in the state, which falls to bits if the king or father is weak or absent" (quoted in Nightingale, *TSR*, 848). Certainly what Miller says is there *is* there, but some would argue that there is *more* there than Miller says, including, one infers, the directors of three very different productions of 1990.

The Branagh *King Lear* opened at the Blackstone Theater in Chicago in May 1990, after it had an engagement at the Mark Taper Forum in Los Angeles. It was touring in repertory with *A Midsummer Night's Dream*, and would end up at the Dominion Theatre in London's West End in August.

Because the company was on tour and would play in auditoriums of different sizes and shapes, Branagh used the same set for both productions. A thrust stage emerged from under the elegant proscenium of the Blackstone Theatre, which was built at the turn of the present century. A semi-circular walkway circled in front of a raked disc on which most of the action occurred. The set suggested, to Tom Morris, "world, castle, and wheel of fire" (896). A moat lay between the walkway and the stage, telling us, as David Bevington said, that "we are in an island kingdom" (*SQ* [41:4]: 501). Actors entered through two side doors or, for big and sometimes backlit entrances, through central double doors. A metallic backdrop looked as if it had been punctured by gigantic backstage arrows, or in more modern and mundane terms, "like the inside of a giant beer tin used as target practice for an air gun" (Morris, 896). The stage, then, was a contested space threatened by the pressure of attack from armed giants. A large circle recessed into the backdrop could become a moon or a partial eclipse. Certainly the stage had its symbolic values, as Shakespeare's original spaces also had. Alfred Weiss suggested that "*King Lear*, more than most of Shakespeare's other tragedies, takes place simultaneously in a microcosm, a geocosm, and a macrocosm . . . the actors in this production . . . convey human, microcosmic aspects, the stage . . . mirror[s] geopolitical aspects, and the total set with the lighting and sound systems . . . suggest[ed] natural, macrocosmic aspects" (462).

In other words, language radiated outward from the semicircle, picking up meaning as it touched concentric lines. The problem, of course, is that we can never be sure what meanings are echoed back upon the individuals, since we are never sure what the cosmic facts are, as Roy West argues. What is the cause of thunder? Is there any cause in nature that makes hard hearts? The sense of surrounding layers of meaning that had something to say—other than just what the rings of a tree may report—

was itself deceptive here. Branagh seems to know as much, as evidenced by "his evident devotion to working from the text outward. [He] refuses to impose the kind of grand 'concept' that frequently owes more to the designer's invention than to any discoveries made by director and actors in the rehearsal room" (Russell, 503). Branagh eschews, then, the question that Thomas Clayton has a hypothetical director ask: "How can I make the play sufficiently Mine that Shakespeare's subsidiary role is recognized, by suppression, for what it is?" (Thompson & Thompson, 237).

The playing space both served the continuous action that the script demanded and framed the symmetrical groupings that Branagh favored. "Branagh," said Russell, "places his cast in conditions that are . . . close . . . to those of Shakespeare's own stage. . . . [He] returns the play to the actors" (503) Jon Lindstrom's lighting defined space effectively, so that intimacy could be achieved even within the Blackstone's huge opera-house format, as in, for example, one of the greatest scenes Shakespeare ever wrote, Gloucester's meeting with Lear (4.6), downstage center. The only "special effect" other than variations in lighting was the actual rain that fell from pipes in the flies and landed in the trench between the outer walkway and the raked semi-circle of the stage.

Richard Brier's Lear began at full pitch. But it was shouting without a subtext and the opening scene was flat until France knelt to Cordelia and asked to take up "what's been cast away." The sudden change in tone gave us a way of *valuing* that Cordelia herself had not established and that served as an emotional guide for what followed. The production got better as it went along, as did Briers, who hit his stride with his curse of Goneril in 1.4, which brought a gasp from the audience. It may be that Briers was himself gaining control of his acting space and getting into contact with the energy coming back from his audience. The Mark Taper Forum, which he had just left, is a thrust platform in a space with a much lower ceiling than the cavernous Blackstone. The Taper seats 737, about a third as many as does the Blackstone. Part of our experience on the opening night in Chicago was watching the actor learn his space—and that was appropriate to the character he played.

The hovel and Dover scenes were superb. In the former, Edgar rose suddenly from a hellishly lighted cellarage, giving the audience the shock he gives the characters on stage. The encounter in 4.6 between Lear and Gloucester was quietly managed and intensely moving, full of pauses and half-awarenesses, very subtle acting in so large a space. Lear "saw better" here, even if Gloucester could not see and, inevitably, Lear's comments about Gloucester's eyes drew laughter—laughter *with* as opposed to *at* Lear with some directed at Gloucester, laughter that allows us to humanize the scene, "make it our own" as we respond to these two old men, one moving within the rhythms of a subdued comedy, the other about to reconcile with his daughter and then to lose her forever.

Edward Jewesbury's Gloucester reminded us of Lear, but drew the contrasts well: a remarkable performance by a veteran actor whose "old fashioned" approach to his craft made Gloucester's victimization by the next generation very credible. He half expected this response, it seems. No kindly old man, he grabbed Edmund by the back of the neck as he demanded to see "Edgar's" letter and then threw Edmund to his knees. David Bevington objected to the laughter "at the wrong places" and "couldn't tell if Branagh's company was playing consciously to [a] taste for sound bites" (*SQ* [41:4]: 501–2), but surely "Goneril, with a white beard"—one of the lines that got a laugh in this production—does deserve one in response to Lear's biting, only half-mad irony. It would be awkward to play the line without a laugh.

The production nicely delineated what a modern *King Lear* must project to a television-saturated audience—a sense of "family." That is hardly all that the script contains; however, this must be there or the play becomes an exercise in sound and fury. *How* the family is depicted is something the actors have to work out— on the basis of their own experience and on the basis of the dynamics that a particular group of actors create in rehearsal. Here, Cordelia (Ethna Roddy) was doing well enough with her spare recital of her "bond" until she ridiculed Lear's quantitative approach to "love": "Why have my sisters husbands, if they say / They love you all?" She had suddenly insulted the rest of the family, brothers-in-law included—and in public! Goneril and Regan, who, the script suggests, are not friends to begin with, were brought together by the threat that Lear poses. They were young and inexperienced in politics, as the script can suggest, (if we see Gloucester and Kent as Lear's primary officers). Russell said that "one major focus of the production [was] power relations, especially among those at court" (503–4). Jay Halio noted that "Lear's 'Come not between the dragon and his wrath' became visual as Kent stepped between Lear and Cordelia" (20). Upward changes in status were signalled, as Russell noted, by entrances from the great double doors, upstage center. "Cornwall and Regan stride on to open the second 'act,' pushing forward the hapless Gloucester" (Russell, 503). Then, in a telling reversal of the convention that had been established—and yet a shocking display of a kind of "power" that denies convention—"in 5.3 Lear enters backward, dragging Cordelia's body" (Russell, 503). Neither Goneril nor Regan knew how to function within the confusion Lear created by redividing the thirds into halves and by giving the sons-in-law the *symbol* of power (the coronet) even as he seemed to give the land to his daughters. The stage itself was a great pebbly map over which contending powers marched and counter-marched, obliterating lines so that Britain indeed became no more than "a conspiracy of cartographers." Goneril turned to Lear on "my flesh, my blood, my daughter," as if to say, "So I am!", but turned away, hurt, as it seemed she had done many times before on "Or rather a disease that's in my flesh." This Goneril (Siobhan Redmond) was unlovable precisely because she had been unloved. Hers, obviously, had been a political marriage and thus her attraction to Edmund was well-motivated. Patricia Donahue argued to the contrary, however: "In its effort to be absurdist, to reveal the meaninglessness of all action, this performance ignored the play's domestic issues" (25). David Hare's production did much more erasing of issues than did Branagh's, assuming that Branagh was aiming at an exhibition of the meaninglessness of all action. While the Branagh was a strong and credible production, Hare certainly made Branagh look good. It may be particularly true of this script that one looks at a new manifestation of it through the filter of one's experience of the previous production. The reason may be that the archetypes are so embedded that their outlines, however inadequate, are indelible. The pattern is suffering, rebirth, *then* crucifixion with "no breath" beyond. Shakespeare shifts the counters in the old story, Christian and pre-Christian, and the results are invariably powerful even in a world that retains only a trace memory of the narrative. The play, of course, tells its own story through specific characters played by specific actors.

Where the production lacked power was in its concept of evil. It was not, as Donahue suggested, that "the emotions [the characters] displayed were for the most part exclusively destructive . . . [They] were ambitious, greedy, or lustful, [and even Cordelia and Edgar] were incapable of love or tenderness" (25). It is very questionable that Edgar's is a role that *does* show love or tenderness, since his allegory with Gloucester is so unnecessary. But here we needed an Edmund who embodies the dark, unsanctified moment of his conception, a blind-spot of energy that grows to eclipse the bright disc of this stage or the space of any *Lear* world. Simon Robert's Edmund was a playboy who had not calculated the risks of the game until it was too late—he thought he was *playing* the wheel as opposed to placing himself *on* it. That approach worked well for the character, but the production needed more to Edmund than a chap toying with the frustrations of married women. It needed evil *here*, particularly within this script, an eclectic version that seemed edited towards optimism. Halio, however, found Roberts the best of the Edmunds of the summer of 1990: "He combined humor with sinister intent in a way that became irresistible" (*SB* [Winter 1991]: 20).

Some of the timing was curious. What sense could Regan's "Put in his legs" make when Kent was already securely stocked? Why did the Captain say, "If it be man's work, I'll do't" when he had already mimed his objections to Edmund's order for Cordelia's execution? The ending, however, hit an effective rhythm. Edmund died on "belov'd," Albany rushed to the central doors on "The god's defend her!" As the doors opened, Lear dragged Cordelia in. He knew that she was dead. The mirror and feather carried no conviction. His second "look there" was the repetition of an old man with nothing to say to the external world. The ending was brisk, but not rushed. The bodies of Goneril and Regan were not produced, so the production missed an opportunity to repeat, in a tableau of death, the scene where that ending became inevitable—the opening division of the kingdom.

Emma Thompson played the Fool in a dark shroud and a white mask—antic, skull, plague victim, the face in Munch's *The Scream*—and moved with increasing deformity, finally pulling painfully "into her grave" after reciting Merlin's prophecy, placed as an eerie epilogue just before the interval. The Fool moved down into the place from which Edgar had emerged, signalling the Fool's alienation from King Lear. This editing gave Thompson a complete characterization within a sequence that moved from the Fool as ambassador to Lear from the Court of Death, to Edgar, whom Lear incorrectly believes to be "the thing itself," to Cordelia dead, where a second "look there" moves as a tiny wave of sound meaninglessly into a sightless universe. Thompson's remarkable Fool—"a skull on a bent pair of tweezers" (Morris, 896)—made this a production worth attending. Russell commented that "this Fool showed Lear the skull beneath the skin. Far from striving 'to outjest his heartstruck injuries,' Thompson's pushy, edgy Fool was determined to educate, not console, hammering home key worlds like 'fool' and 'nothing.' Not entirely sane, Thompson's Fool was an alien and helpless pet, clearly incapable of providing for herself, yet showing a courage near to folly. In the middle of Lear's tense and very public confrontation with Goneril in 1.4, the Fool answered Lear's 'Does any here know me?' by slyly raising her hand: her 'Lear's shadow' thus became as much a definition of herself as of her master" (504)—as, of course, in the Jungian sense of that which is repressed from consciously created *persona*, the Fool is and must be. A Fool made up of that which was unrecognized by a king became, as the King would in another way, one "whose suffering seemed to derive from and be directly related to the suffering of all nature, of the state, and or those around her as well as from her own physical and mental anguish" (A. Weiss, 463). Given a performance that was at once unusual and somewhat against the grain of the rest of production, it is not surprising that Thompson's Fool was not greeted with universal acclaim. This "fool," said Donahue, "gave us a way to read Lear (he's 'nothing'), but she remained inaccessible both to Lear and to us" (25). Robert Logan suggested that "clearly, her Fool, instead of providing a clue to the overall conception of the play, too often merely led us to reflect on the achievements of the actor playing him. In showing up the lack of technique in her fellow actors, it also gave the production an unwanted unevenness" (7). The Fool's role is unique in this world of rationalizers and rationalists, and therefore Thompson's bizarre power provided a profound sense of suffering that needed to be balanced by a sense of *evil* that was not to be found here. One can see, then, how the performance might have been seen as merely a tour de force. Thompson enforced the point that Enid Welsford makes in discussing the Fool's role in this play: "If *Lear* has something of the structural simplicity of the morality play it has none of its moral triteness. Where the medieval playwright furnishes answers, Shakespeare provokes questions and reveals ambiguities" (Kermode, 501). The Fool is "the thing itself" and not feigning Edgar to whom Lear points. The "thing itself" will become Cordelia, living and dead and linked, of course, to the Fool early and late. Deborah Warner's production drew this link in another way, as will be seen.

The performance that drew the most attention, and the most praise and blame, was Briers's. Noted as a comic actor, and the Bottom in the alternating *Dream*, Briers "astonished many by his moving rendition" (Halio, "Three *Lears*," 20). By "the time he finds Kent in the stocks," said Morris, Briers "is thoroughly in his element. He brings to the ghastly rocking of Lear between his rejecting daughters a tragic timing as impeccable as his comic" (896). Jeremy Kingston found Briers "a deep-voiced Lear . . . where the finest moments come in the quiet exchanges with Emma Thompson's excellent and eerie Fool" (*T* 10 August 1990, 18). He was, according to Sylvie Drake "an arrogant tyrant whose descent into insanity seems remarkably sane" (F10). Donahue also found Briers's Lear "a remarkably sane madman" (25), suggesting that she, like Drake, found Briers's underplaying convincing. Logan said that "the production as a whole lacked the cutting edge that the barbaric, primitive elements of the text suggest," and perhaps any production focussing on the "Father Knows Best" theme would be hard put to find that prehistoric resonance, what G. K. Hunter calls "a monolithic and rough-hewn grandeur as if it were some Stonehenge of the mind" (New Penguin, xiii). Logan tended to blame Briers, who, "although clearly a comic actor of skill . . . often lacked the force, intensity, and heroic stature required of the enraged, crazed king" (6). "In the scenes that could be solved by sheer intelligence," said Russell, "like the mock trial in the hovel or 4.6, the 'mad' scene at Dover—Briers did just fine . . . [finding] a new intention for every line, making the twists of Lear's mad logic as comprehensible as he had in the hovel" (505). The frightening "logic" of insanity came through and was more powerful than would have been the over-the-top ravings of a character who could convince us that he was madder. Russell added that "much of Lear's role, however, calls for the kind of terrifying rage that, from available evidence, is simply not in Briers's register. When he could do an end run around the evidence, as when he was at first simply *amused* by the storm, he shone. [But] something of the import of the role was simply missing" (505; his emphasis). Alfred Weiss suggested that the stage itself played a compensatory role in Briers's performance: "In the storm scenes . . . Briers looked and sounded as weak as he had from the very beginning of the play. The full force of the words, which he seemed barely able to rasp out, was expressed in dramatic lighting and sound effects . . . and by a sudden curtain of heavy rain pouring down into the void surrounding the stage. The rake of the stage itself, threatening to tilt Lear into a flooding nothingness, helped to magnify to tragic proportions the pathos of the infirm little man" (463).

Other than Weiss, no other critic praised the semi-circle of rain. "If you're going to indulge in this kind of . . . unnecessary bravura," Drake said, "you'd better be prepared to carry it through for more than one scene" (F10). An effect used once—at great expense—becomes a gimmick only. And, as Kingston said, "it woundingly distracts attention from lines capable enough of conjuring up the sense of hurricanoes with the aid of the odd thunderclap and flash of light across the cheese-grater" (*T* 10 August 1990, 18). Shakespeare's stage, of course, had *only* the words and the offstage sound effect, unless a storm drenched the Globe, or when the English weather drops in on Regent's Park, as in the summer of 1992, when an excellent *As You Like It* somehow squeezed itself in between obliterating soakers (12 August). David Bevington was right to condemn the gimmickry of Branagh's *Lear* and to feel, when an audience responds to it, "the effect . . . of television drama played to an audience whose sensibilities have been defined by watching sitcoms" (*SQ* [41:4]: 501). To suggest, however, how close the judgment call on any given production can be, Weiss, so sensitive to the concentricity of the set, said "had it been performed in a neutral setting, this *King Lear* would have been an excellent and exceptionally well-acted soap opera with no resonances beyond the immediate concerns of the families and their associates. The powerful and evocative set, however, served as a constant reminder that the drama was being played out amid crises of politics, war, and nature and was affecting and being affected by those factors" (463). Branagh said that he hoped to evoke "a rough, raw world, reflecting elemental conflicts," with costumes that reflected a Hogarthian look, when "cruelty and a certain harshness was accepted, and you had to be fit to survive" (Nightingale, *TSR* 23 June 1990).

The issue of *depth* remains debatable. "Branagh's instinctive directing," said Morris, "produces story-telling of crystal clarity and a series of theatrically arresting moments" (896). That was not enough, however, for Drake: "[It] explodes, [it doesn't] dig deep [or] touch us deeply. For 'Lear,' which is a muscular, clear reading of the play and fiercely acted on the surface, [that] means the absence of subtext or of the possibility of tragic dimension. It is a workmanlike, respectable, unboring, capable presentation, that never moves us. It cannot make up in energy what it lacks in maturity" (F10).

Halio noted astutely the production's "vindicat[ion of] the Folio and the quarto's omission of an exit for Edmund in 1.1., [resulting] in a stunning coup de théâtre. Most modern editions have Edmund leave with Gloucester at Lear's command early in the scene to attend the lords of France and Burgundy. . . . Branagh had Edmund placed so that when Gloucester opened the

large double doors upstage center to exit, Edmund remained behind one of them. At the scene's final 'Exeunt,' after the sisters'
departure, the doors closed again, exposing Edmund, who then
began his soliloquy. . . . He had apparently heard everything,
forgotten by both characters and audience alike" (20). This approach provided continuity between scenes, of course, and it also
set up Edmund's repetition of the "Lear Thesis"—that fathers of
a certain age should give their wealth and lands to their children—for a Gloucester unsettled enough by events to believe that
it comes from Edgar. In this instance, Branagh suggested that the
opening scene is also the trigger of the Gloucester subplot, as
well as everything that follows in the story of Lear, his kingdom,
and his daughters.

Two other productions were playing simultaneously in August
1990: the RSC (in Stratford) directed by Nicholas Hytner, with
John Wood, and Deborah Warner's version at the National, with
Brian Cox. Each production was more daring than Branagh's and
each Lear took greater risks with his interpretation than did
Briers. The results were often startling *and* moving, but neither
production achieved, finally, the coherence of the Branagh. Like
the Branagh, these productions "accentuat[ed] the tormented
father-daughter infirmities of age [thus emphasizing] the decline
of a domineering patriarch over the fall of a powerful king" (Frank
Rich, *NYT* 8 August 1990, 11).

But with a difference! Warner's production began with a private, post-reign party. Brian Cox's Lear was already over-the-edge,
behaving with a childishness that had apparently characterized
his kingship. Cordelia (Eve Matheson) blew her paper "hooter"
at Lear, after her speech, believing it was still a game. But, as Alan
Dessen suggested, "Suddenly, the rules of a game that Cordelia
thought she understood had changed" (*SQ* [42:2]: 222). The good
humor that Lear had encouraged was not permitted to turn its
edge on him. In contrast, within the more formal RSC opening,
Cordelia (Alex Kingston) had said enough to satisfy Lear—a bare
minimum, true—but then went on, *in public*, obstinately to object
to her sisters. She was, according to Robert Smallwood, an "angry
and rebellious teenager [who] refused to play the parental game,
her rejection of Lear at least as strong as his of her" (*SQ* [42:3]:
352). Lear's outburst as dictated by Wood was a response to a
nastiness that others had witnessed. Cox's outburst came sudden
and unbidden from a Lear who had not even slenderly known
himself. Cox's Lear was wounded, said Dennis Staunton, with

something "like the sting of jealousy" (*European,* 9). Lear's rebuke was all the more stinging for its not being a reaction to public humiliation. "This tiny rejection," said Benedict Nightingale, evoked "a mighty tantrum, the reaction of an overage baby to a chum who refuses to play" (*T* 22 June 1990, 20). He was, according to Jill Pearce, "acting out his second childhood as he curries favor with his daughters by giving them his kingdom" (*CE* October 1990, 99). In response to Michael Billington's objection that Warner's opening was "eccentric," in that the first scene *is* a "public ritual," Brian Cox said that Gloucester is sent off before the love test, after all, and that France and Burgundy do not enter until after it has exploded (remarks, August 1990). The love test, then, is meant to be a *prelude* to a larger, court sequence that never occurs. The opening here worked as a kind of synedoche, as Cox explained to Alan Dessen: "if we get it wrong in relation to our children, we will get in wrong in relation to our kingdom" (*SQ* [42:2]: 222). This opening was different than any other *Lear,* perhaps, but, as with most of Warner's choices, defensible on the basis of the conflated *Lear* text. It may have been "eccentric" when compared to other versions, but it was interesting, even shocking in its quick shift in mood and mode.

The RSC opening was more conventional, but was, says Dessen "as strong an opening scene as I have ever witnessed" (*SQ* [42:2]: 219). As Stephen Wall said, "Wood's Lear . . . makes it immediately clear that the old man is becoming—has probably long been—impossible to live with. . . . His long pause before asking which daughter loves him most indicates how much he relishes making a scene. His rapid oscillations of mood, rushing to console his children—and the banished Kent too—for what he's just done to them through the impulsive abuse of his own power are an early sign of an irresistible instability" (*TLS* August 1990, 848). Burgundy was momentary unable to remember Cordelia's name. Lear said "take *thy* reward" to Kent, fitting the latter into a pattern Lear was still imposing on this disaster. The value of the formal opening was that it could be mirrored in the mock trial (3.6—a Quarto scene imported by Hytner into a Folio script, in this case a scene that nicely suited Wood's intentional inconsistencies) and in the last scene, where Albany's command that the bodies be produced was followed. As Peter Holland said, "the mock-trial set up two stools and two chairs in a deliberate echo of the arrangement of chairs for the daughters and for Lear himself in the love-test of I.1 . . . a nightmarish reworking of the opening. With the placing of the bodies at the end of the play again made care-

fully to echo the opening scene . . . the mock-trial became a crucial mark of dramatic shaping, the mid-point of the play's journey,
a sign of the distance traversed and that yet to come" (*ShS* 44,
179–80). This emphasis showed that "the trial scene (III.iv) is, in
fact, a parody of the initial love test, the 'justice' of the second
reflecting the 'justice' of the first in an ironic mirror, delivering
indictment rather than reward. . . . Implicit in the trial scene is
the silent Cordelia" (Coursen, *Christian Ritual*, 277). The production showed that the opening scene must result in negative reflections of the decisions made there—"anti-ceremonies" that
demonstrate the disorder inherent in rigidly imposed "order."
The family was reunited in death in precisely the spaces they had
inhabited for the opening scene. Warner also produced the bodies, but to illustrate the pathos and product of Edmund's "love."
That was to make a smaller point about how all this had happened, perhaps, but a valid one, nonetheless, in that so many of
the characters in the play equate "love" with a material "cause."

Warner's production defined the daughters in a "feminist"
mode—according to Lear's response to them. Regan (Clare Higgins) was the "pretty one," whom Lear chased in a mock sexuality
that delighted her and, later, in a rage that terrified her. Again,
the game showed its sharp edges. The daughters were at once
spoiled and despoiled by Lear. Cordelia went off too willingly
to prison with Lear. This was forgiveness without conviction or
perhaps was the scene without the reassumption of patriarchial
control that can be discerned there. No one had won, regardless
of Lear's rhetoric to the contrary. Kingston's RSC Cordelia went
off with Lear at the end because she had come back to him,
having failed to find a life in or with France. She had learned
only to be a daughter, futurity canceled by the "bond" she had
reluctantly admitted at the outset. Warner's Goneril, Susan Engel
(Regan in Brook's production years ago) was "a formidable society
hostess," as Nightingale said (*T* 22 June 1990, 20), and displayed
an "air of well-bred distaste" at Lear's antics (Osborne, *DT* 30 July
1990, 17). Her fury at the Fool in 1.4 was convincing, and her try
at belated sexuality was effectively inept, a maiden aunt essaying
Theda Bara. Her "If not, I'll ne'er trust medicine" was directed
right at Regan. Clare Higgins's Regan had to be restrained after
Kent's insult about "better faces" and was thus insistent that Kent
stay in the stocks "all night *too*." Her "What need one?" might
have been directed at the Fool, as another target of her rage, but
David Bradley's character was trying to stay out of sight. His long
silence had found no point, which was apparently, the point. The

Fool's voice was silenced before it is silent in the script. He froze to death, just before the interval. "By taking the break here," Dessen argued, "at the death of Bradley's abandoned Fool, the first half of the show was given a focus and shape strongly linked to what Lear had lost or destroyed" (SQ [42:2]: 223). Thus, in a way, this Fool was grouped with Goneril and Regan, but his loss created the vacuum into which Cordelia stepped in the second half, and thus was Bradley's fool also *linked* to Cordelia as he is in the script.

Hytner made a sharp distinction between Goneril (Estelle Kohler) and Regan (Sally Dexter). The former knew what the game was all about and was eager to get to play. She had a chance to escape a dull, arranged marriage. Perhaps Edmund could "Conceive" a child for her. She wanted to participate in a recreation of Edmund's history. As Robert Smallwood noted, this Goneril had been "goaded by her father for her childlessness—'to thine and Albany's *issue*, he said—and cursed by him with what she dreads most, sterility" (SQ [42:3]: 352). She, then, *would* "make [Lear] mad," that is "certify . . . him insane in modern terms," which is how Holland heard Wood reading the line, "do not make me mad" (ShS 44, 182). Regan, neither the oldest nor her father's favorite, did not know who she was, and was fascinated and horrified at what she discovered. She went bonkers during the blinding scene, asking *Gloucester* "How is't, my lord? How look you?" and wiping her hands like Lady Macbeth. Later, she offered a rose to be delivered to Edmund ("Pray you, give him this") like the mad Ophelia. Her obsession with Ralph Finnes's "thoroughly unerotic, thin-lipped scheming Edmund" (Staunton, 10), had to be compensation for her father's neglect of her. Holland offered a Freudian reading of Dexter's response to Gloucester: "The torture of the old man made her scream, releasing the violence of her hatred of her own father. Her bizarre concern for Gloucester in the redirected line ["How is't, my lord? . . .] represented her attempt to dissociate herself from the scene and her concern for the father in pain . . . Everything Regan had done so far and everything that she would go on to do pivoted on this moment" (ShS 44, 182–83).

Warner was criticized for what Sheridan Morley called a "spare, sparse academic reading" (IHT 1 August 1990, 11) and for what Billington termed a "studio aesthetic" for a main stage event, "visually dull and intellectually tame" (G 13 July 1990, 36). Holland said that "Warner's method of work ought to leave the action and particularly the actors a generator of emotional power," but he found himself "often bored, engaged as often in thinking about the production as watching it, able to stay serenely indifferent to the events on stage even while admiring much of what was being done" (*ShS* 44, 179). "It seemed," he said, "a studio production awkwardly metamorphosed" (186). Billington found the RSC version "thrilling" and called the set "excellent" (36). For Michael Coveney, the RSC set was "a revelation" (*O* 15 July 1990, 35). Holland, who worked with Hytner before rehearsals, found that "Hytner's work, as operatically opulent and inventive as ever, succeeded because the invention, fresh and revisionist, cohered, local effects growing into dramatic architecture" (179). Hytner used a revolving onstage cube that could scarf up rooms or other scenes and then present these locales to the audience. Sheaves of wheat, for example, stood at attention for Lear's mad review as he handed out spoons filched, one assumed, from one of the daughters to whom he had given "all." The cube attempted, as Smallwood suggested, "to epitomize the play's presentation of human puniness against the elemental immensities beyond" (*SQ* [42:3]: 350), but "the division into 'inner stage' and 'fore stage' was not one that the director explored with any discernible coherence," (351). Furthermore, and crucially, the moving cube obliterated the spoken word—Lear's "reason not the need," for example, and just about everything that Linda Kerr Scott's Fool tried to say. As Halio said, "many spectators found the device distracting, robbing the strong performances . . . of their effect" (19). The set did work well when it displayed Goneril's Chippendale dining room, candleabras flaring and a formal dinner toward, *three* place settings showing that Goneril expected to dine quietly with her husband and father—just in time for the arrival of Lear's young retainers. They wiped their muddy boots on the rug and grabbed rolls from silver bowls. The place had become a locker room awaiting Coach Lear's analysis of the hunt. The serving women disappeared deftly and the scene spilled downstage into the space of Goneril's anger. In the Brook version, the knights were uncouth *and* a military power driven by the whim of an angry and still vigorous ex-king. Here, they were a nuisance but more than enough to disturb the fragile tranquility of a newly-founded household. Wall was correct to suggest that David Fielding's design for Hytner "exerts no purchase on history and derives no urgency from it. [The revolving cube] relates uneasily to the sometimes underlit forestage, and its connection with the text seems arbitrary. Where Lear's contention with the elements is concerned, it doesn't help either the actor or our imagination to box him in. The sense of restriction is characteristic of an attitude to the play that in the end, and for all its insights, evades the tragedy's almost intolerable extremism" (848).

The bare Warner set worked best as Cornwall and company hurried in from the coming storm, long shadows defining the stark area they were deserting, a space without shelter for those they were locking out. Dessen, who argues cogently for some awareness in modern productions of Shakespeare's stage conventions, argued predictably in favor of Warner's spare approach:

> For some playgoers four hours facing such openness translates into dullness. For others, such an expanse of space encourages an intense focus upon what *is* there and what the actors are doing and saying. . . . [I]n practice, this empty space meant an absence of clutter, with the result that no emphatic design concept stood in the way of the text. The actors therefore were free to work from the script with few preconceptions. . . . [T]he choice of space and spacing emerged as *the* major image in this production, one that reinforced the overall interpretation of the story and the play world. Was the result visual monotony or inhabited, enriched space? Wherein does or should lie theatrical excitement for the eye or mind? (*SQ* [42:2]: 221; his emphasis)

Given Hytner's busy and upstaging cube, Warner's stage was more effective, even if a lot of the space functioned as it does in a Hardy novel, where space makes for a lot of walking. Martin Dodsworth, however, discovered theme in that space:

> The dwarfing effect is momentary; what persists is a sense of each character as an individual separate from all others . . . Lear's violent speeches are an attempt to overcome the gap between people that frustrates his affections. The play's gigantism, its expansiveness, which is the expansiveness of its characters, has to do with distance, the need and the failure to fill emptiness, to get close to some other. Lear surrounds himself with followers—reason not the need. In this production it is perfectly clear what he needs them for. (*TLS* 10–16 August 1990, 848)

Branagh's static but suggestive set may indicate a compromise in the direction of Shakespeare. His stage, after all, had its heaven, and hell, and fellows crawling between. When he mounted a challenge to the inherited cosmic system, as he does in *King Lear,* Shakespeare knew that the structure and concept of what he was critiquing were emblematically visible to the eyes of his spectators. Brook's empty space, or Warner's, does not necessarily capture the solid allegory of Shakespeare's stage. Dodsworth said that "the play endorses hierarchy as a social virtue, but Deborah Warner is not very interested in what there is of the play's society. Whole areas of the drama remain unassimilated to her view of it . . . anything that has to do with relationship rather than non-relationship suffers in this production" (848). Dodsworth apparently meant by "relationship" that which defines placement within a hierarchy. Whether the play supports hierarchy is questionable, since Shakespeare does not support *social* structure with cosmic underpinnings or overarchings in this script. Branagh's suggestion of concentric circles of meaning did provide a modern equivalent of Shakespeare's hierarchy of temporal and ultimate issues. It may be that Warner's usual choice of dull and eclectic costumes that refuse to tell us "what time it is" erased the visual element of the play—Aristotle's "spectacle." The *result* may have made the stage an "enriched space," and certainly some of the power of the script came through. But was it *because of,* or *in spite of*? Hytner's cube erased much of the verbal richness of the script in exchange for a visual effect, which *never substitutes* for the language. For some, however, like Billington, the bare stage can finally present only "family tragedy" (*G* 13 July 1990, 36) and thus is a thematically reduced area, no matter how vast physically.

The two Lears, Cox and Wood, naturally drew much of the commentary. Billington praised Wood for maintaining a "permanent state of moral schizophrenia" (*G* 13 July 1990, 36). Cox achieved "sudden, soft, intense insights," said Benedict Nightingale, and was "less rich and complex than [Wood] but . . . more forceful and, crucially, more vulnerable" (*T* 27 July 1990, 20). Wood's strength lay in his ability to leap between extremes. He was at the outset "the barbarous Scythian" who had consumed his daughters. The softer Lear emerged in the reconciliation scene (4.7), where Wood integrated Cordelia's voice into his nightmare, which eased as he saw her *there* as "spirit" then opened his eyes to "Fair daylight?"—as if he could still not believe what his dream had told him an instant before. The extremes worked potently in Lear's alternating tenderness and tantrum as he moved from Goneril to Regan and from Regan to Goneril in 1.4 and 2.4. Rich noted Wood's ability to alter his vocal approach: his "cries of 'Howl!' boom through the large Stratford auditorium even before his final entry from the wings and are then followed by grief-stricken odes to Cordelia just as impressively pitched at the pianissimo end of the range" (*NYT* 8 August 1990, C11). Cox did something *very* different, as Holland noted: he "went quietly up to a number of people onstage, urging them to howl, speaking the word as if in some perplexity as to why they are not howling, offering the sight of Cordelia as one that ought to have an automatic response whose absence is incomprehensible to him . . . the playing revivified the line" (*ShS* 44, 184). If Cox, as Staunton said, "successfully convey[ed] a sense of shared history with his family" (9), so did Wood. It was, however, a different family.

"Cox was the most impressive" of the three Lears, said Halio ("Three *Lears*," 20). Gerald Berkowitz found Wood's Lear gradually falling apart. "The loss of [his] ability to adjust and react instantly," said Berkowitz, "particularly in 2.4 seems to shake him more than anything else" (*SB* [9:1]: 9). What Lear lost, then, was "just personal," and, as Berkowitz saw it, "the process of his decline is unclear, and there is no real sense of approaching madness until it has finally arrived . . . and Wood can generate no pathos in the second half of the play" (9). Jean-Marie Maguin said that Wood's Lear "fails to move. . . . Too many tricks of the voice are used by this impressive master of voice technique. It results in a disintegration of the text and much frustration for the audience when the low tones simply fail to reach many parts of the theatre" (86). Stephen Wall said that "the insanity that John Wood so intelligently signals proves disappointing in the theatrical event because it becomes increasingly difficult to distinguish between the self-regard of the character and that of the actor playing him" (848). Holland suggested that Wood at times displayed "a self-regarding display of technique [and] cannot allow for . . . the play's shattering moments of simplicity" (181). Cox, however, "was, as if inverting Wood's work, most effective in such moments of quiet control" (184). Smallwood found Wood's Lear, "tall, gawky, and erratic, mov[ing] from start to finish in the borderlands of sanity. It was a brave, risk-taking performance, with violent shifts of mood from moment to moment [incorporating] senile forgetfulness, an inability to concentrate attention for long . . . qualities [that] created a believable—an all-too-believable, perhaps—aging parent, forcing us to sympathize with his daughters for what must have been a terrible upbringing" (*SQ* [42:3]: 351). A great moment occurred when Oswald rolled in a wheelchair for Wood, who turned it over and sat on it as if it were any chair. "At your choice, sir," said Goneril with a frigid correctness that ignored Regan's more direct demand that Lear "being weak, seem so." Wood sat on the upturned chair as he said "Patience I need." For Smallwood, however, two major elements were lacking—the kingly "Authority" of the character and his ability to move us. "Pathos, sympathy, pain—should they not be some-where to the fore, even if one is determined on an intelligent and thoughtful reexamination of the play?" (*SQ* [42:3]: 352).

Osborne said of Cox's Lear, "It's a wonder his daughters haven't had him committed" (17), but that is to grant them some control *prior* to Lear's "retirement." Others agreed, suggesting that, for them, Cox's Lear conveyed even less "Authority" than Wood's. "His Lear was a fond, foolish old man from the start and it was hard ever to see him with the mantle of authority" (Pearce, *CE* October 1990, 98). "Cox [was] more often akin to Bottom [than Lear]," said Morley (*IHT* 1 August 1990, 11). Nightingale asked, "How are we to take seriously so undignified a figure? How to believe the spiritual and moral regeneration of someone who seems not just immature, but suffering from near-psychotic infan-tilism? How respect denunciation of the superficial splendors of royalty which come from a man who looks as if he would have trouble landing a job as caretaker in a kindergarten?" (*T* 27 July 1990, 20). The answer may lie in a tiny moment that Cox created when he giggled on "crawl towards death" in 1.1. "The wheel-chair," Holland suggested, "was in I.1 a sign of age but also of resistance to being old" (184). This Lear had yet to learn what life was about, and it was *that* lesson, learned in the soaking storm and the journey to the underworld of his own psyche, that he hoped to share with Cordelia after their capture. The progress of this Lear culminated when he turned to Kent and said, "Do not laugh at me; / For as I am a man, I think this lady / To be my *child*, Cordelia." Only by being who Nightingale said he was at the outset, could Cox have made this Lear as vulnerable as he became. He sacrificed some of the elements that Wood retained, no doubt, but, as Nightingale said, "if Cox's great scenes with Cordelia are no more painful [than Wood's] they somehow con-trive to be more touching" (*T* 27 July 1990, 20). At the end, Cox tried, as Staunton said "to cajole Cordelia back to life" (10), by putting the Fool's red nose on himself. He then placed the red nose on her as he said "my poor fool." He died smilingly, not quite with A. C. Bradley's "unbearable paroxism of joy" but re-united with Fool and Cordelia in an instant. The final moment was not universally appreciated. Holland suggested that

it is crass for Lear, cradling Cordelia's corpse, to fish around in his pockets, find the same red nose [that the Fool had placed on Lear's nose in 1.4 ("a mark of the transfer of folly")] and try it first on himself and then on Cordelia as if somehow to explain his thinking behind 'my poor fool is hanged' (5.3.281). The business simply detracted from the actor's power to create desolate despair, leaving me wondering how the red nose had been transferred through Lear's changes of costume. (184)

Such are the risks in a gesture that will be either remarkably moving or extremely silly, with no neutral zone between the extremes of response.

Frank Rich suggested that Wood "looks as much like Don Quixote as Mr. Cox does like Sancho Panza" (*NYT* 8 August 1990, C11). Each played *against* such "typecasting," however, Wood being a more hardheaded old man, Cox less in control of himself, less sure of his surroundings. Irving Wardle gives a splendid and balanced account of these two Lears:

> Choice-taking cannot be appraised on a numerical scale. What counts is vitality and staying power, not quantity. Some actors build a character through pointillist detail, others through broad continuous brush strokes—two extremes memorably illustrated by the RSC and National Theatre productions of *King Lear*. John Wood, in the RSC version, broke the role down into a multitude of tiny performance units, sometimes changing emotional tack half a dozen times within as many lines, but never losing his central idea of the character as a man of passionate nature but short attention span, continually dragged back to face an unendurable reality. A physically and emotionally agile artist, Wood thus took possession of a part which traditionally belongs to theatrical heavyweights. Brian Cox, in the National version, is a heavyweight with correspondingly restricted mobility. A tirade once launched by Cox has to follow its given arc with no digressive zigzags on the way up or abrupt cut-offs on the way down. Every choice has to be calculated over a long range so as to reflect passing changes of feeling without disturbing the central momentum. In the first half of the play, Cox settled on the idea of Lear as an ancient child: establishing that image by arriving in a paper crown, playing party games, and then firing it on an impassioned trajectory which finally brought him down to earth between his implacable daughters, pleading to be allowed to keep his one hundred knights like a wretched little boy stunned by adult injustice. According to your temperament you will prefer one of these readings to the other, and the reviews duly split over them. What is unarguable is that both enforced your attention by personal choices that made the familiar text thrillingly unpredictable. (*TC* 102–3)

Dessen, for example, "came away [from the RSC *Lear*] conscious of a series of discrete moments and images rather than any sense of the whole" (*SQ* [42:2]: 219–20). Cox's trajectory was towards

the use of that red nose—a tiny moment from the opening cele-
bration brought forward to an instant for which it was radically
inappropriate and powerfully right. Cox had entered for 1.1 in a
wheelchair that rocketed around like an MG. At the end he
pushed Cordelia in the wheelchair, as Halio called it "a kind of
wheelbarrow for her limp body" (21).

The most moving version of the finale, however, in the summer
of 1990, was the two-person performance by Tony and Madeline
Church for Homer Swander's Theatre in England group in Stratford. Madeline Church doubled as Fool and Cordelia so that Tony
Church could hold Cordelia as he had held the Fool earlier, on
"You houseless poverty," saying, at the end, "my poor fool is
hang'd." Church was a Lear of remarkable authority. He knew
Cordelia was dead and turned her face to the audience on his
second "Look there!" He died with his eyes open.

Halio summed up the experience of the three major versions:
"Three powerful productions, all different, all absorbing, all eminently worth seeing and comparing. . . . If anything, they enhanced and enriched the viewer's experience of Shakespeare's
extraordinary tragedy" (21). Can a production in the 1990s or
beyond restore the cosmic sense of the script or even evoke a
feeling that we live in "a time of breaking of nations"? The gener-
alized present or timeless limbo approach *does*, whether the directors intend it or not, tend to close in on family issues. Perhaps that
is inevitable and perhaps that focus is to some extent a product
of an audience accustomed to the measurable rooms and family
contexts of television. Clearly, the Warner production *began* as a
"family affair," and then Cox demonstrated "the progressive loss
or disintegration of the restraints by which the presumably civi-
lized live. . . . The depth of the loss makes the recovery and subsequent loss of Cordelia all the more poignant. It is not a
performance that tidies the emotions" (Alter and Long, 23). Cox's
version, then, at least touches the theme of homelessness and
may remind its spectators of the legs they have stepped over near
the steamvents as they wended to the theater. Wall complained
of the Hytner production that it "is visibly happier to present the
division of the kingdom as a family row rather than a convulsion
of State" (848), and Michael J. Collins saw that potent wheelchair
that Oswald wielded as proof that "Hytner's production had chosen to understand the dissention between the King and his
daughters as a private . . . rather than a public affair" (22). What
should the play be doing in the 1990s? Does it have a "social
purpose" beyond intelligent and perhaps moving productions? If

it is well presented its "almost intolerable extremism" (Wall, 848) will make its point. What we can then make of that point is another question. Collins said that Edgar at the end of the Hytner production could not "turn *Lear* into a morality play," and "admits" that much. The words, Collins said, "sounded particularly appropriate here, for they seemed to recognize that the production, by refusing to take sides or to play for clear or univocal responses, had freed its audience to encounter the script in all its complexity, to live with and through the uncertainty that it never, even at its close, puts to rest" (23).

6

Winter of the Scottish Play

MODERN directors apparently no longer believe that the "holy-supernatural" element of *Macbeth* can be transmitted to an audience. One of the last efforts to do so was Trevor Nunn's superb production of 1976–77, where Griffith Jones (Duncan) prayed fervently in a futile effort to dispel a looming storm of evil and where, later, liturgical music washed ironically against the wreckage of Macbeth's "last supper." In that production, the discrepancy between the loving cup that Ian McKellen (Macbeth) passed around and the blood on the Murderer's face was made clear, and Judi Dench's Lady Macbeth was not *at* the table. Thus the production enforced the distinction that Shakespeare's script makes in basing the scene on the Eucharist—the "notorious evil liver must not presume to approach the Lord's Table until he [or she] hath amended his [or her] former naughty way of life." Nunn considered that the Christian heritage was still available to an audience of the late 1970s. If not, the production educated its audience about a world where even those who would "cancel" the world's order must express the possible destinations of their victims within the inevitable terms of inevitability: "Hear it not, Duncan, for it is a knell / That summons thee to heaven or to hell": "Banquo, thy soul's flight, / If it find heaven, must find it out tonight" and where the murderer is chief victim, rendering his "eternal jewel" to "deep damnation." All of that is there in the script. The Nunn production was spare and fast-paced, playing through its two and a quarter hours without interval. Its "depth" came from the great acting *and* the resonance of "deepest consequence" of the antique world view vibrating under the vivid actions of characters striving to live in a different, "modern" world.

None of the three productions of *Macbeth* in Great Britain in early 1992 made any effort to depict or to develop the sense of the positive supernature that the script describes at length, and, it follows, none of these productions could make much of the "instruments of darkness" that the script also treats at length. These were not "tragedies of damnation," in which the fall of both Macbeth and Lady Macbeth can be charted against the huge dimension of an ethereal sky whose brows overlook the smolder of bottomless perdition, but narratives of political disaster and failed personal relationships. Yet the exploration of even a limited sector of this script shows how alive it still is, and produced radically different productions, two out of three of which were excellent: the Schiller Theatre production at the Mermaid and the Buttonhole Theatre Production at the New End Theatre in Hampstead. The English Shakespeare Company subjected its actors to a nightmare out of *Das Kapital,* overpowering their work quite literally with machinery—the rationale being, one assumes, that Marx's great work was written in England only about 250 years after *Macbeth.* That the latter is hardly a critique of even "The Elizabethan World Picture" is of no matter. The script was reduced to banalities like equating Lady Macbeth's "violent delights" to "the most contemporary case of child-abuse" (Holderness, Program Notes, 2). The search for explicit modernity can reduce the script to irrelevance and incoherence, and here the effort at "intertextuality" was an invitation to a nihilism that the theatre can *depict* but that it should not *represent.*

The Schiller *Tragödie des Macbeth* was in German (Dorothea Tieck's translation) and was "obviously not Shakespeare Stratford-style" (Billington, G 1 February 1992, 21). It received a standing ovation from a full house. Given the reverential treatment Shakespeare usually gets in England—Deborah Warner being a positive exception and Michael Bogdanov usually a negative—it was not surprising that this iconoclastic production, full of Brechtian alienation devices, multimedia effects, and explicit sexuality should be greeted so enthusiastically.

The response, however, was not just to something new and strange. Director Katharina Thalbach's staging was brilliant. The set incorporated two basic playing areas: a large platform, with a staircase that could open down to it and fold up again, and the apron around the platform. This format threatened the actors with the "Desdemona's Bed" syndrome, where a central object inhibits maneuverability, but movement, both physical and chronological, was quick and fluid, except where pauses were built intentionally into scenes. A third playing area was a rope network, a horizontal spider's web, to which the Weird Sisters climbed "into the air" and from which they chirped through a miked-up link to a synthesizer. They sounded like 33⅓ speeded up to 45 rpm but contrasted effectively with the shrieks and moans that made up the "vocal orchestration" of this production. Thalbach said that the idea for this rope network came from the alternative title for Kurosawa's great film, *Throne of Blood,* which is "The Castle of the Spider's Web."

The platform proved versatile. It served as heath, the site of the Bleeding Captain's epic tale, the empty space around which the thanes sat in terrible silence after the murder of Duncan— with Banquo staring accusingly at Macbeth—and the table at which Macbeth enticed the two Murderers, motioning that they come closer and closer to him in a wonderful mime of entrap-ment. Marcus Vollenklee (Macbeth) explained that the primary function of the platform was to suggest that "power is handled on tables." Deals fall apart on tables as well. The platform was the table for the banquet, for which Lady Macbeth spread a huge white cloth. The platform became the Macbeths' bed, the table cloth becoming the sheet with which they engaged in a tug-of-war as they wrestled with uneasy slumber. As Macbeth struggled with the image of Banquo for the red robe of kingship during the Apparitions scene, the lights suddenly came up, showing Mac-beth tossing in nightmare, the red robe his "insecurity blanket." Banquo had melted into the surrounding darkness within a se-quence that represented a splendid "special effect." The platform became Dunsinane, buttressed by ten huge panels that were pulled up to face outward and "laugh a siege to scorn." It became a wrestling ring in which Macbeth and Macduff engaged in a parody combat that spilled, of course, into the space around the ring.

The best integration of platform and outer stage was at the end. The format allowed Siward and his soldiers to arrive outside Dunsinane even as action continued within it. The sense of "sur-roundedness" was augmented by the ropes that dropped down around the central platform, the ropes a metonomy for Birnam Wood and a reminder that the Sisters' prophecies were even now dropping around Macbeth. Young Siward challenged Macbeth by knocking down one of the elevated panels. As Young Siward was killed, Macbeth tipped the panel up again, sliding the body back into space outside Dunsinane. Macduff launched his attack on Macbeth by knocking down another panel. As Macbeth was about to deliver a prophecy-defeating death-blow, another panel fell, catching Macbeth's sword on the upswing. Later, Macduff freed that sword and used it to decapitate Macbeth. This final sequence was a brilliant, miniaturized emblemization of action that pulled our imaginations forward even as we marvelled at the skill and timing of the stagecraft.

Yet another playing area was a small platform, stage right, on which the scene in England was played. This area—up right— associates itself with distance and romanticism, and here Malcolm was an effete tea-drinker, listening to songs from another play ("In the spring-time, the only pretty ring-time"). In the meantime, Macbeth had become the gross, fat-legged politician of German cartoons of the 1920s, so the rugged Macduff had no options but was, like many people of integrity in any system, faced with equally unacceptable choices for leader. Malcolm was a reluctant victor. He turned away from the bloody farce of combat and had to be forced by Macduff to accept the crown. Macduff lay red hands on Malcolm, making Malcolm's tunic of Macduff's "color." The new king bore, as Paul Taylor nicely put it, "the *stain* of succession" (*I* 1 February 1992, 30; emphasis added). Malcolm's final "We shall not spend a large expense of time," in which he "anglicizes . . . the thanes . . . as earls" (Brooke, 49) was delivered in English, as if the change in language could somehow placate the hungry tiger of power facing him. His were panicky words tossed into a rising cacophony of sound and fury.

Thalbach's smaller platform also became *the* stage, as when Lady Macbeth came down the stairs, sweeping them in prepara- tion for Duncan's visit. She recited Macbeth's letter, which she had almost learned by heart. She pulled it from her apron pocket to finish reading it and held it to us for our verification. (The kingship, Thalbach said, is *their* baby.) She then tore the letter up. Its fragments, however, remained in view, at once a visual incrimination and a reminder of sundered expectations. One of the best moments on the smaller stage occurred when Macbeth descended from the murder room. After "I have done the deed," he and Lady Macbeth stood side-by-side in front of the red-lit stairs, absorbing the impact after all of their nerving-up *for* the deed. They felt their own relationship crumbling into emptiness. Another good moment in this space was the line-up of three candles in darkness—Waiting Woman, Lady Macbeth, and Doc- tor—in the mad scene, an echo of the three flashlights the Weird Sisters had used earlier.

Two other excellent moments were Lady Macbeth's "faint" and Banquo's arrival at the banquet. Her collapse was fraudulent, and even she recognized that it had been a silly effort to appear but as a "gentle lady." The issue was political, not moral or legal. Everyone knew who had borne the knife. When Macbeth said of

Banquo, "would he were here," Macbeth spread his cloak wide to suggest how complete things would be then. When he dropped his arms, Banquo stood at his left shoulder, here indeed! It was yet another of the stunning transitions in a production that splendidly suited word to action, action to word.

At the end, downstage of the freeze-framed "coronation," the Three Sisters flashed their lights over the audience, "We need not NEW masters, but NONE!" This effort to go beyond Caliban was gratuitous—the excessive verge on which this production trembled time after time as it made its subtextual commentaries on the actions the script dictates. It was, however, the end of the show and it suggested, as Polanski had done in his film, that evil is a separate entity. The script does not support Manicheism, but that is a quibble when poised against such a vibrant and inventive production—the kind of revivification of a script that we always hope for but seldom get.

A major problem with the production was a rock music inset for Hecate, complete with a revolving globe that sprinkled reflections against the walls of the auditorium. The visual effect was splendid, incorporating the audience within the space of performance. But this was a performance quite apart form the pressure of drama, diverting us from the ways in which the Macbeth myth was being redelivered, yanking us from the sequential rhythms that were being so vividly recreated for us. The idea, of course, was to show that even the scripted world of the play is subject to attack by disintegrative forces. The interpretation showed at least that much, even within the narrowed focus of a purely political world that showed, as Michael Billington said of this production, "power seems not from the brain but from an area squarely below the belt" (G 1 February 1992, 21). This Duncan, for example, was no sainted king but a skull-faced old lecher who peered at Lady Macbeth's bosom (admittedly open for inspection) and, knowing that Macbeth was busy elsewhere, grabbed a final kiss that she could only half-refuse. Little did he know that, as he planned assignation, she plotted assassination.

Thalbach said that she had reservations about the rock interpolation. She saw the moment as a kind of "time tunnel—to our time and back again." She suggested that the music created a break in a production without an interval. She said that the management in Dublin (where the production had been before its three performance stop in London) had insisted on an interval, perhaps because the bar trade had been brisk before the performance and presumably would be during an interval.

The rock interlude was a gratuitous imposition on a postmodernist production from which the "Elizabethan World Picture" had been excised and replaced by a bleak, existential vision, as Thalbach's editing made clear. Duncan's "This castle has a pleasant seat" got a big laugh, it being so inconsistent with the shabby truth. Banquo's subsequent description of "procreant cradles" was cut—though Thalbach had bird-sounds twittering fatuously during Duncan's speech—as was, inevitably, the apotheosis of Edward the Confessor in 4.3.

The scene that got the biggest laughs was the murder at Fife (4.2). Lady Macduff was a grotesquely pregnant hag who lugged her huge, idiot son from place to place and spoon-fed him. The audience's laughter was cruel—endorsed by Artaud—and uneasy. Lady Macduff scuttled with her youngster, piggy-back, away from the murderers, unaware that junior was dead. She was stabbed in the belly, so that the play's preoccupation with infanticide was visualized and, with the splendid duplicity of this production, Macduff's announcement of his own bloody entrance to the world was anticipated.

The scene at Fife is, of course, a culmination—from much reported bloodshed to its enactment and, from there, to the counter-pattern of nemesis and Macduff's revenge. It is easily the best scene in the BBC-TV version, and is powerful even in the Polanski film, which by then has splashed a lot of gratuitous blood at us. Polanski's Murderer pauses to admire an exotic bird and shares his appreciation by smiling at its owner, Lady Macduff. In the Thalbach production the scene was a locus of absurdity, as if two characters from Pinter discussing the merits of fried bread were broken in upon by agents of the Holocaust or of Hell itself. Macduff's memories were revealed as necessary rationalizations. All my pretty ones? Perhaps he had had hopes for the unborn child.

As might be expected, the reviews were mixed. Billington rightly argued that Thalbach's Weird Sisters, or "victorious vamps" tended to deny that "evil works . . . through the agency of human will" (G 1 February 1992, 21). But Billington, whatever his struggle with memories of Macbeth as tragedy, correctly called this manifestation emblematic of "a savage . . . force that constantly equates power with sex." And he remarked that the production "brings out, in a way British productions rarely do . . . despotism's mixture of moral ugliness and farcical absurdity" (21). Paul Taylor recognized that "there's precious little that's tragic" about the production (I 1 February 1992, 30). If "tragedy" involves an "error in judgement" (*hamartia*), one must have a context against which to project the error. Here Macbeth's decision was a slightly more violent reiteration of the inherited way of doing things. Taylor found the production "bracingly iconoclastic," even if "rudely flattened into a brutal, black comic strip" (30). Malcolm Rutherford felt that the London run was too short and that "such a pyrotechnic performance . . . really ought to have been given a run of several weeks at the National or the Barbican." Thalbach, he said, tended to make *Macbeth* "a play without feeling [or] development. That's Brecht: all symbols and no individuals" (*FT* 1–2 February, 23).

Attacks came from Irving Wardle and Michael Arditti. Wardle wondered "what is to be gained by reducing a moral tragedy to a brutal comic strip?" The production proved only that "the German stage [is] over-funded, director-dominated, and swimming in blood" (*IonS* 2 February 1992, C-21). Arditti, again, played Thalbach against the script's ostensible genre. This production, he said, "subscribes to the post-war shibboleth that tragedy is dead. Her *Macbeth* is Ionesco's rather than Shakespeare's. [The] production is constantly played for immediate effect rather than for dramatic truth" (45). No "catharsis" occurred, no release of pity and fear as a result of our vicarious sharing of humanity with the tragic hero. Arditti applied a pre-Kottian thesis that does not account for a Central European projection of the script as a condemnation of the modern political system. The depiction of an authoritarian—or totalitarian—government through the medium of *Macbeth* satirizes our own constitutional systems. That harsh satire—as if the play were directed by Swift—is the production's "truth," and we are free to reject it. Macbeth, down left—negotiating with his conscience—found his dagger not in air but in the auditorium. We were his alter egos, as hungry for power as he was and as willing to achieve it by any means as long as we did not have to face "judgment here."

This was existentialist drama for which this script can work. Peter Brook's bleak stage and film versions of *King Lear* drew criticism similar to Arditti's, and that is a script that supports a nihilistic vision better than does *Macbeth*. Shakespeare's scripts *must* emerge from the confines of academic definition, which will perpetuate only coteries that make Shakespeare "elitist" (if that has not already happened). Shakespeare *must* escape the restrictions that Aristotle, defining tragedy on the basis of Sophocles' *Oedipus*, or A. C. Bradley, emerging from Hegel in a age of ponderous proscenium productions, might impose on the ongoing energies of a given script. It may be that the larger aesthetic dimensions are no longer available to a culture in which "tragedy" now equates to everyday events. It may be that since the egalitarian trends of the late eighteenth century a great man's fall can be only political. Certainly the need for personal appearances and the ubiquity of the television camera have broken down the distance between the common man and "greatness." The politician as "star" is now a commonplace. Where distance still applies, as in the Royal Family of England, there is no corresponding power, only ceremony. It is still possible for a production of one of Shakespeare's plays to educate us to its "world view," which in the case of *Macbeth* is very conservative. Nunn's *Macbeth* is an example. But it is not necessary for the world view to be a "given," nor is it necessary for a production of a classic play to reflect older critical theories. A director who has a new vision of a script—a Brook or a Warner—as opposed to the trendy surfaces with which most directors cover their *lack* of vision—can force us to look at the script anew, in light of what it has always been capable of saying but which it has not communicated until the historical circumstances and the imaginative director coincide. We suddenly discover that "our times" have been there all along and the text in the museum's glass case comes alive one more time. Thalbach's production takes several steps in the right direction, as objections to it based on "classical" approaches to Shakespeare prove. Thalbach's *Macbeth* takes the play's view of the world seriously by mocking it. The caricature characterizations, the "staginess" (at times dazzling), and the editing of the script emerged from a skepticism that took none of the inherited material for granted and that was calculated to offend those who, as Chomsky says, "learn about the world from the doctrinal framework that they are exposed to and . . . are expected as part of their professional obligation to propagate" (14).

The audience did respond to "bracing iconoclasm." Thalbach insisted on a reconsideration of what the Scottish Play means and of what "tragedy" means. The word is generalizing towards what happens in "real life" as opposed to "on stage." A good production invariable challenges our preconceptions about the script, its genre, or the *Zeitgeist* in which the production occurs. Arditti saw Thalbach as a Wizard of Oz, working with "an empty box of tricks" (45). Tricks aplenty here—and they did not add up to some unified "vision" or "single, powerful effect." But the production did show what Central Europe learned long ago and what the rest of the industrialized Western World is learning now.

Regardless of the apparently affirmative closure of the play, the world around it moves in a history without *telos*. Here, no line of kings marched solemnly but surely into the seventeenth century. Instead, Macbeth awoke in a sweaty fever, aware that he was just a player in an endless sequence of murdered and murderer kings. That can be said of Macbeth. Whether it can be said of *Macbeth* is another question. Thalbach's is a *radical* interpretation and certainly her thesis can be debated, perhaps even refuted, but her interpretation results in a splendid production. That is what the script is there for.

The Buttonhole version was in many ways the opposite of the Schiller, and, again, the two productions help define the spectrum across this script can play.

Space defines what can occur within it. The Buttonhole's New End Theatre, in Hampstead, seats about one hundred people. The play was modulated to a conversational level that did not clash with the World War II costuming. It takes actors of great skill to cool the language of this heated script, but the Buttonhole company did so, pulling the audience forward towards their admirably understated performances.

This was "micro-acting" modulated to the "cool medium," but, as seldom or ever happens on television, this acting created a powerful continuum of energy in the theater, a system that is the product of our inhabiting the same space as the actors. The field of energy was particularly noticeable during the first half of the play (with the interval after the banquet scene) and during Lady Macbeth's superb sleepwalking scene.

Unlike the Schiller production, the Buttonhole stressed the development of character as opposed to the mocking of politics. This Duncan was not a pale, dirty old man, an object of ridicule because he *is* king, but an older general, in fact the only person over thirty in the production—thus in the world of the play—until the same actor (Bernard Lawrence) doubled later as Siward. Lawrence was an affectionate Duncan not sufficiently aware of the ambition of the rising generation. One powerful effect of this casting was that, once in power, the Macbeths were tentative and unsure of themselves, having knocked off their mentor and role model. More might have been made of Siward, given Malcolm's youth and Macduff's personal agenda. Siward might have reminded us of Duncan and suggested through the filter of retrospective irony that not all old men block the young from reaching their goals.

This was not some tragedy where crimes smash against the face of the cosmos, but it was a powerful narrative of a failed relationship. Sally Mortemore's Lady Macbeth was a woman whose life and being were predicated upon her husband's career. Certainly the script supports that approach to the role. This Lady Macbeth, thin and icily reserved (her reserve a shield for her shyness), had nothing of her own and no one to share anything with—except Macbeth and his ambition. Her goal was to promote his desires even if that meant poisoning the milk of his human kindness and, in a future she could neither forsee nor consciously experience, her own.

Macbeth, however, as chillingly delivered by Ian Reddington, began to enjoy his evil career, smiling at the language he discovered as he contemplated vivid inner imagery and began to perform deeds without names. True, he got in over his head, since the ghost of Banquo—or whatever it was—went beyond even Macbeth's imaginative constructs ("Take any shape but *that* . . ."). But Macbeth wouldn't share. Lady Macbeth asked eagerly, "What's to be done?" Let me in on it, please! But she was rebuffed, treated as a stereotypic woman, as Macduff had dealt with her earlier ("The repetition in a woman's ear . . ."). Once more she was alone, and, in retrospect, we realized that the only moment when she achieved her goal was when Macbeth descended from the murder room and she exclaimed, "My husband!" Immediately, she had to take those daggers back into that terrible room where her alter-ego father lies in his blood. Having attempted to create a future for her husband, and thus for herself, she was thrust forever into the past, as 5.1 shows. The previous scene ends with Malcolm's "The night is long that never sees the day." Good direction like that of Chris Geelan swings us instantly into the next scene, which shows that Lady Macbeth has indeed found an endless night: "Hell is murky."

The banquet scene is notorious. It is the moment in the script where a chuckle can begin to bubble in a single bosom, grow to an undercurrent of communal amusement, and expand until people are stamping their feet and begging handkerchiefs of strangers in order to mop up the wild tears of their hilarity.

Here it was powerful. An offstage piano played "Strangers in the Night" so that some of the tension of the ambush scene could be siphoned off. Geelan chose not to have an apparition appear, a choice appropriate to a scaled-down, modern world where the supernatural tends to be attributed to the disturbances of a single psyche. But this was a much more potent treatment than that

which Dessen attributes to televisual visitations from the supernatural, which are also narrowed to the psychological (*SFNL*, 1
and 8). The absence of the thing in the Buttonhole production
made Macbeth's sudden starts even more effective than had he
been sharing them with a bleeding Banquo. Macbeth has been
enjoying the dark world of his invention and has been inventing
himself within it. He has forgotten what he once knew—how
terrible it is to kill someone. He is now reminded—as Lady Macbeth will be from the resources of a deeper repression and a
deeper understanding, from an Augustinian standpoint, of what
she has done to herself. The minimalist approach of this production gave remarkable impact to the suggestion of larger powers
beyond the manipulative reach of the protagonists.

Lady Macbeth mustered some final energy in the banquet
scene. In a wonderful manipulation of point of view, we watched
Macbeth watch Lady Macbeth "sit" on the Ghost as she said,
"What? Quite unmann'd in folly?" We could almost picture the
Ghost as Macbeth cried out at the terribly dangerous thing she
was doing. Macbeth recovered and taught his guests to moan and
shake their hands, like children pretending to be afraid of the
boogieman. They responded with sound and gesture when the
Ghost reappeared and Macbeth shouted "Avaunt, and quit my
sight!" Again, our point of view was nicely split—partly with
Macbeth within his zone of terrible knowledge, and partly in the
"natural" world of his wife and guests about which Macbeth can
wonder even as he trembles at what he believes they must see
too. Our own sense of humor could respond here, and we could
chuckle when Macbeth, having toppled table, food, and wine
onto the floor, said "Pray you, sit still!" to his scattering guests.
The scene struck a balance between our responding *as* Macbeth,
as the intimate style had earlier invited us to do, but which we
would have had to refuse to do as we laughed at him, and our
responding *to* his wild behavior, as his movement into singularity
insists that we do as the drama continues. We were asked to give
a complex response here, and that response did allow for some
wry laughter, but not the paroxism that, in other productions,
emerges in occasional outbursts even during Lady Macbeth's mad
scene. Geelan's direction of the banquet scene was so skillful
that description of it in no way captures the complicated response
he elicited from his audience. With the exception of Dr. Johnson
and Poe, criticism is seldom as good as and never a substitute for
that which is criticized. That is particularly true of live theater,
which is its own unique experience occurring at a moment within

the continuum between stage and spectator. Those moments can be savored later and the recollection in tranquility *is* part of the experience, just inside the outer parenthesis that encapsulates the event of a live production of one of Shakespeare's scripts.

Other arresting moments in this production included Banquo's soliloquy ("Thou hast it now . . .") delivered under the stage's long upper platform on which Macbeth and Lady Macbeth, backs to us, acknowledged the "cheers" of the people. Banquo's fears were all the more authentic for the background of mechanically reproduced sound, which was a response to the "false face" of Macbeth's kingship. Macbeth's manipulation of the nervous and scruffy Murderers (Clive Kendall and Gerard Heys) was amusing, showing us how beautifully this sequence can work on stage. He invited them to sit in the two thrones. They put their fannies down very gingerly while Macbeth leaned his arms against the back of the thrones and chatted with them. Later, First Murderer (Kendall) was disappointed not to be invited to join Macbeth's dinner guests. He thought he had earned a knighthood within this debased dispensation. Ideology must be careful about whom it pretends to befriend. After 4.1, Macbeth found a doll abandoned by one of the Sisters. It cued his attack on Fife and, later, he touched it with his sword when he told Macduff, "My soul is too much charged / With blood of thine already." In 4.3 Macduff, having said "No, not fit to live!" almost killed Malcolm with the latter's own bottle of Scotch. Malcolm's escape, it seemed, was as lucky as Fleance's.

Modernizations of Shakespeare invariably run into some problems, and this "most medieval" of Shakespeare's plays is never an exception. Two problems were not disabling but were unnecessary. First: we may not bow to kings anymore but we sure as hell salute generals. Neither Macbeth nor Banquo knew how to greet Duncan after battle (1.4), and the meeting was awkwardly conducted. Second: towards the end, Macbeth, buoyed by false promises, sat in Dunsinane as if it were a health club. He scrawled "FEAR NOT" on the wall and relaxed in his sweatshirt and shorts. He had put on cat's whiskers with grease paint to show that he had nine lives to go along with his three ears. One could argue that by this time Macbeth has sundered his links with humanity, having become the beast that the metaphors, including his own, make him, and that he lives within the illusory security of the allegory he has constructed of surface meanings. But the alienation devices were stylistically inconsistent with the production's earlier muted and naturalistic values and robbed us of the sense of horror that we might have shared with Macbeth—this time—at the loss of a humanity so convincingly evoked for us earlier. Those brief and barren later soliloquies are lost if the character delivering them is merely ludicrous. Eric Porter, for example, shouted "It is a tale told by an idiot!" in the Classic Theater television production of 1974 as the camera rose judgementally above him and the words echoed down around his ankles, indicting *him* for idiocy. But that curse of God, one of the stages in the Kübler-Ross pattern, created a complex moment in which Macbeth recognized meaninglessness but still needed something to blame for what he had done to himself. Such complexity is not easily created from behind cat's whiskers.

At the end of the Buttonhole production, Malcolm stood on the platform above the main stage. This was a young Malcolm, frail alongside his stalwart colleagues. He also favored a potation—not the tea of the Thalbach production but Johnnie Walker Black. While the sounds of dubious battle were not as thunderous here as in the Thalbach version, the restoration in the Buttonhole seemed at best perfunctory and temporary, unless Malcolm proved to be a quick read. And he might. Malcolm (Steven Elder) paused on "we" in the final speech. He was speaking for the first time as "King of Scotland"—a title absorbing heredity, as the elective title, "King of Scots," would not. He thus erased the consistent "I" of his previous detractions. We were left with the hopes and fears that accompany any beginning.

The Weird Sisters, malicious schoolgirls from some nightmare of Stephen King, remained to repeat the opening scene in an undefined space soon to incorporate another play. They pulled another name from the First Sister's purse. Two and a half hours before, the paper had said "Macbeth." This time it said "Michael Bogdanov."

In the notes for the Bogdanov production, Graham Holderness asserts that *Macbeth* "never . . . presents . . . a moral order" to us; therefore, none can have been violated. That means that Macbeth misperceives the world he is in, and does so *in soliloquy*. If so, we must reexamine the soliloquy convention, in which, up until now, we have believed that the character speaking believes what he or she is saying. Moreover, we must reexamine everything in the play that alludes to "a moral order" and conclude that Lady Macbeth is faking her sleepwalking, for some obscure motive of personal gratification, as she may have faked her faint to somehow get Macbeth to stop talking. We are left to second-guess the error Macbeth admits he is making in killing Duncan. That error is defined in the dimensions of a moral order, even if he is only playing at similes (*"like* angels . . . *"like* a naked newborn babe . . ."). Macbeth would not agree with Holderness that "Macbeth is not in any sense 'evil,'" nor would Macbeth defend himself by claiming that "the individual cannot be blamed for the self-destructive contradictions of a divided society" (4). Macbeth may lack modern psychological and sociological language, indeed expresses himself with metaphors with which Dante would have no difficulty. He may confuse himself, but he is not confused about his role in society or about the role of society within a purposive cosmos. The play does not allow us to see him as "victim" of contradictions. He is not the marginalized character of modern existential drama, even if he can be played as "sub-tragic," as Thalbach certainly treated him.

To explore the script as modern drama that no longer creates links with some grand cosmic design is one thing. That approach keeps the script alive for us even as Jacobean England recedes into unrecoverable "historicity." To falsify the script is something else. The cultural materialist argument, for which I have great respect, collides here with what the script tells us, or, to put it another way, the critical thesis conflicts with what the characters believe to be the personal and cosmic *facts* of their world. To take the script and press it into a reexamination of politics, in which apparent virtue becomes merely a cover for malice, is one thing. Certainly the script supports that thesis on its existential level. But to impose upon the script the shallowest of recent jargon and taboos is to make for a pointless evening. The cultural materialist approach can be very helpful with the text of *King Lear*, where the cosmic facts *are* ambiguous, or in plays where history—"the event"—is arbiter of a "truth" that is itself the murkiest of constructs. The facts in *Macbeth* are a single *fact*—unless we argue, as we can argue in the case of Richard II's murder of an uncle and seizure of a cousin's inheritance, that certain actions have sundered Scotland *permanently* from God's aegis. If that is the case, then we have to dismiss a lot of evidence to the contrary. Perhaps we consider the play's expression of its *fact* just metaphor—Lady Macbeth's madness as evidence of repression, for example, and her expression of it as merely more metaphor: "Hell is murky." The play itself is metaphor, imitation of an action, but it is metaphor that does present a moral order to us. That order must be dealt with—even if only to be scorned, as in the Thalbach.

Having said that it isn't there at all, Bogdanov simply ignored it. Yet the absent "moral order" kept pestering the production that denied it. Interestingly, Holderness did not deal with Malcolm's elevation as "King of Scotland," a position beyond election, although Malcolm receives the necessary *collaudatio* in response to Macduff's "Hail!" Malcolm's elevation, combined with his virtue *and* political canniness, would seem to suggest that a reign has been restored, one that is destined to carry into the moment of the play's presentation before King James I. *Macbeth* is not a play that fits the cultural materialist categories, or, if it does, we need a better case than the assertions of the program made. We need the kind of challenge that Thalbach launched, a resketching of what is there into new and, as some critics complained, simplified outlines.

Bogdanov's was the weakest of the three Scottish Plays of early 1992. That is unfortunate because, with a world tour after the opening at Warwick in February, this is likely to be the most influential. The "set," visible as the audience entered the theater, was a huge pile of trash, looking like the set of the Bogdanov's seventies *Shrew* after Jonathan Pryce had demolished it. The dump was dominated by a huge crane. "If its purpose," said Wardle of the crane," [is] to drive home some message on the evil of stage-sanctioned violence (as argued in the programme), it is as ineffectual as Lepage's mudbath" (*IonS* 12 July 1992). Lepage's mudbath will be treated later on these pages in chapter 8.

Three hags entered to prey on garbage. We watched this dull and unedifying process almost interminably until a modern battle broke out. We were supposed to be shocked from the lethargy induced by the search of the dump by the hags. Lights simulated rocket launchers, men rushed about in fatigues brandishing modern weapons, and aircraft fired missiles. We lived again the grandeur that was the Falklands, the glory that was Desert Storm. The actors, we were being told, would be buried in "concept," rather than allowed to play out the ideas that modern directors and actors still find in this early-modern encoding.

It was also clear that we would endure long and pointless pauses while stagehands changed sets. Pauses within scenes for emphasis or reaction? Of course. But never *between* scenes. Shakespeare knew how to swing from one place to another instantly. He brought a new set of actors on, had them identify themselves and tell us where they were, and did not allow the audience to lapse back to an identity separate from that which is participating in the dramatic continuum. One of the worst examples of the many in the Bogdanov production was the exchange of banquet for billiard table for the discussion of Lennox and Lord (3.6). This brief scene requires no set, certainly no set change, and surely no game of pool. Spectators talked unabashedly during the long set changes, and some of the actors had difficulty pulling them back to the ostensible drama being enacted. The supporting cast was weak, but it was also undercut by this unforgivable direction. The actors became Bogdanov's marginalized victims.

The production got some unfortunate laughs, or perhaps this seeming ineptitude was a postmodernist effort to create some intertextuality between the script and animated cartoons. Duncan ascended the catwalk and sat on the golden throne on top of the crane. His feet dangled ludicrously over the edge, so that his promotion of Malcolm to Prince of Cumberland was greeted by laughter. The pistol shots fired at a fleeing Fleance got another laugh from a startled audience, as did the rising of the ostensible victims without benefit of blackout at the end of the scene. There may have been a technical glitch at the beginning of the run of this production, but it looked like another play, where ghosts rise on the churchyard paths to glide. The end of the scene at Fife got a similar laugh for the same reasons. This approach may have been meant to alienate us from *over*involvement, but it forced us to reject what the script presents as factual event. We are willing, as theater audience, to suspend our disbelief in response to a consistent style and tone. We got no consistency here. If the production's purpose was to replace "tragic heroism" with the heroic efforts of actors against an upstart machine, it did, indeed, succeed. But that is another play and one hates to see Shakespeare's play destroyed in the service of a far lesser one. In caricature and political cartoons the person depicted remains in view, however distorted for the sake of a particular emphasis. The process will bring howls, as did the Thalbach production. It was, however, inventive, exciting, and validly within the School of Brecht. It showed how a postmodern vision can reignite the script. But reignition and incineration are two different things.

Michael Pennington and Jenny Quayle fought free of the wreckage created for them to do some superb acting, and "theirs," as Wardle said, "is a powerful and well-designed partnership" (*IonS* 12 July 1992). Pennington is known as a "performer"—that is an actor who works most effectively by himself, as opposed to in situations requiring ensemble work—and his soliloquies were brilliant. "If it were done" was performed in the shadows leading down from backstage right, "Is this a dagger?" in the similar corridor coming from stage left, and "To be thus is nothing" from center stage, as he sat isolated on his uneasy throne. The irony of insecurity coming from the position on stage reserved for *power* was itself powerful. Quayle's first soliloquy, after she had read the letter, was partly whispered and pulled the audience forward in intense concentration. Pennington even pulled us into the banquet scene with a moving "Blood hath been shed 'ere now." Then we were forced to watch Banquo climb to the top of the giant crane so that Macbeth could see him as Macbeth tried to toss back a needed jolt of wine. The guests did not see Banquo, of course, but they must have wondered what that crane was doing up there above the chandelier. Were they renovating battlements in anticipation of a coming siege?

As the run continues, the actors are likely to surrender to the machine, recognizing that it takes too much energy to keep pulling the audience back to the issues that Pennington and Quayle are wonderfully capable of exploring. Let the ticket-buyers contemplate the trash and watch the crane, as if staring through the peepholes at a construction site. They will walk away, suitably uninspired, and think, "Well, that's Shakespeare after all, and isn't it too bad that it no longer means anything."

But it does, it does. Schiller and Buttonhole proved that even this old script retains energies that still communicate powerfully to modern audiences. But, then, it takes no ghost come from the early seventeenth century to tell us this. If Bogdanov had had the decency to let his actors come onstage and downstage and *act*, this winter of the Scottish Play would have been a season of great content.

The reviews of Bogdanov's production touched on some of the problems that emerged early in the run. Peter McGarry called it "a stylish enterprise," but did say that "problems arise when the actors fail to project over the sound effects" and that the production "verges on being too technical at the expense of text" (*CET* 20 February 1992). Robin Thornber described the "clouds of smoke, strobe flashes and the sound of a helicopter [and the] three old bagladies . . . scavenging in the rubble for the boots off a corpse." He claimed that "the style is brilliantly effective at making Shakespeare accessible to young audiences." Perhaps—if the youngsters live in Belfast or Brooklyn. Thornber did, however, find that the "analysis of feudal monarchy" was a "dubious theory" for the production (G 27 February 1992).

The production arrived in Chicago in June 1992 and received unenthusiastic notices. It was, observed Hedy Weiss, "overwhelmed too often by its scenic hardware . . . the reappearing crane, the cracked-mirror lid of a toxic waste tank where the witches cavort and the metallic clangings of John Leonard's synthesized score all prove more distracting than consuming . . . [The production] feels as if each of the scenes was rehearsed in a vacuum, with little thought to how they would flow together as a whole" (23 and 26). That effect could well be the result of a concentration on setting and "concept," as opposed to what the play might mean as an interconnected dramatic entity. M. S. Mason said that "the production itself was uneven, not all the cast came up to the mark, and director Michael Bogdanov got a bit carried away with his central prop and symbol—an electronic crane" (*CSM* 26 June 1992). Joe Pollack reported that the production was "overproduced and overdirected . . . understanding went out the window when Macbeth and Macduff tossed aside their automatic weapons and picked up swords for the climactic duel. The major intrusion came from a shiny cherry picker, the contraption used by telephone linemen and others to work high above the street . . . too many times it appeared to be in use just to show it off" (3 and 6).

The problem is not just a single weak production. The problem is that such a production represents "Shakespeare" to audiences, as do bad productions in Washington, D. C., New York, and the "execrable productions of *The Taming of the Shrew* and *Romeo and Juliet* which toured [Great Britain] in the summer of 1990 with well-respected professional touring companies" that Peter Holland mentions (*ShS* 44, 158). Better audiences may help drive such productions and companies off the boards, but if the audiences are told that bad productions are "good"—as they are told too often—the loser will be good productions and good companies, because, having been lied to once too often, no audience will pay to see them. At least the Bogdanov *Macbeth* is getting the bad press it deserves.

7

Measure for Measure at Stratford, Canada, 1992

THE space in which a play is produced makes almost all the difference: as J. L. Styan says, "the shape of the stage affects the acting and the response to it, even controls the play and the experience of it" (Thompson & Thompson, 209). The Stratford, Canada, main stage is a platform with several levels, an upper stage, and several entrances. The stage sits below the raked auditorium, with three sides of the stage open to view. This format has great advantages over the Stratford, England, main stage, a giant proscenium that at once dominates its huge auditorium and is in turn dominated by that outer space because of the inflexibility of the stage.

But altering the sightlines at the Stratford-on-Avon main stage by building a thrust out from under proscenium would, according to Adrian Noble, involve changing the "sightlines [so that] we would have to close the entire balcony and therefore lose 485 seats" (letter, 3 November, 1992). Assuming a full balcony, that would come to some $20,000 per performance, a figure that even the cultural materialists might gasp at, even if they did not applaud what performance may be losing to a balcony. Furthermore, the Stratford-on-Avon main stage, incapable of "metadramatic" possibilities, invites "reliance on the auxiliaries of staging, on the technicians of lighting , sound, design, and special effects" (Berry, *SQ* [1985]: 595); in other words, on the notorious elements of "director's theatre" at its worst. No wonder so many directors there prefer the Swan, with its long apron and balconies that encourage actors to come out and to look up, or the intimate Other Place, which can incorporate even a "big" play like *Richard III*.

It is possible to squander the opportunities provided by an attractive playing area, as Michael Bogdanov proved by squashing a "concept" down on *Macbeth* at Warwick in February of 1992.

His fine actors, Michael Pennington and Jenny Quayle, could escape his giant crane only fleetingly and only often enough to show us how well they might have done had the director conceived of his stage as a place where actors can *act*, as opposed to a space for the display of his own misunderstanding of how plays work. Ideally, Shakespeare's stage, as Styan says, "is primarily and properly the target area for imaginative thought and emotion." We, the audience, are "the sharers who allow the actors to act" ("Stage Space," 196, 197), and the director must assist in that process, not interfere with it, as Bogdanov seems so consistently intent on doing.

Robert Shaughnessy rightly suggests that "the likelihood is that the RSC's main house [at Stratford, England] is going to look increasingly irrelevant to what is exciting and innovative in Shakespearean performance" (100). In the year that the RSC was bequeathed its stage—1932—John Drinkwater, a proscenium playwright, discussed the limitations of the proscenium stage as a site for Shakespeare:

> The difficulties of the proscenium stage in the matter of action are usually overcome in the more intelligent kind of Shakespearean production, [but] those of intimate contact between the stage and the audience are not. Here the loss has been serious. [T]o . . . visualise . . . performance at The Globe, however dimly and imperfectly, is to realize what impoverishment in this respect is nearly always suffered by Shakespeare when he is acted in the theatres today. . . . There was no effective frontier between the play and its public. Nothing like the convention of the fourth wall had been dreamt of, and the players neither could nor wished to pretend that they were not being overseen and overheard. . . . In the proscenium-stage theatre [we] miss half the secret of [Shakespeare's] dramatic art. (89–90)

The truth of what Drinkwater says about the erasure of frontiers can be felt even in a production that makes no direct allusion to its audience but occurs on a stage with dimensions and perspectives not framed behind a fourth wall. *Measure for Measure* is a script that does not call for any direct reference to the audience. Certainly the Duke's sermons-to-self and other ruminations are not meant to create the "relationship" that Hamlet establishes with his audience (cf. Berry "Hamlet and the Audience" and Pennington) and are often shifted around, as in Langham's production, where "the sword of justice" replaced Vincentio's telling concern with "place and greatness," a brief speech invariably defined as a textual problem, when it really illuminates one possible motive of his plan—the reburnishing of his own tarnished image. Styan notes the desire of the actor playing Hamlet "to step out of his play, even outside his part [to be] alone on indeterminate space" ("Stage Space," 198). The characters in *Measure for Measure*, however, although they engage in soliloquy, cannot escape to some extrapolated plane where they can ponder universals (cf. Beckerman, 48–49, on the Duke). If Isabella, for example, complains *to* us, she erases the tightening nature of the trap she defines, and diminishes rather than enhances our response to her dilemma. In this production, Angelo's "What's this?" would have been a public embarrassment if addressed to us, since he was discovering, as David Prosser said, "an unexpected erection" (*Whig & Standard*).

If anything, Langham used his space to distance us from the action. It was a dark zone reminiscent of Fagan's final cell, a grim city in police-state central Europe, although placed in Freud's time, in which even Lucio wore somber clothes—a narcissist dressing as he believes successful people dress. Lighting shifted the scene from ducal chambers (marred only by an unnecessary psychiatrist's couch) to convent façade, to jail, to street, all bound grimly together in scene individable. After his first meeting with Isabella, for example, Angelo remained in shadows, down left, as the Duke examined Juliet. Her "injurious love" bit into Angelo, who then swung onstage with "When I would pray and think, I think and pray / To several subject." It was a superb sequence, showing that Angelo had been up all night and could be expected to lose control when next he saw Isabella. This production did not use the levels, steps, and corridors, or gesture towards its audience, as did the same company's *Love's Labour's Lost*, where a golf ball was actually driven into the balcony, but it provided a continuity and resultant tension that would have had to be achieved by other means, if at all, within proscenium premises.

When director Langham said "I don't think that *Measure for Measure* is an appropriate play for this theatre" (6), he feared that this large auditorium might overpower "an intimate play that requires mankind to be put under a microscope and does not require the sort of sweeping movements that the Festival stage usually asks for" (Langham, 6–7), but Langham underestimated the versatility of his stage and his own skill in using it. Alex Suszek accurately described the "scene flow": "as seamless as a film" (*GPN* 3 September 1992).

The interview with Langham was conducted early in the rehearsal period. Designer Desmond Heeley showed a little more confidence in the process when he said, "In *Measure*, there are many different directions in which the visual line can go. . . we've had to wait for awhile, until things could appear. And what is marvelous is that this place allows us to do that" (10). The "permission" is part of a process that resulted in a coherent narrative sweep that pulled the play's conflicting elements into that dynamic space that Shakespeare invariably turns towards his audience, but that proscenium stages turn off more often than on. Writing of the Stratford, Ontario, stage thirty years ago, Peter D. Smith said, "when an audience is confronted by that stage, it prepares itself, almost by a reflex action, to exert its imagination to a unique degree" (526).

Langham was not asking for a proscenium, but for a smaller theater like The Other Place, which might well have closed his production in to a greater intimacy. What Heeley did create within the large auditorium was an "ambiguous canvas [with] different pictures on it rather than [anything] very specific." Heeley found "that the more abstract [he] can make the shape, the more focus . . . it can produce for the actors" (9). Actors people the space, providing the specificity, with the invariable assistance of the language ("And have you nuns no farther privileges?"). And, of course, the audience participates in and completes the process. That is one reason why, as Richard Hornby says, "excessive historical accuracy is a mistake when setting or costuming Shakespeare; a certain ambiguity about space and time is usually a virtue" (*HR* [Summer 1988]: 431).

Jonathan Miller's Greenwich production in 1975 was as grim as Langham's though more grey than black, and set interiorily in the Vienna of the year of *The Interpretation of Dreams*. But there, the long narrow stage, perhaps all that Greenwich provided, emphasized the narrow path these characters trod. It captured the pinched nature of Julian Curry's repressed Angelo and of Penelope Wilton's Isabella, intent on the veil and incomprehensibly capable of attracting both Angelo and Vincentio. She shook her head at Joseph O'Conor's Duke and strode back to her convent, leaving him alone on stage at the end. That was a powerful ending, but it was primarily "intellectual." The shape of the stage itself did not pull emotional energy forward. Stratford, Canada, insists on that involvement, whether the production explicitly invites it or not. The stage is open to us so that it pulls us towards it and creates a continuum of energy that proscenium stages rebuff. Suffice it that Langham and Heeley drew us towards what Styan calls "a fluid stage that encouraged not merely the leaps of place and time, but also the quick changes of time and style designed to expose the areas of the mind where conflict and paradox lie" ("Stage Space," 197).

The rejection of the Duke may be falling out of fashion, as certain elements of the feminist movement achieve a conciliation with the male world (but see Rosenberg on the ambiguous ending, à la Barton, Thompson & Thompson, 84, and J. Cook, 95–101). Kate Nelligan could hardly refuse Kenneth Colley's Duke in the BBC-TV version of 1979. Television was then a "Father Knows Best" medium and is, even now, not a site for ambiguity. Things must be wrapped up in the final few minutes and the defiance of that norm leads only to a smashing of picture tubes. Carla Mendonca's 1990 Isabella at Oxford accepted a kneeling Duke, humbling himself as he had asked her to do. She was thrilled at what he had done—for *her*—and saw him as the exception among men and therefore worth embracing. This was particularly the case when this Duke was contrasted with Terence McGinity's Angelo, "more than usually repressed and unselfknowing. He trudges on stage with an armful of official literature, and the rumpled suit and pinched, scrubbed face of some middle-level Rotarian . . . but there is no missing the excitement blazing in his eyes or the promptness with which he dumps those books . . . and his behind on to the throne. . . . Suburban savagery is implicit throughout his performance" (Nightingale, *T* 7 July 1990, 25). Juliet Stevenson at Stratford-on-Avon in 1984 (main stage) gave the Duke an enthusiastic, if chaste, kiss when he divulged his stratagem ("The image of it gives me content already"). She was meant, according to David Massey (Duke) to participate at the end in "the miracle of what [everyone] is seeing in each other" (Jackson & Smallwood, 30). Stevenson believes that the Duke "manipulates [Isabella] unconscionably" (Rutter, 29), but says

> Our director wanted [the play] to end as comedy—he meant comedy as defined by a resolved ending. But we discovered that a resolved ending really depends on the Duke. . . . I stood and looked at him. Watched to see what he would do. Because unless the Duke takes on the trial of *himself*, which involves bringing himself to let Lucio off the hook, to exercise forgiveness he hasn't learned the capacity for mercy from Isabella, and there is no justification for a 'happy' ending. Nothing mutual has been established. He watched me watching, turned back to Lucio, and reprieved the death sentence. (Rutter, 51–52; her emphasis)

This ending convinced Michael J. Collins:

[Stevenson's] long walk down the stage was simultaneously the seal
of her goodness and generosity and a thrilling, entirely convincing
confirmation that, even in Vienna (or in the world just outside the
theatre), men and women can sometimes be more noble, more heroic,
more loving than we have any right ever to expect. When the Duke
then moved toward her as she spoke, the audience saw confirmed as
well the love of these two extraordinary people, who had struggled
together to bring some measure of justice to the world, 'whose relationship,' to use the words of Gary Taylor, had developed 'gradually,
naturally, and irresistibly' though the play (*TLS* 16 August 1985, 905)
. . . the play seemed not only to have earned, in the tangle of an all
too familiar city, its comic ending but also to affirm, in their closing
embrace, that we may yet, in our own cities, find some measure of
justice and joy. (26)

The Stratford-on-Avon production, then, was meant to be *comedy*, in the deepest sense, and not problem play. Angelo put his
arm around Mariana. Isabella untied Claudio, who joined Juliet,
and the Duke's "you all should know" was directed to us, even
in the Stratford-on-Avon main house, so that we could participate
in this miracle. Only Lucio's violent objection to marrying Kate
Keepdown shadowed this reconciliation, but Lucio's was the
"truth" that Shakespeare poises against his comings-together:
Jacques, Malvolio, Antonio (in *The Tempest*), and, of course,
Shylock.

Massey says he "never minded" the laugh that his proposal to
Isabella got (30), but Roger Warren called the laughter "derisive,"
"an inevitable consequence of the production's loss of any sense
of direction. The sheer integrity, consistency, and power of this
Isabella enabled her to survive the collapse of the production; but
I heartily wished that this distinctive individualist had . . . turned
the Duke down" (*SQ* [1984]: 457). While the production built towards this conclusion with what N. W. Bawcutt termed "a sense
of steadily ripening intimacy between [Isabella] and the Duke"
(40)—she had hugged the Duke and called him *"good* father"
earlier—her acceptance was unconvincing. Can the script *ever*
lead to "miracle"? Did the ending sentimentalize the experience,
somewhat as Coleridge's Mariner does ("he prayeth best . . .")?
Was it that the proscenium and the precise geometrical patterns
of the earlier part of the production and the suddenly introduced
"State Pen" prison, along with the stagey mirror that Adrian Noble was using in his productions of that period and an Angelo
who, as Irving Wardle said, was already "an old hand at criminal
seduction" (*T* 5 October 1983) had alienated one so completely

from the production that he could only participate in Lucio's response? Or did he hope with Warren that this Isabella would scorn an "incompetent maneuverer" (457)? This ending sharpened response to the script, and is dealt with thus at length because several excellent discussions of this moment in the script do not deal with this production (cf. Dawson, McGuire, Nicholls, and Williamson), in some cases, of course, because their analysis predates it. (But see Shrimpton's positive response, 201–4.)

Brian Bedford's Duke at Stratford was a bumbler. Lawrence Devine nonetheless found this a "Duke-centered" production, as opposed to the Angelocentric, one of 1975, when Bedford essayed Angelo (*DFP* 17 August 1992, 3E). Doug Bale noticed the same shift in emphasis, finding that "the play [does] seem to revolve legitimately around the duke, not Angelo" (*LFB* 19 August 1992). (See Adrian Noble's analysis of the shift in dramatic emphasis from Angelo to the Duke: Berry, *Directors*, 167–69.)

Bedford almost gave the game away when he knew who the Provost was and when he anticipated the Duke's return to applaud Isabella's participation in the Friar's plan. He had no idea why he was absenting himself, a fact underscored by Escalus's anger at being passed over, "Though first in question." As Hornby argues, "whether characters have motives or not, they always have conscious objectives" (*AE*, 34). Here, the intention seemed to be a curiosity that made the sure-fire scenes with Lucio work with splendid focus. Whether Lucio's defamation is accurate or not, this Duke was asking for it. (I notice in audiences recently a great enjoyment of disguise and mistaken identity, perhaps because 'realistic' television does not provide us with the superior position of 'dramatic irony,' as Shakespeare so consistently does.) Perhaps Langham decided that the "once upon a time a duke decided to disguise himself and go out among his people" folk tale was sufficient for the opening narrative drive. This approach made sense of the Duke's fumbling effort to explain to Friar Thomas, indeed to insist that the Friar ask Vincentio why "I do this." The Duke seemed to be asking himself, "Why *am* I doing this?"

Langham did not know, when interviewed, "how the play is going to end" (7). The energies worked out in rehearsal, particularly with a young actress working with this company for the first time, would dictate the ending. And that approach could give the scenes a tentative, provisional feeling, like those in *Casablanca*, where Bergman did not know as she was playing the scenes whether she would end up with Bogart or Paul Henreid. Eliza-

beth Marvel's Isabella was angular, even awkward ("a bit un-
gainly": Prosser: having "a tall powerful-looking frame": *New
Yorker*). She took her cue from Lucio. "Touch him!" She did, until
a discomfited Angelo pulled his hands away. This Isabella had
yet to master the hiding-of-hands technique that the Sisterhood of
Saint Clare demonstrated in the first convent scene. This Isabella
needed to reach out and touch, like the hapless Wing Bid-
dlebaum. It was her "psychological gesture," as Michael Chekhov
calls it, and she had the Duke's hand to take at the end. This was
a "natural" result of the energy the actress had created with her
naive Isabella. She, like Stevenson, had hugged the Friar earlier,
and had touched the man beneath the robes, as Bedford showed
by registering puzzled pleasure. The dribbling dart had found an
incomplete bosom. At the end, she found a comfortable "father,"
particularly as contrasted with Colm Feore's taut Angelo, the ultimate product of an externally dictated environment. Counter to
what this ending communicated, an observer can see a *comparison*
between Angelo and the Duke suggested by the script, in that
each man wants to use Claudio as a bribe to achieve Isabella:
"This Isabella," said Kenneth B. Steele, "was not an eager, expect-
ant bride, but a woman startled to be caught once again in a man's
trap" (17). Daniel Watermeier's version was more consistent with
the tone of this production: the Duke "seemed at the end a genu-
inely good and wise ruler, worthy of Isabella's admiration and
love" (21). That makes the play sound as if it were directed by a
critic of the allegorical school, but it was accurate about the ending. Whatever the Duke "intended," he did expose the hypocrisy
of his own police state and perhaps moved it towards a body
politic a trifle kinder and gentler. Watermeier saw Angelo at the
end of this production as "the serpent still lurking in the garden"
(21). Perhaps so, but not personally so. This Angelo had been
destroyed, but the possibility of the fascism he represented still
lingered, as it shadows all governments that affect benevolence.

It is to the play's "modernity" that the program notes by Elliott
Hayes's pointed: "In light of current attention being paid to
charges of sexual harassment, particularly the Anita Hill case
. . ." (11). That emphasis might have been inevitable, but it was
unfortunate, since it tended to dictate critical response: "Ages-
old hypocrisy still rings true" (*G&M*), with the subhead, "The
duplicity and confusion characterized in *Measure for Measure* bring
to mind the televangelist scandals and allegations of sexual mis-
conduct against the U.S. presidential candidates." "Bard's blast at
harassment timeless" (*WS* 17 August 1992). "Bard casts sharp

eye on today's mores" *(TS)*. "Yesterday's play brings home today's issues" *(BPP)*. "Dark comedy relevant in today's climate of sexual harassment" *(KWR)*. "Measure for Measure addresses matters of concern relevant now" *(SO)*. One critic even lost the production for a moment in the march of sociology: Angelo "sensuously rubbed his hand over [Isabella's] close-cropped hair. It was a fascinating image of harassment, made all the more repulsive by today's statistics and headlines on violent acts against women" (Watermeier, 20). The act was either repulsive (it was) or it wasn't and the bow towards political correctness invited by the program notes did not make it more so, anymore than a statistic makes more horrible a single death at Dachau.

It becomes too easy, then, to exclaim about how modern and timeless the old Bard is—surprise!—and not to notice what this production actually did. A weak Claudio, for example, was not helped by an Isabella who upstaged his "Ay, but to die!" with her anxiety about his constancy. Here, both young actors needed help from their director, and the reviewers should have noted the lapse in energy in an otherwise powerful production.

The production's great strength, along with its subtle use of the acting space, was to balance its serious and amusing elements. The critics proved this by disagreeing about the production's tone. The *Thunder Bay Chronicle Journal* found the production "almost unrelentingly dark and dreary. . . . It's uncomfortable to watch. It's frightening, it's also thought-provoking" (20 September 1992). "As if to emphasize the tone," said George Mathewson, "the characters are dressed in browns and greys and move though an autumnal light. A set of cobble-stones and rusty iron bars adds to the gloom" *(Ob* 17 August 1992). Daniel Watermeier responded to tonal changes during the production: "Michael J. Whitfield's marvelously plastic lighting evoked various moods of chiaroscuro gloominess, of cold, bleak starkness, or, in the contrasting final scenes, of warm glowing hopefulness" (20). Robert Reid found that "Desmond Heeley's black set and sombre costume designs suggest a country where sexual licentiousness is a complex symbol encompassing political corruption, moral depravity and spiritual bankruptcy" *(R* 15 August 1992). Marion Duke, on the other hand, felt that this production "highlights the comical aspects of the play," but that "This emphasis doesn't always work. . . . The characters are too dark, too duplicitous" *(LB* 26 August 1992, 12). Brad Reaume detailed the subjects of the plays jokes and said, "it doesn't sound funny. But it is" *(CC* 9 September 1992), and Matthew Smith added, "What might get lost in all this is that *Measure for Measure* is a very funny play" (*IT* 19 August 1992). Edward Hayman suggested that "Langham's droll production finds fresh fun at every turn" (*DN* 18 August 1992). Lawrence DeVine found it "charming . . . a much funnier 'Measure' than we usually get" (*DFP* 17 August 1992, 3E). Those who hold with gloom have the edge, because, as Liam Lacey noted, "the humor is set in a context of brutal state oppression" (*G&M* 17 August 1992).

Suczek remarked on "the highly effective musical score underlying almost the entire course of the action" (*GPN* 3 September 1992) and the *Chronicle Journal* called the score "by turns foreboding and decadent" (20 September 1992). Stewart Brown pointed at "a constant edgy undertone of music" (*HD* 17 August 1992). Watermeier found the score "especially effective during 2.4, when a subtly pulsating, repetitive rhythm underscored Angelo's advances and Isabella's terror" (20–21). Composer Stanley Silverman likened his score to Schoenberg, an appropriate composer not just for the dark setting, but one whose challenge to the traditional major-minor tonal system, unresolved dissonances, and contrasting lyrical or dramatic progressions seem appropriate to this script—as the critics in their diversity of response seemed to suggest.

Modernization seems to insist on the updating of the language. (But see Robin Phillips's defense of using Shakespeare's language, including "codpiece" in his 1912 setting for the Stratford, Ontario, 1975 *Measure:* Berry, *Directors,* 106–13.) In the current production for example, "unbuttoning" substituted for "untrussing," "apt forgiveness" for "apt remission" and "wall'd up" for the lovely word "circummur'd." Why? The loss of the latter word represents a loss to the language, even if our comprehension is (possibly) aided by the emendation. Why must Ragozine, a perfectly good "pirate" become a "smuggler"? The "prenzie" Angelo can become "pristine," but must "viewless winds" become "invisible"? "Viewless" winds are not just incapable of being seen but have no point of view, no motivation, only the "intention" of aimless movement and the movement of whatever the wind encounters—like the dust of Francesca Rimini in Dante. In mere randomness can exist eternal punishment. Much was lost here for the sake of dubious "clarity."

Langham suggested that what he has learned as a director is how to help the actor be "private on stage," so that we can think, "he really is by himself, he doesn't know we're here" (7). It may be that the script of *Measure for Measure* calls for that isolation. If so, the Stratford stage created a powerful medium for our response to the closed-off nature of these characters and thus to their coming together both in script and curtain-call at the end.

Fifty years ago, Margaret Webster touched upon the element that Langham's approach to the script emphasized: "This . . . is a play which has possibly grown more comprehensible as the audiences have become educated to . . . the importance and complexity of the subconscious mind" (190). That sector was available to us in this production because the space became what Thomas Clayton calls "a theatre of sharing primarily through the script and its enacting that makes that [sharing] not only possible but inescapable" (256). Here, the curtain calls argued at once the new-found if tenuous unity of Vienna and the unity of the company that had imitated this Vienna on stage. Thus the final bows permitted us at last a physical sharing which is one of the benefits and joys of good theater everywhere.

8

The Good, the Horrid, and the In-Between

FIVE productions of 1992 and one of early 1993 demonstrate the range of quality available in Shakespearean production today: the *Richard II* at the Mark Taper Forum (May 1992), the well-staged *As You Like It* at Bob Jones University (November), the Lepage *A Midsummer Night's Dream* (August), and a *Hamlet* at the Shakespeare Theatre in Washington (October), which was weak with Tom Hulce in the lead but better with Gary Sloan in the title role. The critical response to the *Richard II* and the *Midsummer Night's Dream* suggests that one purpose of Shakespeare production is to provoke disagreement. No one was neutral about either production. Regardless of what the critics say, the author's lack of neutrality in the case of the *Richard II* and *A Midsummer Night's Dream* emerges from the guidelines announced at the outset. A special instance of "reading Shakespeare on stage" emerges from Tina Packard's production of *Twelfth Night* in April 1993.

Robert Egan's powerful *Richard II* in Los Angeles was hammered by the reviewers, primarily, it seems, because the reviewers took the program notes seriously and could not permit the values of the production itself to take hold of them. It is probably wise not to read that "literary" material until later, if at all. No explanation in a program accounts for what happens on stage, where tone of voice, movement, and gesture go far beyond those printed words in the "text." It is also possible that a spectator from the East Coast, long accustomed to Joseph Papp's racially-mixed productions, settled easily into watching the *play*, as opposed to the colors or lack of colors of the actors's skins.

In a pretentious and politically correct essay in the program ("Performing Arts"), a professor claimed that "a multi-cultural production can become a profound example of the way Shakespeare's play confronts the real uses of images in *realpolitik*, while also prodding us to imagine history as an ongoing rebellion against the illusive power of images" (Little, 9). A play can be used, of course, to make a number of statements, as in the notorious case of *Henry V*, which becomes pro-war or anti-war, according to *the Zeitgeist* and a director's angling of the material at his audience—cutting the scene with the traitors, as Olivier did in his film, having Henry "space out" as a host of repressed material flooded him, as Branagh did in his film. Henry V shows us how to manipulate images once Richard II has eradicated the *symbols* of kingship, in uneasy cooperation with Bolingbroke. But how does multiculturalism in any way relate to the issues of the *play*? That the issue may bear on the nature of theater today and on the politics of a particular production is true. Having seen productions over the years with interracial casting—Joseph Papp's powerful *King Lear* in 1974, with James Earl Jones, Raul Julia, Paul Sorvino, and Lee Chamberlin, and an excellent, though underappreciated *Cymbeline* at the Arena in D.C. in 1983, with black actor Peter Francis James, as Posthumus, for example—one asks with Richard Hornby:

> What will it take for race to move . . . into the background on our stage? "Color-blind casting," as it is often called, is clearly not possible unless our society itself becomes color-blind, which is not only unlikely but probably undesirable. Besides, there are cases when race is at issue in a play (a white Othello would indeed be a distortion), which is why Actors' Equity makes them an exception to its recommended color-blind casting policy. What we *can* aim for is color *neutral* casting, in which we accept the conventionalized nature of the stage, and suspend concern about the race of an actor unless the play itself stresses it. (*HR* [Autumn 1989]: 460; his emphasis)

Unless the *play* is dealing with race, then, it is illegitimate to force the production to do so. What happens to a production like David Chambers's *Cymbeline*, at the Arena a decade ago, is that the race of the actor becomes irrelevant at some point, melting into the issues the play is exploring, which in *Cymbeline* is not race. As Hornby says about Jones's performance as Judge Brack in Ibsen's *Ghosts*: "if [spectators] were honest with themselves, they would have had to admit that they soon forgot about Jones's race in *Ghosts* because his performance was so strong" (460). With a black actor playing Aaron or Othello, race is always an issue. It is there in the text, regardless of protests to the contrary (cf. Jonathan Miller).

The *Richard II* program went on to say that "Multiculturalists share the view that . . . unified approaches to history are—despite their longevity—a mere phase of history, not some transcendent and always present cultural truism." For Bolingbroke, "history is neither anarchic nor confined to a single hegemonic order" (Little, 9). This is, of course, to set up a straw-person. Who since Henry Adams has espoused unified theories of history? Hitler. Ronald Reagan, who made a destructive effort to get back to a time that he thought he understood. Can *Richard II*, that very "ambiguous" script, be *effectively* reduced to propaganda? The play may be showing, through its movement "From Richard's night, to Bolingbroke's fair day"—a statement doused with the acid of irony—that a king can shatter the totalizing mythologies that support his "Body Politic" (which incorporates a unified approach to history superbly articulated by John of Gaunt) by murdering an uncle and seizing the inheritance of a cousin. A king can destroy the premises that sustain him and radically alter the nature of the office. Shakespeare's "discourse" is not conducted with the murky metaphors of political correctness but often within the "contextualizing" imagery of the theater itself, as in *Richard II*. We are asked as this script moves by to see it as *conflict* not *message*. The play is, as I have argued elsewhere, a clash of historical interpretations, but Bolingbroke's pragmatism can hardly be seen as superior to Gaunt's medieval vision. Indeed, Bolingbroke would like very much to get back *into* the world he has conspired to destroy. For that, he is a model for later usurpers—Claudius and Macbeth.

Richard II is "about" a lot of things. It is "about" Watergate and that analogy was used when Ian Richardson in 1972 discussed the extraordinary reaction of American audiences to John Barton's famous production. "It's Watergate!" he exclaimed. Well, yes, the play, like history, depicts a man named Richard engaged in an increasingly desperate effort to retain power. But the murder of Gloucester and a second-rate burglary are not analogous crimes, and have only a "cover-up" in common. The effort to coerce a Shakespeare script onto a narrow wedge of *Zeitgeist* usually fails, and it is unfortunate that the Taper production was judged on the basis of the assertions about multiculturalism in the Program.

The production was about power. It vividly depicted the paradigm shift from Richard's concept of a divinely premised kingship to the reign of the pragmatist, Bolingbroke. The latter, exponent of conservative values, ends up leading a revolution. Here, Bolingbroke cradled Richard's body ("a dying Richard," as one caption said) in his arms, aware that Richard had taken with him all the intrinsic and valuable qualities of kingship and that he, Bolingbroke, had sacrificed a vital segment of his own humanity in

attaining the crown. We could believe his "mourning here" because he had cooperated in destroying the world that had nur-
tured him and the system of values which he had, ironically,
defended in launching an attack on Richard. It did not matter
that this was an Afro-American Bolingbroke. He still spoke the
words that the script provides him.

Richard II must be stylized on stage. Richard insists on that
from the opening line about "time-honored Lancaster," even if
we will watch Richard violate "time" as it pertains as a kind of
"timelessness" to the premises of his kingship. Here, the narrow
backstage area of the Forum's semi-circular stage featured Elizabethan costumes on dressmaker's dummies. This was the past, the
heritage of history and of the theater. Since the production played
to the audience, in soliloquy and direct address, the effect was of
history itself driving its azimuths directly at us, webbing us
within its making of charts. As people were killed, cloths were
placed over the headless dummies, suggesting that not only were
people dying but that concepts and traditions were dying as well.
The past was hardly monolithic here and it did contain value,
even if that value was not discerned by "modernist" agendas.
The murder of Woodstock, imported into the production through
a fragment of "Woodstock," was mimed. A dummy took the actual hits. This alienation device showed us that this was far more
than a drive-by killing. It also predicted the mimed killing of
Richard at the end, so that the Cain/Abel equation that the text
applies to each murder was emphasized with a visual reinforcement of the spoken words. In a splendid touch, Exton covered
Richard's body and left it downstage for subsequent presentation
to Bolingbroke. As the latter entered to conduct a dynasty-
confirming pageant, the fact that would confute him and turn the
scene to funeral was already there, but not yet perceived. Richard
lay heavy just under Bolingbroke's consciousness and just below
his physical sight. The scene was visually a synecdoche for
Bolingbroke's reign, as Richard is forever being disinterred, psychologically, and physically, in the blood scraped from Pomfret's
stones which becomes a relic endorsing a rebellion. Henry V will
actually reinter Richard's body, as he tells us, bemoaning the lack
of efficacy of his remorse. Egan's suggestion was far more effective
than John Barton's in the RSC version of twenty years ago, where
Bolingbroke became the Groom who visited Richard in prison,
and where Bolingbroke, very prematurely, got the "Uneasy lies
the head" speech from the middle of II Henry IV.

Here, the stage created images and relationships for us without the gimmicks—snowmen with carrot noses and stilts for the up-stage crow, Northumberland—that Barton imposed upon a defenseless script. The Forum's semi-circular thrust stage became the "concept," as Egan deployed circularity to echo the oft-mentioned and oft-seen crown. Persons in the center of the circle might send subordinates powerfully outward, or the person in the center might be threatened with an implosion. Richard exploited his vulnerability and complained from within a knot of followers after his uncomfortable trip across the Irish Sea. York was coerced into "neuterness" by a circling group of Bolingbroke's faction. Being in the middle was in an ambiguous position: *some* power was also *some* danger, since the center could not hold. The production signaled that the script is "an inextricable tangle of right and unright," as Bradley said long ago (*Oxford Lectures*, 255). In the deposition scene, Richard's "centrality" was at once the place of his erasure *and* of his powerful demonstration that now the center—kingship—cannot hold.

The production was costumed in the "indefinite modern" mode that works so well with this script. The opening scene and the deposition featured microphones, as if for the Senate or the hard-of-hearing Supreme Court. Characters broke away from this decorum, as did the Mowbray and Carlisle, powerfully doubled by John Vickery, to launch accusations directly to Bolingbroke, or to us. Richard's "Conveyors are you all" indicted an audience looking in upon the making of the forces that were absorbing and would engulf the witnesses to his deposition. We were guilty participants in usurpation and the "silent majority" that would become fractions in the numbness of consensus with our yellow ribbons and jokes about the spotted owl and self-serving conviction that "If I saw a rape occurring on campus . . . ." We, like the headless mannekins, were headless history looking in. That it was a *king* being deposed, and a *bad* king at that, did not matter. The small theatre and its thrust into our space insisted that we be a defined audience to what came close to being an actual "event," as opposed to an imitation of an action.

Excellent smaller moments included Bushy's speech on "perspective," a piece of "courtiership" often cut but here splendidly developed by Tim Fitzpatrick; the Queen's scene with her Ladies played as a solo, which could have moved further towards Ophelia's madness to have been absolutely chilling; Richard's entrapment of Bolingbroke into the courtier's role, and Richard's nailing Bolingbroke with "I have a king here to my flatterer." The expansion of the point about the inversion of the male game of hierarchy was precisely made (cf. Tannen).

One thing that did not work was the discussion of blank charters, imported from somewhere. Intended to show how nasty Richard is, it sounded more like an idea whose time has come, indeed one espoused recently in the populist campaign of Tom Harkins and incorporated into the winning strategy of Bill Clinton.

Kelsey Grammer, Frasier Crane on the television show *Cheers*, played Lucio in Egan's *Measure for Measure* five years ago (Provensano, 4). His Richard was first powerful, then pathetic, his early aggressiveness a shell that cracked to reveal hollowness, self-pity, and sudden humanity at the center. Grammer did not do much with the middle position of cynicism that Derek Jacobi developed so brilliantly in the BBC-TV version, but Grammer's approach was dictated by Bolingbroke, a psychological foil in the script, and, as interpreted potently by Robert Jason, a man so cynical that he recognized himself only as he held the dead Richard at the end, when it was too late. This production showed what the script does, that it is too late once Gloucester is murdered. If that profound crime produces a *black* king in Jason's Bolingbroke, then that is a sign of deep disruption in body politic and cosmos, one the casting makes emphatic.

This was a great production—intelligent, well-paced, brilliantly acted, and aware of the role of its audience. It was in a class with the other great modern stage version of history play—Terry Hands's monumental version of *Henry V*, with Alan Howard. If the production *is* an argument for multiculturalism, it shows us something we should have learned long ago, but apparently have not. Good actors took on one of the most difficult scripts in the canon and succeeded brilliantly in a color-neutral production.

The reviewers tended to disagree, though they can be pardoned to some extent, since a 6.1 earthquake rocked the Forum on press night, 22 April 1992. The actors paused, a few spectators bolted, and then Kelsey Grammer said, "I think we're okay now," and returned to script with "Nay, Uncle, dry your eyes." Stephen Wolf said that "Like some waylaid 'Star Trek' episode, the Taper's *Richard II* timidly goes where politically correct plays have gone before. [It] is wayward . . . severely flawed and redundant . . . a one-dimensional political allegory . . . Lost in the multi-cultural shuffle is the development of Richard's moody heroism" (*DN* 27 April 1992, 15 & 17). Hoyt Hilsman indicted the effort "to draw political lessons from the piece," and found the production "hol-

low and airless." The "generally uninspired cast and limpid direction result in a listless evening [with this] dry and almost
academic production" (DV 24 April 1992). "Academic" and "dry-
ness" create an oxymoron, of course, even if some admire "limpid" production. Candy Carstensen saw the production as a
"hodge-podge," and said that Grammer looked "as if he just rode
in on a motorcycle. We already know . . . that corruption and the
notion of absolute power is a never ending problem . . . And the
people who don't know this are the people who would never set
foot inside the Mark Taper. So what's the point?" (BHC 24 April
1992, 35). The question, then, is the irrelevancy of theater itself.
If theater is already preaching to the converted, that group must
recognize the flaws within its structures of power and status—
and do something. But as the production went on, a large segment of the city had just been burned down. But, again, Carstensen seemed to be responding to the notes, not to the
production. Bruce Feld reacted to what he called the "break-neck
speed" of the production, which looked "like a military drill,"
in which the actors "race through their verse at high volume."
Interestingly Feld indicted Egan for "miscasting" (D-L 30 April–6
May 1992). Feld would have exchanged Bolingbroke and Richard.
The Barton production alternated Ian Richardson and Richard
Pasco as Richard and Bolingbroke in what some feel was an illegitimate conflation of opposites. Before each production, Richardson and Pasco decided who would play which role, one handing
the crown to the other, in a mime that suggested that it didn't
make much difference. It does, however. Richard and Bolingbroke
are not interchangeable. To cast a black actor as Richard might
have made a point about victimization, but it might have confused
the issue of kingship, unless color became neutralized fairly
quickly. Jones used color in the King Lear, when he brilliantly
played an older generation "Negro" against his militant daughter,
Cordelia, who had marched at Selma. It was a remarkably powerful subtext in the mid-1970s.

Welton Jones suggested that "whatever contemporary relevance
[Egan's] casting device generates is at the cost of the points Shakespeare wishes to make," whatever those points may be. Jones
commended Grammer's "nicely contrasted aspects" and said that
after awhile "skin pigment becomes irrelevant" (SDU-T 24 April
1992, E-9). Sylvie Drake found the production "meddlesome, ex-
peditious, occasionally intriguing . . . entirely too politically correct." "How much can a text be bent," she asked, "to suit different
ends?" The production was "highly conceptualized," a tendency

which has a "sterilizing effect." Grammer did not show "enough vulnerability" to balance "all that muscle" (*LAT* 24 April 1992, F-1 and F-18). For Tom Hatten, "the blend of style and periods didn't gel" (KNX). For Linda Rose, "The problem is that *Richard II* isn't really much of a play" (KWNK). Having solved *that* problem, Linda gave the production two and a half roses out of a possible four. Daryl H. Miller accused the production of "wanton anachronism," but credited "the actors' firmness" as the earth shook for "calm[ing] the audience and . . . probably prevent[ing] a panicked dash for the doors." The "play resumed," she said, "at exactly the same intensity level at which it had been interrupted" (*DN* 24 April 1992, 23). If so, that is an excellent job of reporting! Jay Reiner suggested that "When Shakespeare's plays are made 'relevant,' it's not unusual for his language and complexity of character to suffer." He found that Grammer did not show Richard "revel[ling] in his own self-pitying fall from power" (*HRep* 24 April 1992). While this Richard did enjoy his surrender to Eliot's Fourth Tempter—that was indeed one of the strengths of Grammer's performance—Reiner's insight into the role as scripted is excellent. Thomas O'Connor found the production "sometimes muddled," and said that "self-consciously Brechtian . . . silliness [creates] a distracting current" against which Grammer "swims with remarkable strength" (*OCR* 24 April 1992). Any glimpse of Brecht seems likely to rouse antipathy.

Just as this reviewer was beginning to question his own criteria and/or wonder whether a different rationale governed response to drama in Los Angeles, he found Sandra Kreiswirth's review. She said "*Richard II* is a play about power." She found Grammer "royally moody" within a "clear and accessible production." While the multicultural point was "obvious," she said, it "plays well in a showy production that doesn't get in the way of Shakespeare's rich and forceful language." The production "is both intriguing and interesting, thanks to Egan's vision and Grammer's performance" (*DB* 26 April 1992, D-5).

All of these reviewers grappled intelligently with the problems which the program tossed at them. The program, however, became the filter through which they looked at the production. Some might have found more tremors within the production had not an earthquake shifted plates beneath an already trembling Los Angeles. In the following weeks, Macbeth's line about "Thou sure and firm-set earth" became a prayer. The production could not help but absorb some of the events that were happening below the Taper and south of it, but it was one to which this observer wished he could have returned, even if he cannot say the same for L.A.

One way to make a proscenium space work with a Shakespearean script is to build out from it, creating a thrust in front of the arch. This process apparently will not work for the Stratford-on-Avon main house because it would eliminate sightlines from the balcony. It works splendidly, however, at the huge Rodeheaver Auditorium on the campus of Bob Jones University.

For William Pinkston's *As You Like It*, in November 1992, an apron emerged from under the skirts of the gigantic gold curtain, so that the play could occur within the ample proscenium space and also on the several levels downstage of where once the footlights had shone through the fourth wall.

The proscenium area worked splendidly for the "court scenes," played in front of a shadowy chateau, with balanced topiaries on the left and right defining a formal and rigidly controlled political system. The space permitted not only the strolling, private conversations of Rosalind and Celia but the trumpet-accompanied entrances and exits of Duke Frederick and his large entourage. The apron in front of the proscenium accommodated the wrestling, which was outdoors, a point that no one would bother noticing had not the recent RSC production placed the contest ludicrously within the polished marble of a room of state. The downstage apron also served the powerful banishment of Rosalind. Duke Frederick stepped down-center, often the place of harshness and formality, and turned to point at Rosalind, down right, the zone to which our sympathy is drawn. The tonal qualities of each playing area combined with the closeness of the action to the audience to make us feel Rosalind's vulnerability and the whimsical absolutism of Frederick's power.

The two playing areas were combined brilliantly by use of a scrim in front of the proscenium arch, on which the trunks of giant trees were projected. The downstage apron became the edge of the woods, into which Rosalind, Celia, and Touchstone trudged, and into which Orlando helped the weakened Adam. We got a splendid sense of "edgeness," what they call "interface," as the two playing areas balanced against each other as the script suggests they do. The travellers will find behind the scrim a world they do not anticipate, where not all things are savage but where, indeed, exists the energy that will permit the conflicting worlds of the play to harmonize, so that the zone at the edge of the woods becomes a space through which the banished Duke and his party will return to the world of other people. The concept was perfectly realized at the end by having Rosalind in her wedding dress deliver the Epilogue down center and, of course, to us, the other people. She was surrounded by the many celebrants of Arden. The feeling projected from this position can be (as in the Duke's banishment of her earlier) one of harshness. Here, it was softened by the words themselves and by the fact that her authority was backed by her having, in a sense, pulled the spaces of performance at once together in reconciliation and marriage *and* towards us physically so that we were invited to create our own countermovement of emotion and applause, back in the direction of the production's flow of language, music, motion, and of space itself. The Epilogue, then, was a demonstration and culmination of what the production had done and was doing. Everything led to the moment when Rosalind, now the woman who had been playing the androgynous Ganymede, "conjures" us. We must yield to this white magic and the white-gowned magician or there will be no magic. In this play, perhaps more than any other, with the possible exception of *The Tempest*, Shakespeare *includes* our response within the energy system of the play itself. There is not some separate moment when our identities "come back to us" as the stage and its fictions fade. Our identities have been changed and the fiction is in some way our truth, unless like a Jacques it will serve only to thread the fabric of our melancholy.

When the scrim was raised, the forest primeval ranged off into blue distances. The banished Duke occupied a rocky outpost that echoed the gray shapes of the apron. The trees moved on tracks, with a facility that would have made Malcolm of Cumberland envious. The background altered, to reveal wide lakes with forests beyond, so that we observed several semi-civilized areas within a vast and uninhabited world. The feeling was of a supportive something "far more deeply interfused" underlying this human activity, in spite of the occasional snake or lion, or Jacques who turns his back on the dance. When light was allowed through the scrim, some trunks remained, column-like, upon it, while others loomed upstage. We glimpsed a tableau of the Duke and his followers through the scrim before it rose for the first forest scene to begin. The actors, then, were "in the woods," particularly when Orlando, behind the scrim, pinned poems to trees. His words were recorded, not spoken directly, so that we had a sense of his being wrapped up in a self-created fantasy, only partly visible to himself, as to us. This was to "live by thinking," that is by the imaginative (and silly) constructs that obscure the flesh-and-blood Rosalind. The technique also permitted us to place some retrospective irony on the banished Duke's "adversity" speech. He is not fantasizing, of course, but he *is* rationalizing and would like very much to get back through that screen that divides him from the court and its comforts.

Director Pinkston and scenic designer Harrell Whittington showed how an inherited proscenium format can be redesigned so that the size and scope of the "framed stage" can be employed to create vivid "pictures" while the downstage apron can be used to bring the energy of the script out of the merely pictorial and into intense contact with the audience. The versatility of the playing areas gave the actors a liberating and uninhibiting environment in which to enjoy their work. It also gave us the opportunity to experience the remarkable variety of theatrical techniques inherent in this and any Shakespearean script.

This was, then, a production that understood the nature of the theatrical transaction and which paid its audience the compliment of assuming that we understood as well. Beyond that, the production had the ability to educate us to the necessity of our interaction and away from our less vital response to television.

Can a reviewer review a production if he walks out of it after half an hour? This one headed for the bracing Thames twilight as Peter Quince slopped through the mud of Robert Lepage's *A Midsummer Night's Dream* at the National Theatre. Quince said, to great laughter, "Here's a marvelous convenient place for our rehearsal."

It had been a terrible experience for this spectator, even though he had not been in one of the first two rows and thus had not been required to wear a plastic slicker to protect his garments from the mud being splattered on the stage. As we entered, Puck sat like a frog in the middle of a mud puddle of the type engendered by severe sewer leakage in some shanty town. She invited us with a wave of the hand to join her or it. When one is Calvin's age one might have splashed on in, to appear later to a horrified mother. "Where have you *been?*" And "*What* have you been in?" The production appealed to the Calvin perhaps, but not to the theoretical adult.

The opening scene was delivered primarily from a bed being poled about in the glop. Egeus delivered his accusations of Hermia while standing in a chair, so that no sense of relationship *or* conflict could develop. The pace was slow, deadly slow, as the bed plied the mud and revealed more and more people on it, as if it were the last floating object left after the sinking of the *Panay*. Subsequently, the actors slithered and slid, perhaps in scripted ways, but possibly involuntarily, on a surface that resembled that of the 1934 Giants-Bears championship game. The actors got muddy and lost their clothes amid the chill of the air-conditioning. Distinctions between the characters got lost under the foul caking, as did, inevitably, contrasts between what used to be called "the worlds of the play." Strange music drowned out what lines might have reached the auditorium. This was a case where one *knew* he was supplying the lines from his own head, unwillingly but inevitably, in a one-man interior reading that had cost some sixty dollars. The stage, meanwhile, had suffered the fate of the "nine-men's morris" and crystal was muddier than even imagination could have rendered it. This reviewer reviewed with his feet.

Action is probably prior to language in theater as Aristotle argues, and as one can learn by watching Shakespeare in a language not accessible to the watcher. Language, however, is a significant aspect of the script, as is acting, or the bringing to each role an ability to speak the verse and to make it at once a vehicle for personal intention and a medium for relating to the other characters and, possibly, to the outer audience. Neither language nor acting was a component of Lepage's production. Furthermore, *pace*—the rapid driving of the script through the playing area—that permits an occasional pause for emphasis, and thus establishes *rhythm* was totally lacking here. Lepage, like so many ostensible directors, refuses to learn the first lesson and never will. Since this production was obviously rejecting the basic criteria announced in the introduction—language, acting, and rhythm—and only promised more rejection, this auditor walked away from it as he would from a destructive relationship. He was tempted to shout, as had an enraged departee during Joseph Heller's *We Bombed in New Haven* years ago, something about what Lepage eats, but he assumed that the audience would have believed that the obscene allusion to cuisine was just part of the show.

The critics were actually divided on this one, many seeking for a middle ground amid the mire on which to place their pros and cons. Some critics tried hard not to be stick-in-the-muds, as it were, by suggesting that, while this production was not *their* cup of goo, it was, nevertheless, this or that good thing. Many cited objections but found them unformidable. Sheridan Morley found Lepage's "performance-art gimmickry . . . weird and wonderful," and praised the occasional "image of stunning beauty." Yet he admitted that the actors were "condemned . . . to a mud bath" and that "some have trouble with the plot, some with the poetry and some with the English language itself. This is not the place to start if you have never before seen the 'Dream'. . . . [The] evening seems to have more to do with Lepage and less and less to do with Shakespeare" (*IHT* 12 August 1992, 14). Steve Grant provided another mixed review: Lepage "has quite rightly connected with the piece's sexy, Freudian undercurrents . . . resulting in] a swirl of imagistic and cultural reference-points." But Puck's "French accent is so impenetrable that the verse may as well not exist." The production "can be in turns breathtaking, ponderous, revelatory, amusing and downright boring. But how much of it is really concerned with Shakespeare's original, and how much would someone who hadn't see or read the play learn about its structure, meaning, and beauty?" (*TO* 15 July 1992).

Here of course, the reviewer made assumptions that Lepage apparently did not—that the play *has* structure, meaning, and beauty. Ian Shuttleworth found that Puck, like a number of the cast lacked the acting strength to do justice to her lines. Lepage's "dirty, sexy, violent and unique production will alienate a number of people whose idea of dressing up for the theatre doesn't include a complimentary waterproof cape if you're in the first two rows. . . . So be it. The rest of us cannot afford to miss it" (*CL* 16–23 July 1992). Clare Bayley said that "Lepage's visual prowess is not . . . best served by Shakespeare's text. . . . His meanings, though endlessly ingenious and desperately beautiful, don't shed new light on Shakespeare's play." The verse speaking, Bayley said, is "not always good," but claimed that Angela Laurier's "French-Canadian [accent] endows Puck's speeches with a new clarity." "A seductive and technically flabbergasting production, then, stronger on wizardry than illumination, though no doubt subsequent generations will ask us eagerly, 'Did *you* see Lepage's Dream?'" (*WO* 15 July 1992, 56). And one reviewer will say, "A piece of it." Michael Coveney praised Puck's ability to make her feet into ears for Bottom (Puck was a contortionist of considerable skill) and found her "brilliant invention . . . characteristic of the show's slithering plasticity." He discovered in Bottom "the ultimate, triumphant cultural misfit in a world that gives reptilian consistency to the shared ancestral psyche." The problem, however, was that "Lepage has stretched the action to last three and a half hours not because he needs to, but because, as Peter Hall would say, the actors speak the words not the lines" (*O* 12 July

1992, 54). Again, does one go to the theater to be reminded of that ancient reptilian stem of brain quivering into the escape mode? And, if one wishes to hear the music and not just the notes, good jazz does exist. Shakespeare does not necessarily exist so that a Lepage can place the script within what he considers to be his cultural heritage and afflict us with the result. French-Canadians should be murderously indignant.

Nicholas de Jongh, however, came "away bewitched" by "an astonishing mud-bath comedy," in spite of his assertion that "the acting lets the production down [with] too much rhetoric of mere rant and too little of the anguish of sexual jealousy." "You may be entranced or repelled by Lepage's imaginings. You are unlikely to forget them. . . . [He] has given the play a new dimension" (ES 10 July 1992, 7). Clive Hirschhorn said that the production "throws up [sic] images that hauntingly redefine this bewitching comedy," but found that the mud "cool[ed] the magic" and created for the actors "what has to be the most physically uncomfortable production of their careers" (DE 12 July 1992). Charles Spencer felt that "the delivery of the verse is often atrocious, and at three-and-a-half hours the evening is too long." "Some," he was sure, "will believe this show to be a perverse act of cultural vandalism." He found himself "longing for the bright, sunlit certainties of a more conventional production [but found themself] sliding ever deeper into the director's disconcerting world of the subconscious. . . . Far from diminishing the magic of The Dream Lepage has enriched it" (DT 13 July 1992). Benedict Nightingale felt that "those unfamiliar with the play may be distracted by all the wallowing. Some good lines are lost in the physical ado. Comedy is inevitably lacking." The production, however, sought "darkness in the play . . . particularly sexual darkness. . . . There is no more brilliantly imaginative production in town" (T 11 July 1992, Arts, 4). A production of this script can give us its darker tonalities of sexuality without dropping the play into a swamp, as Cuilei's several versions have shown.

Not much else was in town in August: a pallid RSC Romeo and Juliet, a credible The Alchemist, and a strong A Woman Killed with Kindness. The best production was a matinee performance of the Q1 Hamlet in the innyard of the George, Suffolk, by the Medieval Players for Sam Wanamaker's Globe. Patrick Knox was a wonderfully droll Hamlet and the doubling was virtuoso.

It may be, then, that some version of Gresham's Law was darkly at work when critics praised Lepage's glue. Robert Hewison found that "the glutinous acting surface has the slippery quality of dreams, both sexy and horrific. . . . Someone is bound to fulminate against Lepage's Canadian bespattering of our literary heritage. Nonsense. The visual poetry surpasses any music the rhetoric misses. [Lepage] is true to the magic of the piece. This is a must see" (*ST* 12 July 1992, VII/6). The problem, however, as Hewison implied, was that word and action were in competition with each other, as opposed to being complimentary, "suited" the one to the other, as Hamlet suggests they should be. When Shakespeare's play becomes an incidental undertone, not merely rendered hysterical by a competing production, as in some modernizations, but strongly repressed, then something is very rotten in Athens. Puck, for example, gives us Shakespeare's early rhythms of the supernatural—the trochaic tetrameter of the Weird Sisters. The rhyming meter contrasts with the pentameter of the human actors (and of Oberon and Titania, as well) and if it is totally lost, as here, a dimension of the script that Shakespeare "intended" is also lost.

Some critics did condemn the production. Irving Wardle suggested that "the acting convention is that the immortals are at home in the primeval slime and the humans are not." He said of the young lovers that "it is often hard to hear their lines, much less discern any individual character. . . . This set does not transmit a metaphor of self-discovery, or the darkness of adolescent sexuality, or some Jungian archetype. It transmits the idea of mess and dirt, an environment that must be hell for the actors and works havoc with their movement and comic timing." Wardle found the show producing "unexpected laughs," as when Quince waded into the rehearsal space: "Very funny; but it is a joke against the text. Shakespeare's jokes are submerged under the splashing games" (*IonS* 12 July 1992). Wardle praised the Regent's Park version of the play, which was nonetheless superficial, particularly when contrasted with the 1989 edition with Sally Dexter as a powerful and menacing Titania—as opposed to whatever she was doing in the same role for Lepage. Malcolm Rutherford said that "the company plays the full Shakespearean text, if not the verse, but any other connection with the original is tenuous. . . . The production makes a travesty of the play . . . carelessness with the words is a general tendency." He complained of "some excessively slow playing," and concluded that "those who admire the *Dream* for the beauty of its language as well as its comedy are likely to be disappointed. The case for this production is simply curiosity to see something different" (*FT* 10 July 1992). Paul Taylor found the production "leadenly paced and unfunny. . . . Here the design arrogantly obliterates distinctions between various worlds and species. [Puck] negotiates English with all the nimbleness of Inspector Clouseau. . . . As Helena rightly puts it, 'Oh long and tedious night!'" (*Independent* 10 July 1992). For Maureen Paton, the lovers were "almost unrecognizable in their mud-packs [and] the rude mechanicals seemed marooned in this morass. . . . There's enough water here to stage Moby Dick" (*DE* 10 July 1992). Jack Tinker felt that "this is the ultimate actor's nightmare. . . . I have never seen a company called upon to endure so much physical torture in the name of art. . . . What we lose are the separate elements of the play itself when court, fairies and Mechanicals are all reduced to sodden splashing" (*DM* 10 July 1992). Kenneth Hurren found that "Alarm bells ring when plastic macs are dished out to 'front-stalls patrons . . . poetry and meaning nowhere survive [this] show-off Canadian" (*MonS* 12 July 1992). Michael Billington called Lepage's

> the most perverse, leaden, humourless and vilely spoken production of this magical play I have ever seen. . . . With amazing precision Shakespeare . . . shows how the separate worlds of fairies, lovers and mortals gradually converge: a point entirely lost if they inhabit an aqueous universe governed by Puck from the start . . . water also drowns sound and slows down movement: one reason this appalling production takes three-and-a-half hours . . . Doubtless some gullible loon will claim this production is as big a breakthrough as Peter Brook's landmark 1970 [version. But where] in Brook's hands, the play became fantastically airborne, [Lepage] reduces even the best performers . . . to mud-caked puppets. (*G* 11 July 1992).

Indeed, Brook was invoked. Lepage, said de Jongh, "transforms our idea of the play as dramatically," as did Brook. Lepage, said Paton, "has attempted to upstage Peter Brook's landmark 1970 production." "No production since Peter Brook's white gymnasium version of 20 years ago has been so thoroughly conceived as a feast of interrelated transformations" as Lepage's, said Coveney. But the allusion was not always positive, as Grant showed: "Bernard Levin said of Peter Brook's equally radical production in 1970 that 'Shakespeare would have stood up and applauded.' I can't see the Bard putting his hands together here with much enthusiasm."

Brook's squash court, for all of its liveliness, phallicism, and superbly spoken verse, had few if any imitators. That is some solace. Identity and play-erasing mud-baths are not "the wave of the future" for Shakespearean productions.

Two reviewers, George L. Geckle (*SB* 11, 27–28) and Barbara Hodgdon (SAA April 1993) were lured by the quotation from Jung in this production's program, Geckle very cautiously, Hodgdon enthusiastically. Jung says, "The psyche is not of today. Its ancestry goes back many millions of years. Individual consciousness is only the flower of a season, sprung from the perennial root beneath the earth." The program does not give a source for the quotation, but it is a Jungian commonplace. While Jung does deal with the primitive, particularly as a source of "instinct" and as a pre-conscious condition that explains both the Eden myth and our own biological infancy, Jung emphasizes *individuation* and sees regression not as an end in itself but as a way of returning positive libido to the process of individuation. In the Lepage *Dream* we got such loss of differentiation that no individuation could occur. We could not tell who the characters *were*. Jung talks of "seeds of light broadcast in the chaos . . . (the seed plot of a world to come). One such spark is the human mind. The arcane substance—the watery earth or earthy water (*limus:* mud) of the World Essence is 'universally animated' by the 'fiery spark of the soul of the world' in accordance with the Wisdom of Solomon 1:7" (190–91; his emphasis). We got the mud and not the fiery spark of imagination. The program also quoted Rupert Brooke in its journey through Unfamiliar Quotations: "One may not doubt that, somehow, good / Shall come of water and of mud; / And, sure, the reverent eye must see / A purpose in liquidity." The critics made nothing of these lines, perhaps happy to have been spared Joyce Kilmer's "Trees."

The new historicists have ungraciously taken over Shakespearean scholarship. One ramification of their domination is that scholarship has even less to say to the theater than it ever did. If the plays live only in *their* time and if any other text is to be valued equally with the words in the script, thus removing the script from its dramatic and relevant context, then much of today's scholarship can in no way inform what happens to the plays *as plays*. That means that a Lepage is free to inflict any "interpretation" on the script and make it mean what he says it means, in a version of Orwellian nightmare. Assuming that academics cared about such atrocities, they have disqualified themselves from objecting to them. We are left with "Director's Theater" run "amuck."

Lepage does indeed display contempt for the English Language. It may be, as he claims, that he is "very open to English Canada," but his *Dream* betrays the fact that "Theatre programs in Quebec City. . . . have traditionally deemphasized speech training," and, even more vividly, that "in Quebec people are much too respectful of the written text" (quoted in Jacobson, 17). The written text becomes "a wash of word-sounds [as background] for action and emotion" (quoted in Jacobson, 19). He pursues the techniques of "the New Baroque" described by Lise Bissonnette: "Visual effects are taken to extremes, primitive sentiments return, genres are mixed in bold new ways. [Nonlinguistic sound and frenzied choreography are] expedient way[s] of reaching across a border, of gaining access to an audience who may speak a different language" (quoted in Jacobson, 19). The "new Baroque" seems to have some built-in limitations, including its insistence on "frenzy." It may be that another director will apply its tenets successfully to a Shakespearean script. But *no* script will work if the words are, like rock lyrics, just part of the cacophony. If the script is, as Kozintsev says, "a diffused remark" that signals intention to a director's imagination—and that may be true for a film-maker—the signal is for the editing of language to the medium, not for the elimination of the language. (The exceptions might be the silent film, where title cards could create awkward hiatuses between shots, and those annoying subtitles for films whose story we already know).

While the mud would have been an insuperable barrier of soup for many, one free of mud and in *French-Canadian* might have been intriguing. But then it could not have launched its intended attack on *English*. Lepage could not, it seems, have his language and still try to make his cowardly point. Ludmilla de Fougerolles, who heads the Commission for the Protection of the French Language, in Quebec, claims that "we are excessively tolerant. . . . Today we live in French" (7-A). If so, no need for tolerance exists. At the same time, no one need be tolerant of Lepage's attack on the Shakespearean script. He does not reinterpret. He obliterates.

Michael Kahn's production in Washington in late 1992 was a rare *Hamlet* that featured different actors in the title role. The two Hamlets were Tom Hulce and Gary Sloan.

Kahn's production was well-articulated, briskly paced, and blessedly free of any tendency towards the "bright idea" for which Kahn has been criticised in the past. With Sloan in the lead role, the production transcended some of the problems that casting and direction inflicted upon it. The production was designed around Hulce, of course, since he would play Hamlet over fifty times, with Sloan alternating once a week during the production's eight-week run. Had the production been built around Sloan it would have been better in all ways, since the lucidity and occasional power of his performance tended to focus issues that seemed very murky in the Hulce version.

Something central was missing in Hulce's performance itself, as Roy Procter suggested in recasting the old "Our Gal Sunday" question: "Is endearment enough? Can this Hamlet, who might be mistaken for one of the servants in the royal palace of Elsinore, resonate with the tragic stature he needs to get his emotional due from the audience in Shakespeare's most intriguing play? The answer: No" (*RT-D* 24 November 1992). *Time* suggested that Hulce's "ironic, self-deprecating intelligence . . . ought . . . to provide fresh insight into a few scenes. . . . But in a hokey production all too typical of Washington's Shakespeare Theater, Hulce fails to make the words sound sincere and obscures the political and revenge narratives with muddling about real-or-feigned madness" (7 December 1992, 83).

In a recent article, *Los Angeles Times* critic Jan Herman blasted "celebrity theatre," with its "stellar-looking productions with TV stars to match [but] desperately lacking in the one essential that might have made it work: the coherent acting of a unified company" (*Quarto* 2 February 1992, 4). Her complaint echoed that of Caryn James ("Too Oft, Fault Lies In the Stars," *NYT* 6 January 1991), which discussed Mel Gibson, Dustin Hoffman, Kevin Kline, Michelle Pfeiffer, Denzel Washington, Morgan Freeman, Burton and Taylor, and others. Kelsey Grammer and the Mark Taper *Richard II* was much better than Herman says—and Grammer had worked in Shakespeare for his director, Robert Egan, as Lucio previously. Kelly McGillis played a winsome Viola for Kahn in a badly conceived *Twelfth Night* at the Folger that was not McGillis's fault (cf. "Two D.C. Comedies," *Marlowe Society Newsletter* 9 (1986): 8 and *Performance as Interpretation,* 30). Dustin Hoffman played an understated and effective Shylock for Peter Hall a few years ago. More recently, Megan Follows was a beguiling if somewhat underspoken Juliet at Stratford, Canada. Film and television are distinct media calling for different qualities from actors, but neither medium is necessarily good "training" for the stage. Film can do much with its camera and its editing. The nearness of a microphone in each medium encourages actors to ignore the specific attention to vowels and consonants that projection in an auditorium demands. Shakespeare's lead characters demand *on stage* qualities that carefully controlled and meticulously edited media do not—not just the ability to project the voice clearly and conversationally into space but also range and versatility. It may be that Ralph Berry is correct to assert that Hamlet does not demand a great actor, but rather a "star" (Thompson & Thompson, 24). But the star must be many things within the space of the play—lover, graduate student, crown prince, court jester, impresario, playwright, playactor, murderer, attacker of pirates, skilled duelist, multiple murderer, etc. Of these, the only role not requiring "star" quality is that of graduate student. Furthermore, as Michael Goldman points, out, "the play abounds in situations that require the principal actor to shift his mood or mode of action because of a change in audience" (75). It is possible to play "above the role," as Olivier tended to do in his self-directed film version, and "below the role," as Nicol Williamson did in his Round House rendition for Tony Richardson, where he was a snarling, Midland outsider wondering, as we did, what on earth his business at Elsinore could be. What convinced us in Williamson's performance was his hatred of Claudius. Derek Jacobi got *inside* the role as cynical intellectual and, by that declension, as jester, powerfully illuminating vast patches of the script though the persona that "worked" for Hamlet. Mark Rylance did not try for Jacobi's sophistication, but made his commentary on Elsinore by becoming remarkably vulnerable, probably bonkers by any standards but particularly so as seen from the perspective of Claudius's desperate joviality or Polonius's chilly political game of chess (Peter Wight and Patrick Godfrey in the RSC version, as opposed to the much weaker production that Ron Daniels redesigned for the American Repertory Theatre). Rylance brilliantly swung Elsinore around his "politics of tantrum" and at the same time won us to a Hamlet who was absolutely "impossible" within his scripted world

It looked as if this were the Hamlet that Michael Kahn worked out for Hulce. Hulce could not make it work. He lacked vocal range and, in fact, his voice seemed strained. Typical of the contrast between the two actors was that in the Nunnery Scene, Ophelia tried to comfort Hulce's Hamlet as if he were a little boy who had skinned his knee. The same Ophelia tried to kiss Sloan's Hamlet as woman to man. The "relationship" was slightly more believable with Sloan as Hamlet, a remarkable fact given an Ophelia whose motivation was a) to be taken seriously by her father and b) to get rid of her virginity. Sloan was burdened with a concept that he could make work occasionally, when his approach to the character was permitted to jump brilliantly free of Kahn's and Hulce's conception.

The problems here were not those attendant upon having a "star" as Hamlet. The problems were in the concept of the role, a concept born from a notion of *this* actor's range and flexibility. Had one not seen Sloan, however, one would have agreed with Jan Herman that, in this instance, the importation of a star from another medium did undercut "the coherent acting of a unified company." As it was, Sloan could only do his best to make Hamlet coherent within an inchoate production. What he could have done with the role had it been his own is moot, although he deserves the chance within another production soon.

It may be that the production merely borrowed ideas from other recent productions. Kevin Kline's dull New York production had Hamlet manipulate Rosencrantz and Guildenstern physically, forcing them, for example, to lie down beside him to gaze upon "this brave, o'er hanging firmament," and so he did here. But several touches suggested that Kahn was borrowing primarily from Daniels. In the RSC and ART, Hamlet stood with bags packed, waiting for the train to Germany at the beginning of 1.2. For Kahn, he exited the scene rudely, right through the middle of one of Claudius's speeches, went upstairs, and dropped a calf-skin bag from the balcony, narrowly missing a lady-in-waiting. He held his books during Claudius's lecture, so that the latter could tap them on the word "unschool'd," though Claudius got the emphasis wrong. (The distinction he may be making will work if he stresses *un*.) Rylance reached out and touched the Ghost in 1.5, the little boy who had disappointed his powerful father. Kahn's Hamlet knelt, held onto his much taller father, indeed crawled with the Ghost as the latter tugged himself offstage. Hulce did all of this better than Sloan, since vulnerability would seem to be one of the few tricks the former has in his bag, while the latter was stuck with all the business without believing it. One result of this overplaying of Hamlet's response to the Ghost was that our sense of Hamlet's *mission* was reduced, if not erased. For the sake of a single scene, the dramatic pressure of subsequent scenes was lost. One borrowing from Daniels that worked—particularly for Sloan, whose timing was superb—was Hamlet's advice on "*the* speech." Hamlet's advice on using all gently, and neither sawing the air nor being too tame was interpolated into a Player's efforts to memorize the Lucianus speech ("Thoughts black, hands apt . . .") and that gave an amusing pointedness to Hamlet's concern with his own written dialogue. The Ghost's affection for Gertrude here seemed another borrowing from Daniels, although this Ghost did not cradle her. He crossed *to* her, however (in the only entrance he was permitted from stage left) and exited sadly, dismissed by her inability to see him. But, all right—the idea of his continuing love for her is supported by the script. After Polonius's murder, Kahn's Hamlet entered, as Rylance had done, in a bloody white shirt with a bucket and began to wash himself. This approach permitted him to squeeze a sponge as he accused Rosencrantz of being one. Rylance had been covered with blood as he slaughtered Polonius and was then almost drowned by an angry Claudius in the wash bucket. Here, Hamlet dispatched Polonius with a single neat blow (Sloan took two, the first thrust a range finder), spilled no blood, and dragged Polonius off on a blanket, presumably to save Polonius's magnificent Lord Burghley outfit. Were we to infer that Hamlet then engaged in some cannibalistic orgy where Polonius was eaten? If not, the borrowing from the Daniels production was meaningless.

In response to another production, Peter Holland said, "it is sad to see a production borrowing jokes and gags and business and not learning how to copy the energy and style" (*ShS* 44, 178). And that is to put it very mildly as far as the Kahn *Hamlet* is concerned.

If Hamlet is just a little boy who breaks into an occasional adolescent squeak, as Hulce did ("Yet I, / A dull and muddy-mettled rascal . . ."), then we need a powerful cast around him. Rylance gave an intentionally bizarre performance—every syllable thought out—and was supported in the RSC version by a superb troupe. Here, we got a good Ghost (Daniel Southern), although the Ghost should say, "I *am* thy father's spirit," that is *not* a goblin damn'd. We got a good Player (Emery Battis), who was permitted his Pyrrhus speech, complete with a mimed Hecuba by the Boy Actor. We got a good Gravedigger (Eric Hoffman). The Second Gravedigger returned from Yaughan with a stoop of liquor just as Hamlet talked of stopping a beer-barrel. Hoffman gave his assistant a dig in the ribs when the Priest said that Ophelia should have been buried in unsanctified ground.

We got a Polonius (Ted van Griethuysen) who had at least thought about his relationship with his children—a son was a way of reliving vicariously a wild youth, but a daughter was a gigantic pain-in-the-neck, *unless* perhaps she could be used as a political pawn. Ophelia (Francesca Buller) was delighted when Polonius finally listened to her, misinterpreting his response, which was to the seriousness of the Crown Prince's "love," not to her in her own being. Otherwise, one could scarcely wait until she had distributed her damned flowers. She had been to a finishing school where they taught the girls a British accent. It jarred palpably against the suddenly discernible American accents of the rest of the company. If Laertes is played as a young fool, he does not become Hamlet's "foil" (though the word was cut here). Even in a rave review of this production, Hap Erstein said, "Laertes get in some steamy rough-housing with his sister, Ophelia, though it's hard to figure what Mr. Kahn is implying by it" (*WT* 24 November 1992, E5). Indeed, Laertes's leave taking was awkwardly acted, as if the actors were trying hard to follow orders but failing. In Richardson's version at the Roundhouse in 1969, Michael Pennington and Marianne Faithfull evoked a convincing aura of incest—an inevitable activity spreading out from the central example of Claudius and Gertrude.

If Fortinbras is cut, we lose the great "How all occasions . . ." soliloquy. Here, since Hulce and Sloan had established some rapport with the audience by way of soliloquy, we felt the absence of that late rumination and the reasons why Shakespeare put it there. Why did this production give us so much of the background information—Horatio in 1.1. and Voltemand in 2.2, including Norway's request that Fortinbras be given "quiet pass" through Denmark on the way to Poland, the lines that set up Hamlet's encounter with Fortinbras's troops later and, at the end, Fortinbras's arrival at Elsinore? This early material was there, it seemed, to show Claudius's response to the success of his embassy and thus to let us see his defenses relax as the inner threat of Hamlet grows—but better to give us the scenes the lines anticipate than the anticipation without the scenes. This editing suggested that the production itself was aimless.

The Claudius (Jack Ryland) and Gertrude (Franchelle Stewart Dorn) were unconvincing, perhaps because they had not been directed at all. They acted, unconsciously, against the opulence of their costumes. Ryland roared most of the time—including his non-prayer—blew his cheeks, scratched his head, and mugged at the audience after Gertrude corrected him on the name of Hamlet's fraternity brothers. "It had been so with us . . ." was a line in a play, not a sudden discovery of how dangerous Hamlet really *is*. Claudius's emotional reactions seemed to *follow* his lines, rather than be fitted to them and he gave an occasional quick glance at nothing as he finished a line. "Now, out of this . . ." should indicate a pause for thought. Instead, we got the line and Laertes's immediate "What—out of this—my lord?" The actors knew the lines, but not their sense. We got pace, but no rhythm. Where was the director? The exception was when Claudius commanded

Gertrude to "set some watch over *your* son," revenging himself for her defection from him after her description of Ophelia's death. Dorn sulked and shrugged, made several unmotivated movements up and down stage, totally upstaged the Laertes rebellion as she stood down right, illuminated and staring at Claudius, making some point but draining whatever point the scene was making. She got lines from Q1—"It joys me [at] the soul he is inclined / To any kind of mirth"—for some reason, but otherwise could not have been an "objective correlative" for *anyone's* positive response. "Did you assay him / To any *pastime*," she said, as if to say, "For God's sake, what have you been doing all this time?" "What *theme*?" she demanded of Hamlet at Ophelia's grave, one of those "new readings" that makes nonsense of whatever the line is trying to mean. Again—the exception—she realized as she said "do dead men's fingers call" that the allusion represented a blunder, since she was telling Laertes the story of his sister's death. No chemistry existed between her and Claudius, though they smooched unattractively in public, nor any between her and either of the Hamlets. Gertrude can be a great role, as Gertrudes like Eileen Herlie (opposite Burton), Celia Johnson, Elizabeth Spriggs, Jill Bennett, Barbara Jefford, Judy Parfitt, Virginia McKenna, and Claire Higgins have proved. To see this Gertrude with no knowledge of any others one would be to conclude that the role represents one of Shakespeare's big mistakes.

The Laertes-Claudius plot was played in a non-space (midstage, right-center) with the stage as fully illuminated as this one got. The tensions of the scheme and its ominous adumbrations were drained by placement and lack of any support from the lighting. The plot got a little more potent when the characters made an unmotivated move down center. Polonius crawled across Gertrude's bed towards Hamlet, after getting stabbed, and drew a laugh. The bed itself was unnecessary, dictated by the convention established by the Gielgud production of the late 1930s. Both Hamlets made sure that Gertrude was protected by a comforter before the mild bounce Hamlet inflicted on her. Before Hamlet and Gertrude wrestled, Hamlet had to push Polonius off the bed. He lay almost out of sight and one wished that Hamlet had forgotten him during his discussion with Gertrude and the entrance of the Ghost. Hamlet's sudden recall of the murder *he* has committed would have made sense of this awkward staging. As Claudius died, grotesquely entangled in a spiral staircase, his crown dropped to the floor. Being made of plastic, it compressed, bounced three feet, reshaped itself in midair and drew a laugh.

A plastic crown for Claudius? Yes, but is that moment is a good one for a laugh? The same crown was held up as part of Hamlet's coronation–dead march. No one, obviously, paid any attention to how the production actually played. It made no sense to have Horatio address his order for Hamlet's body to us, the audience, as we watched actors behind him respond for some reason to his commands.

The new Shakespeare Theatre is comfortable and small (seating about 450). The playing area is deep with a small apron coming out from the proscenium. The acoustics are good, even for speeches delivered from upstage. It is neither a thrust nor a raked stage and thus represents some retreat towards conventional, old-fashioned formats. The stage at the Folger was not very large, had little backstage area, some bad sightlines from the auditorium, and those two notorious posts on either side, downstage left and right. It called for downstage playing to the audience and little else, since inner stage and upper stage were hard to see and hard to listen to. Still, it was a good place for Shakespeare as long as directors did not try to impose a set upon it. As soon as they did, of course, the stage would not work and everyone had a lot to complain about. The major problem with the Folger stage was the inappropriate uses to which directors put it. The latest production at the new theater incorporated, for some reason, a large, functionless column, against which Hamlet leaned during his first soliloquy. The column would have made sense had Hamlet said, "solid." He said "sullied." In the new space, Kahn's simple inability to know what works on stage and what does not and his willingness to borrow meaninglessly from other productions undercut some talented actors—in this case in the service of a Hulce who pulled the production and its values centripetally towards his considerable weaknesses.

The concept of "doubling" has been dealt with in a number of recent studies (cf. Booth, Berger, King). A good example of how it can work on stage came in Tina Packard's Shakespeare and Company *Twelfth Night* at Waldoboro, Maine, in April 1992.

Many years ago at The Theater at Monmouth, Malvolio exited at the end of the madhouse scene (4.2) to a few chords of "O, Mistress Mine" played on a lute. Immediately, Sebastian entered, giving himself a reality check: "This is the air; that is the glorious sun." This magnificent transition showed us Shakespeare's intention. Malvolio remains in darkness, Sebastian has stepped into the light of Malvolio's dream. Olivia has seized the day with a vengeance and is "roaming" with her "true love."

Packard's production went even further with the "consciousness/shadow" approach to Malvolio, whose sybaritic daydreams of daybeds become Sebastian's waking experience, by doubling the roles. The process was made easier by the actors' introducing themselves at the outset to an audience of mostly high school students, while announcing that some would play more than one role, and interspersing the opening sequences of the play (where, as seems to be usual practice these days, Viola's shipwreck preceded Orsino's ennui).

Tom Jaeger was an excellent Malvolio in a severe, dark steward's robe, with a wonderfully forced smile, a hilarious savoring of the word "fellow," and a splendid array of obscene gestures for Toby, once Malvolio believed that he had achieved a tangible fantasy (3.4.84ff). Sebastian's smile was more natural, of course, and the character wore a loose shirt, cream-colored trousers, and boots, at once costumed like Cesario and free of Malvolio's restrictive formality. Sebastian was what "lies under" Malvolio. The latter had indeed "read" Olivia correctly, even if only in the direction of his own gratification.

The "law of reentry"—where an actor doubling as another character must remain offstage for at least one scene before the other character enters—had to be violated, of course, but the production had introduced itself *as* a play and the very narrow stage of the Waldo Theater had encouraged a downstage acting style that incorporated the audience, as when Viola asked "I pray you, tell me if this be the lady of the house" and a high school student told her. An inner curtain closed in front of Malvolio at the end of 4.2 to facilitate Sebastian's almost instant entrance. Olivia's "fetch Malvolio hither" at the end was to Sebastian. Once Malvolio exited with his angry threat of revenge, Sebastian could reenter to stand with Olivia.

Except for their costumes, Sebastian and Cesario didn't really resemble each other. Sebastian was about six inches taller than she. Our laughter at the end was partly at the characters on stage who could have been deceived into mistaking the one for the other. That, of course, was also an intention of this production— that the awareness of the fictional characters could catch up to ours and thus erase the play at the moment that the fiction on which so much of the plot has been based was also erased. The production, more than any *Twelfth Night* I have ever seen, pointed

Fabian's question (delivered here by Feste) about whether "sportful malice" should "rather pluck on laughter than revenge." Certainly this production emphasized the festive closure, particularly since Malvolio's alter ego was there, Olivia's smiling Count Sebastian.

9

The Directors and the Critics:
Stratford on Avon, 1992

IN his essay on "bi-fold authority in Shakespeare," Robert Weimann distinguishes between *locus* and *platea*. *Locus* involves what or who is represented on stage, *platea* relates to who or what is doing the representing. Weimann suggests that the former was invariably "conservative," or, to put it in his terms, "the Elizabethan theatre was not, by any stretch of the imagination, a subversive institution, hostile to the Tudor balance of socioeconomic forces old and new" (409–10). Indeed, it was that balance of forces that sustained Shakespeare's theater. That status quo, in which the stage tended to ratify the power structure, could be challenged, however, "deeply and profoundly" by "whatever *platea*-dimension Shakespeare's stage tended to retain or, sometimes, revitalize" (410). The present study does suggest "conservative" criteria for production—that the language be clear and that it *mean* something beyond merely our ability to hear it, for example. Those criteria, however, do not necessarily call for "conservative" production values, as the following discussion of the 1992 season at Stratford-on-Avon should prove. The guidelines of the Introduction to this book should be placed at the service of the imagination and daring that goes into the best Shakespearean productions. Too often, however, directors do not even abide by the criteria, much less provide the vision that great productions demand and reflect.

With Deborah Warner no longer on the scene, the Royal Shakespeare Company did little challenging of the status quo in Stratford during the summer of 1992. Given its title and implied mandate, that is not surprising, particularly in view of Prince Charles's recent interest in "teaching Shakespeare the proper way" (as quoted by Terry Hawkes, Stratford, 1992). The best that can be said of the season—with the exception of Sam Mendes's *Richard III*, with Simon Russell Beale, treated elsewhere on these pages—is that it was "controversial." The controversies themselves are interesting, often more so than the productions inciting them, since the critical debate places Shakespeare against and sometimes within the "popular culture" which was competing for scarce pounds on a recession-ridden island in 1992. What the critics failed to notice, responding as they do to individual productions, is that "director's and designer's theater" has returned with a vengeance. And, of course, it was never away. By the time the actors show up for rehearsal, the major decisions have been made. The hapless actor can ask for a line or two back and may even win, since RSC directors seem intent on stretching their productions out to three hours, so that tourists, paying the equivalent of $50 per seat, "get their money's worth." We are paying by the hour these days and often purchasing only tedium. *Locus* and *platea* seemed to flow into each other in the 1992 productions, so that little energy or friction occurred between the two "authorities" that Weimann describes. And again, embarrassingly, RSC has little if anything to take to London for the next season. The only Shakespeare that RSC offered in London in August of 1992 was a pallid *Romeo and Juliet*, a remake of an even weaker Stratford version of 1991.

One of the better productions of this weak season was Peter Hall's *All's Well That Ends Well*, at the Swan, where the platform and the high balconies encourage the actors to look up and to speak up. Like all of Hall's productions, this one moved at a crackling pace, except when Helena summoned magic powers surrounded by the music of the spheres or when Diana's prophecies became echoes from Delphi. Pauses within rapid pacing equate to *rhythm*, which Sir Peter's productions invariably have. Furthermore, Toby Stephens's Bertram really did believe in Michael Siberry's Parolles, in spite of the latter's resemblance to Bert Lahr's Cowardly Lion. Regardless of sneers at "male bonding," it had occurred here, and Stephens's disappointment was profound and convincing. To respond to it did require a trace memory of a society in which young men did share the combat of American football, or rugby, or combat itself. As Paul Taylor noted, "all [Bertram's] military colleagues turn as one to watch his abashed, horrified reaction to the garrulous treacheries of Michael Silberry's Parolles" (*I* 2 July 1991). Dessen suggested why the humiliation of Parolles was so potent here: "clearly, the interrogation of Parolles was an interrogation of Bertram" ("Taming the Script," 6). Bertram ended up, according to Taylor, "a head-hanging, penitent, wreck" (*I* 2 July 1992) or, as Benedict Nightingale had it,

"Stephens may not be wearing rags weirdly plastered with straw, like Siberry; but it is an abject, shattered husband Helena takes home" (*T* 7 July 1992). Furthermore, Barbara Jefford's icily dominant Countess played superbly against Richard Johnson's bumbling grandfather of a King. He got a big laugh when he promised Diana the same deal at the end that had started all the trouble earlier: "If thou be'st yet a fresh uncropped flower, / Choose thou thy husband, and I'll pay thy dower." "It'll work *this* time," he seemed to say.

And he was right. We did not believe that any young man of his court would refuse Rebecca Saire's Diana. We *could* believe Stephens's rejection of Sophie Thompson's Helena: "In such a business give me leave to use / The help of mine own eyes." It was obviously a directorial decision to present Helena as a frumpy Puritan, heavy cross being her primary frontal endowment, shoulders slumped, long mouth pulled to each side in a frown. After her cure of France, she *may* have been meant to enjoy a positive metamorphosis—white gown and new hairdo. But the face tended to take itself at Helena's own low valuation and nothing really had happened to alter Bertram's. His rejection on the basis of class was a rationalization of his fear of a life sentence with a Helena who made him shudder. But he couldn't *say* that and thus prepared the trap that the King completed for him. Helena, then, was insisting on a relationship that could never work, but then people do that, thinking "to wed . . . a bright particular star." At the end, neither Bertram nor Helena seemed to warm to the "sweet use" to which he had put her, as he suddenly realized that he had been the victim of "cozened thoughts." Dessen suggested that "the absence of a kiss [between Bertram and Helena] forestalled any upbeat ending" ("Taming the Script," 6). Bertram was also the victim here of matriarchy, patriarchy, and a virgin's blind intentions. Some saw Helena as pregnant in her white wedding dress—or had she borrowed one of Doll's cushions in order to attract sympathy? "Most people on the stage, Bertram angrily excepted, are for her," as J. C. Trewin notes (186). Most productions of *All's Well* elicit compassion for Helena, as opposed to showing *her* try to elicit it for herself. The latter approach is certainly valid and permitted the production, as Dessen said, to leave "open a sense of problems to come without eliminating all hope" ("Taming the Script," 6).

Certainly this seldom-seen script *is* "problematized," full of options for directors and actors—and audience. Richard Johnson said, "It all seems to be quite a simple story—quite simple stuff—

but it isn't anything like that. We are left with a set of possibilities at then end—'if,' 'if,' 'if'" (Remarks, 4 August 1992). Bertram was left at the end with the same problem he was so frantic to flee at the outset. He had learned not to trust in "the world of men," but that lesson hardly prepared him to love Helena, who had fulfilled a seemingly impossible list of demands, but who merely presented the list at the end, and seemed to have learned nothing.

One interesting aspect of the production was a murky mirror on the upstage side of the Swan's open platform. At times the stage grouping was echoed in an impressionistic version of Rembrandt. The effect was powerful when this did occur, but it seemed random rather than intentional. Only Parolles, appropriately enough, seemed to recognize the mirror and preened before it at one point to admire his magnificent scarlet costume. It may be, of course, that the mirror was a version of "upstage fourth wall," to be observed within a decorum that *only* Parolles violated.

How would the emphasis would have changed had Saire been cast as Helena? Then Bertram would have had a chance to show that he had opened his *eyes* at last. We would have lost Bertram's rationalization at the outset, of course, but we might have picked up a happy ending, as opposed to one that "ended well." Here, Bertram's vision needed no spectacles. Helena had merely sprung the trap for which Bertram had drawn the blueprint. The ending hardly "contextualized" a world-without-end bargain, merely another bad marriage. That institution has seldom been a cure for unrequited love. Dr. Johnson suggests that Bertram is "dismissed to happiness" at the end, but that seemed an unlikely ending here.

The immediate critical reaction to this production seemed astute. Some critics, however, took Bertram at face value: an "ungallant swine" (Paton, *DE* 2 April 1992) and "an immature and unpleasant snob" (Nathan, *JC* 10 April 1992), although Paton suggested that "one could almost feel sorry for Bertram, were he not such a twerp." Others praised Thompson. Paton claimed a "sweet gravity" for Thompson's Helena, while Terry Grimley extolled "Thompson's vivid performance—all innocence and resourcefulness" (*BP* 2 July 1992, II/10). Nicholas de Jongh, however, found a "doleful Helena," who suffered with "relish" (*ES* 2 July 1992) and Charles Spencer an "irritatingly busy and mannered" Helena (*DT* 2 July 1992). Malcolm Rutherford saw this Helena as "a mousy-looking woman, whom one can well understand Bertram wishing to avoid." Rutherford wished that "Bertram's rejection of her [could have been] more inexplicable and therefore more interesting." Rutherford said, "she is an intelligent, inventive woman. Why can't she be attractive as well?" (*FT* 2 July 1992). Benedict Nightingale found "Sophie Thompson not the passionate, handsome Helena of tradition, but an intense girl who sometimes seems awkward to the point of being gawky, and ingenuous to the brink of gormlessness" (*T* 10 July 1992). It is "hardly surprising," said Carole Woddis, that Bertram "bolts, seeking sanctuary in war" (*WO* 8 July 1992). Some, then, disagreed with Jane Edwardes's contention "that if Hall were to start work with an entirely different cast tomorrow, the result would be depressingly similar" (*TO* 8 July 1992). Was it over-all conception *or* a casting decision that dictated what de Jongh called "the prospect of a really grim marriage . . . at the conclusion" (*ES* 2 July 1992)? Perhaps both. As Irving Wardle said, "Sophie Thompson's de-glamorised Helena, a pious dreamer . . . precisely articulates her every move in pursuit of Bertram without inviting sympathy. Given that context, I do not see why Bertram should still be played as a snobbish, mean-spirited brat simply for resisting marriage to a girl he happened not to fancy" (*IonS* 5 July 1992). If, as Lyn Gardner suggested, "Helena's fate is not happy-ever-after but a loveless marriage to a snob" (*MonS* 5 July 1992), it seems only fair to point out that this has been vehemently Helena's choice. Dominic Loehnis said that "at the end, one's chief feelings are of pity for Bertram, trapped by this arrested adolescent. You can't help feeling that he should have fled further" (*STel* 5 July 1992). This Helena, Martin Dodsworth felt, was "quite capable of wanting what will harm her," and gained "the power to impose her childish conviction on others" (*TLS* 10 July 1992, 18).

Critics were mixed on production values. Rutherford believed that the first half "over[did] the literalness at the expense of enjoyment," while Peter McGarry claimed that "The play itself . . . is taken too seriously" (*CET* 1 July 1992). Spencer said that "you get the impression of dogged conscientiousness rather than real inspiration [and] a certain blandness," in that "too few of the characters take on an urgent life of their own and the production seems to hold the audience at a distance. . . . What's missing is a unifying atmosphere, the sense of a coherent dramatic world." Spencer said that "the show never achieves those dramatic bursts of illumination when an audience suddenly feels it understands just what Shakespeare was getting at" (*DT* 2 July 1992), and de Jongh agreed that there were "too few signs of the insights and illuminations once regularly provided by the young Peter Hall

. . . Bland's the word." (*ES* 2 July 1992). "We are left," said Loehnis, "with 20 characters in search of a director, and the resulting experience is a strangely empty one" (*ST* 5 July 1992). "There is intelligence and clarity," said Taylor, "but . . . the details do not add up to a world" (*I* 2 July 1992) Edwardes found the production "admirably clear, pictorially seductive and all too frequently deadly dull, full of statuesque poses and little real communication" (*TO* 8 July 1992). Robert Hewison said that "Hall gives us stagey poses. The actors seem stifled and the style old-fashioned, as the RSC rediscovers its love of shoes and lace and hats and awkward props" (*ST* 5 July 1992). Ian Shuttleworth found Hall "unexcited by the thrusting three-dimensional space of the Swan . . . uninterested in the dramatic journey (a subversion of romance) . . . Hall's company boom the lines of the story. It is all words and no play. By default, it is a reminder of how far modern Shakespeare has progressed. Hall seems unable to take us on the imaginative journey demanded by the new generation of minimalist directors" (*CL* 9 July 1992).

Hall's was a more "minimalist" production than all but one of the other Stratford Shakespeare plays in 1992. Part of the reason might have been the apron stage of the Swan which tends to push any set upstage, off the apron. Hall's *All's Well* was a lot more spare than his elaborate and effective *Merchant* at the Phoenix in 1990. And again, the proscenium Phoenix calls for an elaborated and, probably, an elaborate set.

Others were happier with Hall's *All's Well*. Wardle found that Hall's company delivered the play "with an exemplary clarity that reveals some piercing character insights no less than its grave beauty" (*IonS* 5 July 1992). Michael Coveney felt that "Hall's emblematic, austere approach takes you right to the heart of every knotty speech and twist of plot line," and compared Hall's "most lucidly exciting close contact reappraisal" with Warner's *King John* (*O* 5 July 1992). Michael Billington found that "the elegant formality of a spoken opera staged in Caroline costumes . . . can sometimes seem a touch impersonal but its great merit is that little-noticed lines leap illuminatingly out of the text" (*G* 3 July 1992). Michael Davies said, "It's coherent and witty . . . and has The Hall-mark all over it, from the power of the direction to the pace of the action" (*EM* 3 July 1992). Ann Fitzgerald said, "An almost bare stage and subdued 17th century costumes focus attention on actors and text—spoken with a steady clarity that helps our understanding of the complex psychology of the play" (*T* 2 July 1992). Terry Grimley agreed: "With an intimate, almost domestic, sense of scale, the play unfolds with great clarity and a natural, unforced rhythm" (*BP* 2 July 1992).

Two other points worth emphasizing were noted accurately by the critics. As Edwardes pointed out, "Hall creates a strong tension between the increasingly powerful Puritans and the fading Elizabethan age, encapsulated in Anthony O'Donnell's decrepit, overweight clown, whose lewdness is well past its sell-by date" (*TD* 8 July 1992). And Nightingale noted that "Hall invites a parallel between [Bertram] and his army chum, the cad and liar, Parolles, [whose] humiliation is decidedly uncomic and seems meant to prefigure Bertram's own unmasking" (*T* 10 July 1992). As Dodsworth said, "Parolles's . . . agony of humiliation . . . is an anticipation . . . of the process Bertram undergoes in the very last scene, a kind of burning out of the moral centre," and therefore "a psychic equivalent to the curing of the King's fistula" (*TLS* 10 July 1992). Both of these "structural" connections—one a contrast between two epochs and one a comparison between events within the play—were vividly made and greatly enhanced the production's power.

The weakest of Stratford's offerings was David Thacker's *As You Like It*, on the Main Stage. A play that has music *within* it requires no interludes between scenes. Never, never, but too often at RSC, as in Barry Kyle's lugubrious *Love's Labour's Lost* of several seasons ago. A huge masoleum of a grand salon, a fascist palace featuring a macabre parade that included a one-eyed moll from Chicago and housing a gigantic grand piano does not suddenly become a site for wrestling. We can suspend our disbelief only so far. The heavy emphasis on a heavy set meant that we did not get the back and forth "filmic" effect the script provides. Here, 2.2 had to occur before 2.1. The Arden set was a busy mess, resembling the paper-mâché models that Lionel made for its train sets in the 1930s, and created obstacles and hazards for the actors, (as had Adrian Noble by putting an excellent company on slippery parachute silk in 1985 for his *As You Like It*).

The lighting for Arden was awful. A moon slithered up behind the set's huge tree, but instead of giving the stage a glimmering suffusion of light it merely competed with the spots in full view of the audience. No director who had ever sat in a theater would have permitted these two sources of light to fight with each other. They erased any sense of the forest as an agent of transformation. Nor should a director have tolerated the upstaging whereby Audrey and Martext wiped out Jaques's and Touchstone's discussion or in which Audrey destroyed Touchstone's disquisition on the dueling code. In the excellent Regent's Park version of 1992, John Kane and Samantha Spiro cooperated on Touchstone's response to Jacques's demand for a renomination of the degrees, Audrey cueing Touchstone's panicky and very funny recitation.

A director might exhibit some respect for language. If Rosalind mentions her "doublet and hose" twice, it ought to *be* there. It didn't matter very much here, since Samantha Bond's Rosalind was obviously female all the way, except to Peter De Jersey's remarkably uncurious or blind Orlando. At Regent's Park, a lissome Cathryn Harrison *explored* her disguise, which fit her most featly, and learned vicariously what it was to be a male, what it was to be Orlando. Hers was delightful and totally convincing Rosalind which restored an auditor's faith in the role and in the play.

The Thacker version's chief deficiency was its failure to establish relationships—between the one-on-one confrontations and any unifying concept and, more simply, between the characters. When Jaques finished his "Seven Ages" speech, we got a pause. Then: enter Orlando carrying Adam. Jaques's final line about all that cliché-old-age lacks was *not* linked up with what Adam, however toothless and frail, obviously *has*. Thus were we robbed of the connection that Shakespeare often makes between line and stage direction (cf. "absolute trust" [Enter Macbeth]). Celia's directions to Oliver were aimed at the auditorium and thus she squandered their very amusing effect as she tries to hold him there as she falls in love. This was perhaps the most obvious example of the actors's inability or unwillingness to make eye contact with the other characters.

The production achieved some positive reaction. James Christopher praised the "magnificent sets: the windowless, black marbled court . . . in contrast to the sumptuously naturalistic Arden" (*C'sC* 26 April–9 May 1992). Kenneth Hurren agreed: "Johan Engles's set designs are spectacularly successful" (*MonS* 26 April 1992). Paul Taylor found that Bond "combines a delightful comic flair with a lovely quality of pensiveness" (*I* 24 April 1992) and Charles Spencer said that "she really does look like an adolescent boy." Spencer claimed "great freshness and vitality" for the production, which "confirms Thacker's growing reputation as one of our finest Shakespearean directors" (*DT* 24 April 1992). John Peter discovered "profoundly modern" implications in the production, in that it showed "the human personality being liberated by liberty, and the implied argument that oppression can stunt the soul" (*ST* 26 April 1992). Susanne Williams turned Thacker into a more explicit modernist: "he "managed to create an Elizabethan 'Return of the Jedi,' incorporating scenes straight out of Flash Gordon, James Bond, Robin Hood and Seven Brides for Seven Brothers" (*BM* 24 April 1992). John Gross found the production "fresh, spirited, straightforward . . . all the main elements slip into their rightful place" (*STelegraph* 26 April 1992). Jack Tinker was rhapsodic: "a production that will stand as an icon for time to come. . . . I cannot imagine anyone crass enough not to leave the place bewitched by" Bond, who has found "the role destiny carved for her . . . [Thacker] simply unravels all the play's diverse themes and weaves them into a clear and comprehensible whole. . . . Johan Engles's rich settings fairly throb with rampant nature" (*DM* 23 April 1992).

Others, however, discerned the lifelessness of this offering. Christopher found it "overlong" (*CC* April-May 1992) while Nicholas de Jongh saw Rosalind and Orlando "upstag[ed by] the gorgeous settings" (*ES* 23 April 1992). Irving Wardle found that the "relationships are underexplored. . . . Celia . . . almost vanishes . . . while . . . Rosalind, stronger on languishing than on mischief, settles for a leisurely rhythm that fails to ignite the Orlando scenes." For him, the production provided "precious little electricity" (*IonS* 26 April 1992). "From this fairly heavy-handed start [the grim court of Frederick]," said David Murray, "one waited for some definite view of the play to develop and make itself felt. It never did." For him, the Arden set was "a broad tilted greensward, suitable for displaying market produce . . . [I]t carried no undertones or overtones, nor the least romantic conviction. . . . A few individually attractive performances floated free, unmoored by any whole dramatic conception" (*FT* 24 April 1992). For Ian Shuttleworth, "the whole is unsatisfying; we *know* the world isn't like Shakespeare's festive comedies. . . . Thacker sacrifices the play itself to his over-reductive vision of it, and in the process loses sight of the forest for the trees" (*CL* 30 April 1992). Michael Coveney found that the production "smacks of routine dullness. . . . If an audience does not love its Rosalind . . . the play simply fails to catch alight. . . . I do sense an overwhelming lassitude of intention in this instance. [The] pace is deliberate and slow . . . vitiated by a complete indifference to the intellectual and sexual climate of the comedy" (*O* 26 April 1992). Aidan Goldstraw agreed: "this is a low intensity affair, where enemies lack fire and lovers need to be more ardent. There seems to be a real lack of heart in the show" (*E&S* 23 April 1992). "Largely missing from [this production]," said Michael Billington "is precisely that quality of giddy rapture and insane ecstasy [that Rosalind assigns to love]." Billington found Bond "operating in an emotional vacuum. . . . This lack of emotional detail spreads throughout the production." "Certainly," said Nightingale, Rosalind's "rapport with Phyllida Hancock's curiously understretched Celia could be greater" (G 24 April 1992). "There are wreaths and songs and a rustic dance and high spirits," observed Lindsay Duguid, "which do not dispel the mild feeling of fatuousness which hovers over it all" (TLS 8 May 1992). The main stage does seem to be a daunting space, and it may be hopelessly old-fashioned for critics to ask for "thematic coherence" in a production. But better a wrong vision of how the play may be trying to mean than no vision at all.

Bill Alexander's *The Taming of the Shrew* did have a vision of the script, and one that worked. Many observers did not agree with that positive assessment, however.

In a sloppily written "Introduction," a group of bored, young aristocrats of 1992 found a drunk (Sly) tossed from a tavern. Cruelly, they fitted him out in finery and cruelly was a beardless younger brother forced out of the breeches to be Sly's wife. The "frame"—the aristocrats lounging on a platform behind the Shrew episodes—did indeed upstage the inner play, which became the form and pressure of another time, of 1594, reaching histrionically and anachronistically towards the layabouts of 1992 and failing to be understood. For many, like Gill Robinson, "the movements at the back of the stage distract the audience from the main task at hand—the taming of Kate" (SO 10 April 1992). And, at times, one did read "distraction" and not "interaction." In a nice irony, however, Sly offered some candy to a seemingly starving Kate, Sly missing the fiction but receiving the emotional content that his lordly companions scorn. "Isn't it condescending, though," Paul Taylor asked, "to suggest that you can't trust a labourer to spot the difference between art and real life?" (I 2 July 1992). Perhaps, but this was a production in which the borders between "art and real life" were crossed with increasing frequency as the two plays became one.

Within the inner play, Bill McCabe's Tranio assumed his disguise with a vengeance, sneering at Lucentio with what the East Coast used to call "Locust Valley Lockjaw" and threatening to become Mosca from another play by another playwright, as Paul Lapworth accurately noted (SH 10 April 1992). In fact, Tranio's wooing of Rebecca Saire's Bianca was so successful that it would clearly supersede any financial arrangements worked out by Vincentio and Baptista Minola on behalf of Lucentio and Bianca. McCabe's was, as Michael Billington neatly put it, "a clear intimation of the proxy wooing of *Much Ado*" (*G* 3 July 1992). We got in this Tranio a Sly who believed in his role before he assumed it and assumed it as his "right," by merit, not by birth, and thus a "modern" character commenting also on his lordly audience. As Miriam Gilbert said, "by suggesting that Tranio hoped to win Bianca for himself, McCabe's Tranio turned scenes of comic pretense into something much darker" (SAA abstract, 1). And we got in Bianca a mirror of the bitchiness of the young aristocrats, both male and female.

As a commentary on the "taming plot," Anton Lesser's pint-sized bully Petruchio delivered a vivid slap to the face of one of the aristocratic ladies enlisted to play the minor roles, in this case, one of Petruchio's feckless servants. The young woman was shocked but said nothing as Petruchio dared her to make an unscripted response. "You're on *my* stage now," he seemed to sneer. Billington suggested that "she'd be less likely to dwell on the Pirandellian implications than to phone for the police." The inclusion of the on-stage "audience" as bit players did work a nice inversion, however, as Paul Taylor argued: "it's the modern day thesp who seems to be working off a bit of class resentment in the scene when the ranting hero belabours his 'unpolished grooms,' here performed by the upper-class oiks" (*I* 2 July 1992). At the end, Kate's speech was directed almost exclusively at the Right Honorable young woman who had been enlisted to play the Widow, a role she had already essayed, it was clear, at school. The Widow and woman rejected Kate's advice about surrendering to lord and governor but the young woman joined the acting company, eager to play Kate on stage even while not accepting the submission Kate advocates in that old speech. To escape into a fictive "truth" could be, it seemed, a very enjoyable experience, an ironic mode of freedom for the modern and emancipated woman who would never take her stage character seriously and would be, thus, doomed to inhabit some confusing zone along the regress between 1594 and 1992. At the end, an awakened Sly glimpsed the actors on the street. It was as if he had recalled some fragment of dream now irrelevant to his hangover or the wife he believes he will tame, waiting in some row house down the endless line of chimneys below the pub.

Obviously, Alexander created an "adaptation," although the intentionally overacted inner play was, he said, "faithful to the 1623 Folio" (20). And just as obviously, the inner play was subject to and surrounded by heavy "conceptualization." The issue raised, however, was the relevance of an old play for a sophisticated modern audience. And that is a good question, to which Alexander gave an intentionally ambiguous answer. "What I have sacrificed in terms of what Shakespeare wrote," he said, "I've more than replaced by reclaiming the overall structure of the play," which, he is certain, included a conclusion to the frame. Had he "entirely removed the Christopher Sly framework the play 'would have lost' its central metaphor about people watching a play . . . the way we perceive other people in the way they act . . . It's the job of a director approaching Shakespeare to make an audience . . . experience the play brand new" (20). Dessen, however, argued cogently that Alexander presented a new *play:* to conflate the 1594 and 1623 texts "into one supposedly 'complete' stage version is . . . to create a third entity that corresponds neither to version one nor to version two . . . the existence of *A Shrew* has become a blank check for adaptation at the pleasure of a director" ("Taming the Script," 4). What happens when the Sly frame is completed, as Dessen suggests, is that the emphasis shifts "away from a contrast between Kate-Petruchio and the rest of Padua" (4). In Alexander's production, the frame and inner play became so entangled with each other that the point that the 1623 Folio may make—that is, that the "play within" is now being conducted by Kate and Petruchio—could not be made on the Stratford stage.

The "critics will either love it or hate it," Alexander said (20), but instead, they discussed it very much within the premises that Alexander provided, without necessarily applauding the production. "Why," asked Nightingale, "is the Sly subplot given such emphasis that it almost upstages the play itself?" (*T* 3 April 1992). Edwardes agreed with this question: "The aristos . . . stretch the play considerably, and the flatness of the . . . dialogue does little to add to an evening that is deprived of the high spirits needed to make the schooling of Kate bearable. . . . Her capitulation over the time of day has rarely seemed such a defeat. [The production provides no] sense that Petruchio and Katherine enjoy their battles, and with the line-up of nasty toffs watching from the back, this becomes a drab and depressing evening" (*TO* 8 April 1992). Alexander, however, intentionally stylized the inner play to "look like" a play and put the toffs inside that framework once it arrived at Petruchio's country house. For Charles Spencer, "this production combines the tiresomely modish with the drearily traditional. And it entirely lacks the high spirits and good humor which can redeem the play in performance" (*DT* 3 April 1992). While the play *is* performance, Spencer would be right if each segment of the production—frame and interior—were to be taken at face value. But it is the communication between the two components that either worked or did not. For Spencer, it did not. The frame "becomes increasingly irritating [and] serves as a constant distraction from the play itself." Wardle claimed that "every director of the play . . . sets out to neutralize its crude message on sexual dominance without killing the comedy. Alexander's solution is to pin the guilt on the actors's ruling-class patrons whose crass behavior they are merely reflecting" (*IonS* 5 April 1992). If so, it was strange that the toffs would choose *this* play, unless the males saw it as somehow confirming their superiority. As it was, the inner play became something like "The Murder of Gonzago," and, at the end, one of the young women of the on-stage audience, Lady Sarah, vividly cast off the arm of her boyfriend, Lord Simon, as they exited into the first streaks of morning. Wardle added that "The play always works; but this version comes closer than any I have ever seen to wrecking it." Brendan O'Keeffe found that the concept "goes stale quickly and, like any half-realized, over-schematic dramatic idea, interrupts audience pleasure" (*WO* 8 April 1992). "Like most 'concepts,' it works for and against the play itself," said Robert Hewison (*ST* 5 April 1992). Paul Taylor found that "the trick played on Sly feels too nasty to be at all amusing and this distinctly chills the atmosphere" (*I* 3 April 1992). For Kenneth Hurren, the frame "invades and unbalances the ensuing play [which becomes] a deeply unpleasant affair [and supports]—a touch unexpectedly—. . . that anti-feminist backlash we read about" (*MonS* 5 April 1992). Again, assuming an interplay between the two structures of the production, it did not work for Hurren. but the "unpleasantness" would have to emerge, then, both from Kate's acceptance of the doctrine of submission *and* the Widow's rejection of that doctrine. Hewison claimed that Kate's "submission speech bears no relation to the psychology of what has gone before" (*ST* 5 April 1992). And that may be true, in that it is a speech *to* the on-stage audience, or at least to one member of that audience, and not necessarily *from* the experience she has had. She saw the point clearly on the road to Padua; her words about "mistaking eyes" were directed to Petruchio, not to Vincentio. For Kirsty Milne, also, the "update becomes a source of irritation rather than enlightenment" (*STele* 5 April 1992). Maureen Paton said that "this lamentably gimmicky production limps along until the story of the fiery Kate and her

tamer Petruchio begins," and then, "Alexander is foolish enough
to squander what magic survives his directorial technique and
turn the tale into no more than a hen-pecked husband's drunken
dream" (*DE* 2 April 1992). Billington said of the frame: "Feasible
in theory the idea falls apart in practice. It strains our credulity
. . . the frame seems bigger than the picture. . . . [T]he constant
presence of these toping dopes draws much of the fun and sting
from the comedy" (*G* 3 April 1992). The initial game was hard to
credit because it was too close to us in time and lacked any "once
upon a time" tonalities. For Billington, apparently, the two elements drained energy *from* each other throughout the production.
"The frame draws as much attention as the picture," said Oliver
Reynolds (*TLS* 10 April 1992, 18). Taylor agreed: "It's a production
in which the surrounding action looms large in your memory. . . .
Full of ideas, if not always coherent, this *Shrew* is never tame."

Many critics responded positively to the "ideas" and the way
they worked out on the Stratford Main Stage. Douglas Slater
found the production "entrancing. . . . Alexander boldly and ef-
fortlessly weaves all together in one sweep of action. [It] compares
with the very best [of *Shrews*]" (*DM* 7 April 1992). "At last," said
Andrew George,

> a director has succeeded in marrying the shabby Christopher Sly
> scenes to the lustrous central action [in] a marriage of true impedi-
> ments. . . . As a piece of theatre, it is intelligent, magical, and wholly
> absorbing. . . . Alexander is not hamstrung by the self-censorship of
> political correctness: Kate's final speech no longer *has* to be ironic, for
> she speaks it not to the theatre but to a self-possessed 20th-century
> woman in the closet audience. . . . The production calls up the vis-
> ceral world of the sonnets: 'Thus have I had thee as a dream doth
> flatter'. (*FT* 3 April 1992)

Simon Reade was equally enthusiastic:

> a unique *Shrew* that sets an intellectual standard for all subsequent
> productions this century. . . . [The] Sly scenes . . . provide a coherent
> alienating frame . . . which is wholly engrossing. [The] players deliver
> a sinister, philosophical comedy where all gets wrapped up in the
> reality of illusion—let by a terrier Petruchio and a bulldog Kate.
> Broadside critics have reacted with bardolastrous bluster to this pro-
> duction, which is precisely the mark of its brilliance: to place a great
> question mark over one Shakespearean myth. (*CL* 16 April 1992)

Nicholas de Jongh felt that "this provocative production . . . deals
fascinatingly with the Shakespearean game of changing identi-

ties" (*ES* 2 April 1992) and Paul Lapworth agreed: "The variations on disguise and role-playing are interesting to the end" (*SH* 10 April 1992) Neil Taylor said that "the result [of Alexander's concept] is a most extraordinary experience and one which transforms the play . . . the relationships of Sly to his companions and Sly to the play [are] the bases for interpreting the relationship of Petruchio to Kate" (*PI* June 1992, 23). Marion Brennan also picked up on the interactions between frame and "play": "[The aristocrat's] intention with Sly is to 'mess around with his mind a bit,' a sinister theme repeated in the way the supposedly gentle Bianca manipulates her suitors and Petruchio famously tames Kate. It's brave and clever and worth doing . . ." (*K&S* 2 April 1992). For David Nathan, Alexander "persuasively brings us up to date" (*JC* 10 April 1992).

It is typical of "Director's Theatre" that far more attention is paid to "concept" than to "character." It is also true that the concept of "character" itself is in disrepute, since it doesn't "intertextualize" well at all and unless the character can be interpreted within neo-Freudian terms or as a victim of patriarchy. Interestingly, however, critics did look at the central "love story," or conflict. Wardle found that the emphasis on "class vengeances . . . redoubles the brutality of the role [of Petruchio]" (*IonS* 5 April 1992) Spencer reacted to Lesser's "odious jauntiness" by wanting "to biff the little tyke on the nose" (*DT* 3 April 1992). Michael Coveney suggested that "Petruchio's madness became not a weapon of sexual tyranny but a psychotic condition by which Kate is increasingly fascinated" (*O* 5 April 1992). Milne found "a streak of sadism in [Petruchio] which leads us to expect an answering streak of masochism in Katherine. [In her capitulation, however], she seems not crushed but excited" (*ST* 5 April 1992). If so, she accepted, perhaps, what Kenneth Hurren called a "nasty little money-grubbing Petruchio" (*MonS* 5 April 1992), but that may be preferable to being a "hyperventilating, near-psychotic bag of nerves," as Brendan O'Keeffe labelled Amanda Harris's Kate (*WO* 8 April 1992). Lesser, said Nightingale, was "more formidable than his slight build would suggest. But then he needs to be, for Amanda Harris's Kate is as splendidly baleful a shrew as I can recall" (*T* 3 April 1992). De Jongh suggested that "her chosen identity—that of an angry child—cannot be easily shed" (*ES* 2 April 1992). "We know," said Taylor, "that this is *not* a nature she is happy with" (23). The *Burton Mail* (5 April 1992) found Kate "deliciously demonic from the start," yet "it seemed some of the men in her life were more in need of the taming process [than she. Petruchio was subject] to unbecoming . . . temper tantrums," as indeed Curtis suggests in calling him "more shrew than she." Paton felt that Lesser rose "above the mistakes of this misguided production and create[d] a real sense of tough love in his wooing" (*DE* 2 April 1992). Reynolds found that Harris provided "little sign of how [shrewishness] became [submission]" (*TLS* 10 April 1992). Wardle, also responding to unmotivated farce, found "no clue to who she is or what she is angry about" (*IonS* 5 April 1992).

The inner "history" was, no doubt, exaggerated and might have been cooled to a subtler tone, just as the frame might have been made a bit more vibrant. The inner actors were *not* meant to be members of the RSC, but of an out-of-work Cheek-near-Bone Company, and the outer people were not meant to be actors at all, except for the aspiring Widow. Modifications in this scheme might have diminished the distinction between what Alexander called the "juxtaposition of times and periods on stage" (20). It was that juxtaposition and the interplay between the two periods and the conflicts between the attitudes revealed within them that made the production worthwhile, although it is possible that Jane Edwardes was right to say that it was "more interesting to discuss afterwards than enjoyable to watch at the time" (*TO* 8 April 1992). (For an analysis of Alexander's framing of *Shrew*, that appeared after this chapter was written, see Michael J. Collins, "The Taming of the Shrew," *Shakespeare Bulletin* [Spring 1993]: 22–23.)

Adrian Noble's *The Winter's Tale* was not the triumph that critics made it out to be.

Leontes, it seems, *began* the play with suspicions and set Hermione up. He then prowled the perimeter of his lawn party and watched her gestures, adding the words from his own paranoiac horde. That's not a bad conception, although we tended to be searching for Leontes (John Nettles) in the scrum as Samantha Bond's Hermione persuaded Polixenes. But Nettles went over the top very quickly, leaving him no place to go after Mamillius's death. The more controlled performance of William Wight years ago at Monmouth (Maine) was more persuasive than Nettles's as, more recently, was Tim Piggot-Smith's chillingly "sane" Leontes, as he constructed his fantasy-world without an Iago to cue him: "Kissing with inside lip . . . Is this nothing?" he said, as if educating an ignorant Camillo. "Control" yields intensity, giving the audience something to do beside witnessing a tantrum that must be indulged because the tantrumer is King and the playwright Shakespeare.

Elements to praise in the first half included Gemma Jones's biting Paulina, and the "Our Town" trial of Hermione, under the crow-hover of umbrellas, where Bond's husky and rangeless voice served her well, as if she spoke after months of damp incarceration. The bear was scary, but the sequence lasted for a strobe-blink too long, just edging over into the zone where the audience becomes aware of how it's being done. And then a very hokey angel appeared, telling us perhaps that it has all been a dream. Not for Antigonis! Nightingale saw it too, and found "the hovering mum . . . a bit preposterous" (G 3 July 1992). And isn't Antigonus's line about "Wolves and bears [doing] like offices of pity" meant to be fired straight at Leontes, as the latter "commends" the baby girl to some "desert place"?

The second half was signaled by a note dropping on a balloon and read by Camillo, who became "Time." It was cutesy and unbelievable even in a play that insists on suspension of disbelief. Had Samantha Bond read the speech as a neutral allegorical character, necessarily "He," the effect would have been powerful. The sheep-shearing was a town fête from several periods—a 1911 band, post–World War I outfits for the men, and pre–World War II dresses for the ladies. Not a sheep in sight. Florizel (Alan Cox) might have drifted down from Eton for a dalliance, but he was not about to make his niche in the future quiver for the sake even of Phyllida Hancock's fetching, barefoot contessa of the county fair. Paul Jesson's Polixenes nicely articulated his affinity with Leontes by constructing an unpleasant allegory ("That thus affects a sheep-hook!"). But Bill McCabe's Autolycus was permitted to go on and on—to sing, when he cannot sing very well, to dance, when he cannot dance very well, and to repeat his pickpocketing and watch-pilfering at least one too many times. McCabe is an actor who needs to be controlled by a director. Here, the scene, long enough at some 875 lines, also went on and on. It became, as it is always in danger of doing, the play itself, and did not integrate with Sicily, except through Polixenes. It may be thematically that, as Kirsty Milne said, "Optimism in Bohemia makes reconciliation possible in Sicilia" (STele 5 July 1992), but here the emphasis was on Autolycus's irrelevant business—except for the negative echoes that Polixenes provided.

In the final scene, we faced Hermione's back, downstage center, and were blocked from Leontes's reaction as he gradually comes to life. Since Noble had previously employed a scrim and freeze-frame technique, in apparent preparation for the finale, the shift in perspective was, as Michael Coveney suggested, possibly "a deliberate ploy to render the court itself an apparition, or a weakness in design" (*O* 5 July 1992). This closing did echo the opening, in which Mamillius, downstage, looked at the party going on behind the scrim, but so what? If the play is somehow Mamillius's "tale," how, at the end, has it become Hermione's story? She becomes, one assumes, a stand-in for Mamillius's wish-fulfillment, but does *Winter's Tale*, like *King Lear*, mirror its opening scene with its last? Furthermore, since the village festival had taken so much time, the reconciliation was rushed. Gone, inexcusably, were lines like "Hermione was not so much wrinkled, nothing / So aged as this seems," and "What fine chisel / Could ever yet cut breath?" In other words, the "trade-off" that Noble effected, along with his staging of the scene, drained the finale of what Stanley Wells calls, "the thrill of ritual participation" (*TLS* 20 February 1981, 197). Admittedly, that effect is difficult to achieve on Stratford-on-Avon's proscenium stage. But it was not reached for here.*

Any sense that this was a gimmicky and hollow production was a minority view. It "comes close to perfection," according to Malcolm Rutherford (*FT* 3 July 1992). De Jongh discerned "a thrilling strangeness infect[ing]" an "enthralling, eccentric" production (*ES* 2 July 1992). Spencer found it "spellbinding," infused with "a wonderful freshness of approach" (*DT* 2 July 1992). For him, the finale captured "the heart of some religious mystery, full of grace and forgiveness." "And only the hardest-hearted will be able to sit through its magnificently moving conclusion without blinking back the tears." Billington suggested that "Noble's notion of the play as a child's darkling fantasy even accommodates the

---

*In James Hoban's *Winter's Tale* by the Renaissance Players in Portland, Maine in May 1993, the statue scene found Hermione down center, with Florizel and Perdita stage right, Leontes and Polixenes stage left, and Paulina mobile, able to move between the statue and both Perdita and Leontes, Paulina was, in effect, "Time," capable of movement, fulfilling the allegory of Time as he begins act IV. Paulina was the "mankind witch" that Leontes had accused her of being but was practicing white magic, as she says. We were thus able to experience the entire "miracle"—the "statue" and the responses to it, and Paulina's crucial control of a fiction becoming a "reality" as time and human purpose coincide. James Stephens had been a powerful Leontes, and that alone gave remarkable impact to the scene. This modest local effort was simply better staged, better edited, and better acted than the RSC version.

Bohemian revels" (*G* 3 July 1992). The concept "embraces sacred and profane and gives [the play] thematic unity." Ann Fitzgerald said that the "production finds the broad range of human emotion, the darkness, the beauty and the uproarious comedy in Shakespeare's late play" (*T* 2 July 1992). Hewison said that "Noble has created an imaginative world one warms to . . . the visual and the verbal, the comic and the tragic, all come together in the last act" (*ST* 5 July 1992). Michael Davies felt that "every scene is a tableau of beauty, immaculately dressed and flawlessly executed . . . it's by some way the best RSC production this season" (*EM* 3 July 1992. (That comment was made, of course, before *Richard III* opened at The Other Place.) Richard Williamson found the production "gloriously entertaining [and] imaginative . . . a real gem to add to the already sparkling Stratford season" (*SM* 5 July 1992). Paul Lapworth called it "a marvellous production. . . . Noble walked the high-wire between realism and fantasy with supreme confidence. His eye for balance, parallels, contrast and coherence was remarkable. . . . Only Hermione's *dea ex machina* into the bear episode was a bit of a shock" (*SH* 27 June 1992). Douglas Slater responded "glowingly" to the production, which added to "what is already among the very best of Stratford seasons" (*DM* 7 July 1992).

McCabe was lionized. "I have never seen a better Autolycus," said Peter Porter (*TLS* 10 July 1992, 18). Slater called McCabe "a direct successor to Will Kemp," and there was probably a lot more Kemp than Robert Armin in McCabe's performance. Of the actors, only Nettles drew an occasional negative. "He is quite at sea with Leontes," de Jongh said, "flailing a touch breathlessly and blankly with the king's creshendos of sexual jealousy." "Nettles," according to Coveney, "lacks the size, oddness and metallic edge of an Ian McKellan or Michael Pennington." Wardle felt that Nettles "seems not to have considered who Leontes is (a tyrant or a possessed victim?); and the flinty attack of his RSC work in the 1970s is precisely what it lacks now" (*IonS* 5 July 1992). "He is too inclined," said Paul Taylor, "to register emotion by chopping up the lines into a sort of hyperventilated telegraphese" (*I* 3 July, 1992). Nettles, said Billington, "lacks the flint and spark of true madness" (*G* 3 July 1992). The problem might have been television, where Nettles acted for a decade. Spencer suggested that "after years of working on television, his emotion doesn't seem quite big enough to fill Stratford's main stage" (*DT* 3 July 1992), while Richard Edmonds found Nettles "not unscarred by television [and] lack[ing] projection" (*BP* 3 July 1992). It may be that

Nettles overcompensated in his transition from the "cool medium," where camera and microphone are close by, to the vast
auditorium that confronts the main stage, and thus delivered
what Edmonds called a "manic" Leontes. Peter McGarry said that
Nettles's "ludicrous vocal posturing and generally inept portrayal" contributed to a "somewhat tedious [production] which
doesn't add much lustre to the so-far disappointing main-house"
(*CET* 2 July 1992).

In fairness to Nettles, many of the critics agreed that he was
"more powerful in rheumy, grizzled regret than in rage," as
Nightingale said (*G* 3 July 1992). "He is more arresting," observed
Milne, "as the stumbling broken old man of the second half than
the paranoid tyrant of the first" (*ST* 5 July 1992). "As a penitent
thawing into ecstatic confession," Wardle said, "he is on top of
the part" (*IonS* 5 July 1992). Hewison, Lapworth, Taylor, and Edmonds tended to agree with that assessment, which is a typical
reaction to an actor who takes his Leontes too far in the first half.
Any change is an improvement.

The only critics, besides McGarry, who disliked the production
were Edmonds, who suggested that McCabe's was "an OTT performance [with an] overload of comic business [which] can lose
the text" (*BP* 3 July 1992), and Taylor, who called the production
"external" (*I* 3 July 1992). The "fresh ideas . . . create . . . doubt
when pondered," like Time's message as delivered to Camillo,
"scaling down his intuitive sense of [Perdita's] worth when they
meet at the festival." For Taylor, "not all of [the] novelties, alas,
convince you that the play has been newly felt." *Platea* in no way
challenged *locus*. It is interesting that, while the critics did notice
the elements of carnival and the many balloons featured in this
production, their discussions were rather general. That may say
something about the script, with its fusion of *Othello* and "Cinderella," but it also said something about the production. The production, like infatuation, might well create doubt if pondered.

Joan Byles has recently written an essay on a performance of
Hamlet in Romania that defied the authorities, attracted packed
houses to a cold unheated auditorium, and may even have been
a factor in the anger of the crowds that confronted Ceauşescu just
before his tumble (Stratford, Aug. 1992). There, certainly, we find
a confrontation of *locus* by *platea*, a translation of manifest content
into something subversive. In this production, Horatio was killed
at the end because he would tell the truth. The director insisted
on this ending in spite of objections from the police, arguing the

authority of Shakespeare, even though none of the available texts, as the police apparently did not know, support the summary execution of Horatio. With few exceptions, Stratford seems interested in pleasing the Prince of Wales these days and in subordinating potential *platea* almost totally to *locus*. Is some second coming at hand? Is someone like Brook with his *Lear* and *Dream* so many years ago or Warner more recently slouching towards Stratford to shake us all loose from our preconceptions about Shakespeare and how his plays should arrive on the stage? For the most part, 1992 was a summer of discontent, seldom made glorious except by the blessed sun itself, and otherwise illuminated by the perceptive commentary provided by critics who make these productions the most scrutinized in the world.

10

Richard III: Large and Small

THE first few years of the 1990s offered two excellent versions of this difficult script: a surprising fact in itself, after Anthony Sher's powerful performance of 1984, in which Sher dragged his helpless legs behind him but turned his metal crutches to remarkable use as he blocked halberds or pinned enemy throats between their pincers. That great performance has been amply chronicled, particularly by Chris Hassell and Sher himself. The National Theatre mounted an opulent version in 1990, with Ian McKellen in the title role, and the summer of 1992 saw Simon Russell Beale take the role on in a minimalist production for Sam Mendes at Stratford's new Other Place. Each was a marvelous production, though each probably as different from the other as could have been possible, even if the two directors met and drawn up a list of contrasts they wanted to make. Taken together, the two productions form the ends of the spectrum of possibilities for *Richard III*, suggesting how energetically the same text can produce productions that are different *plays* yet remain faithful to the inherited script.

Richard Eyre's *Richard III* at the National incorporated many of the same actors as Warner's *King Lear*. Eyre showed that the same space can incorporate very different tones. Warner's was a spare and unadorned production. Eyre used the huge National frame to create a panorama of a fascistic rise to power. The staging itself reminded its audience of how fascists use such panoramas: Mussolini jutting his jaw from a balcony as thousands cheered in the square below, or Hitler at the Nazi Party Conference at Nuremberg in 1934 as re-evoked in the monumental *Triumph of the Will*. Part of the production's power was that parts of it had much the same effect on its audience as do carefully orchestrated political events—Party conventions in the United States, for example. Eyre was telling *and* showing, so that Richard's story made for participation—and rejection as well—within the play and within the auditorium. Eyre created a modern world for his script to bustle in, which is always a dangerous approach when that world still lives in the memory of some spectators. The danger is that the world in which the script is set will fight the script itself to become the "play," as in, for example, the Papp-Antoon *Much Ado,* much-celebrated but really a clever little play about a charming little U.S. in the era of Teddy Roosevelt, when wars always ended happily. Eyre's setting was post–World War I Britain, home of Edward the Duke of Windsor, Oswald Mosley, and photographs of Wallis Warfield shaking hands solemnly with Hitler. The concept brought criticism, but was also *colorful* after the drab eclecticism of so much of the rest of the season. Sheridan Morley summed up critical ambivalence by calling the production "flip and flashy," a combination of "brilliant invention" and "dangerous gimmickry" (*IHT* 1 August 1991, 11). Dessen, who was less harsh on this production than one might expect, said that he did "not remember a recent show with more special effects per square inch . . . fog for 1.1; a gurney and a morgue-like atmosphere for 1.2; an elaborate dinner served in 1.3, a massing of the royal family for a group portrait in 2.1–2.2. . . . A toy train traversed the wide stage in 2.4 and then recrossed it at the end of the scene so as to lead into the red-carpet welcoming of Edward IV's sons in 3.1 at a train station" (22)—Waterloo, one assumed. The overall sense of the set was neatly captured by David Richards: "It's a world of endless corridors, vast ceremonial rooms, police stations hung with metal lamps and, way upstage, a door half-cracked to let in a shaft of chilly, white light. In such a society, men *are* insignificant, fodder for a coup or a grilling" ("Three Faces of Richard III," *NYT* 7 October 1990, H 30; his emphasis).

One member of the company complained that the concept for *Richard III* was "schematic," rather than "organic" as it was for Warner's *Lear,* in which this actor was also working. *Lear,* however, explores early decisions that have a "darker purpose" unglimpsed in Lear's conscious agenda—one could call it an agenda of consciousness—at the outset. The script *is* a "working out" and does indeed resist schematic directorial impositions. *Richard III,* however, develops Richard's conscious agenda, however delivered through "drunken prophecies, libels, and dreams," until, in *his* dream, the Augustinian premises of his world assert their primacy. A schematic approach to *Richard III,* in which the characters's roles are assigned in advance, is consistent with the script. The actor, however, rightly suggests that such an imposed vision leaves no room for the script to stretch and develop and, therefore, denies further growth to actors and production. Eyre's approach became a problem on tour, when the production was unable to adjust to the acoustics of, for example, the Brooklyn Academy of Music or the Kennedy Center in Washington, D.C. For Warner's *Lear*, a few re-blockings would probably have solved the problems, but this *Richard III* was already set rigidly in concrete by the time it left the National.

Eyre's approach solved some problems, as Lois Potter reported: "There are two traps for the director and star of *Richard III*: reaching the peak too early, and making Richard nothing more than a comic role model [. This] brilliant production avoids both, but takes enormous risks in the process." A major reason for the production's success, says Potter, is that McKellen "deliver[s] the opening soliloquy in a dry, old-fashioned, upper-class accent that negates any possibility of making friends with the audience" (*TLS* 3–9 August 1990, 825). That is, unless we are dry, old-fashioned types ourselves. Thus Richard was neither "comic" nor able to peak during that tour de force opening, which includes his placing Clarence immediately into the pattern Richard has just described for us. Indeed, Peter Holland found that McKellen's characterization "exacted [a] heavy penalt[y] . . . there was little room for a real language of comedy to surround or be generated by this Richard. McKellen['s] . . . Richard had nothing of the charm of the comic villain, the generic outsider, defining himself instead simply as a wounded soldier" (*ShS* 44, 188). Richard, then, was a more mobile and higher-born version of Wilfred Owen's soldier in "Disabled." That established his bitterness precisely. His wounds became the personal grievance that paralleled the grab-bag of complaints which Hitler used so effectively in the late 1920s and early 1930s.

A second reason for the success of this production, according to Potter, was the way in which the characters fit "the emotional wasteland of which they are a part. The utterly credible Hastings (David Bradley) and Stanley (David Collings) are bureaucrats not only because of their briefcases and umbrellas but in their inability to imagine evil until they are themselves implicated in it" (825). Potter thus explained one of the reasons why the fascist analogy rang so eerily true here. Yet another reason for the production's ability to maintain our interest was its unwillingness to make easy judgments:

> We are denied warmth and humour: the lighting is nocturnal, hard on the eyes and nerves. At Richmond's first entrance, the lighting

changes to golden afternoon sunshine and, for the first time, we see what looks like a realistic backdrop: a panorama of green fields dominated by a church. They'll always be an England, after all. We have waited so long for this visual relief that we want to believe in it. But it is ambiguous: the green landscape may simply be Richmond's own propaganda poster. (825)

In other words, the production did not make simplistic distinctions within its dictated format.

Not all critics agreed with Potter on the second half of the production. Peter Holland remarked "a catastrophic loss of direction in the second half. There was, quite simply, nowhere for the production to go once Richard was crowned" (187). One of the reasons, Holland said, is that the Richmond context *was* unambiguous: "The arrival of Richmond . . . was heralded by a new backcloth, a chocolate-box saccharine depiction of the English countryside, a rural idyll of everything Richmond is fighting for. I desperately wanted to see this vision as ironic but the production left no space for such a reading" (189–90). Propaganda, of course, strives to leave no space for alternative inscriptions. Richmond offered a different set of symbols here, but, after Richard's self-directed, black-and-white newsreels, these were potent stereotypes. The line between the Boy Scouts and Hitler Youth was defined not by the activities in which we boys of the 1930s engaged but by an indoctrination into different systems, one aiming at producing soldiers who would die for Hitler, the other certainly pressing toward an agenda that Pat Robertson would approve.

McKellen's performance drew praise. Holland remarked on one of those "small touches" that characterize the work of this actor: "the grotesque comedy [with the Lord Mayor] was completed by the arrival of Catesby (3.5.19) with Hasting's head in a fire-bucket (into which Richard dipped his hand at the end of the scene, presumably to close Hastings's eyes)" (188). McKellen's "controlled performance reminded many of his recent Iago," Dessen said, "but also, in the latter scenes, had the demonic and despotic energy of his notable Macbeth of the late 1970s" (220). The comparisons are interesting particularly in that both the Macbeth and the Iago were studio productions, each originating in The Other Place, with the *Macbeth* going on to the Warehouse in London. His "Richard," said Frank Rich, "conveys evil with a bloodless equine hauteur, an intellectual aggressiveness that runs roughshod over the foolish and the weak" (*NYT* 8 August 1990, C16). Benedict Nightingale, however, felt that the format hindered

McKellen from "exploring Richard as thoroughly as he did the stealthy, ravenous Macbeth . . . or the dry, cold Iago he concocted" in 1989 (*T* 26 June 1990). The performance was closer to that chillingly detached Iago—as one could argue that the *role* is—and particularly powerful in McKellen's cynical deployment of sexuality. Richard III's brutal use of women for political purposes reflects the Nazi practice, where the puritanical "shalt not" mentality typical of the right-wing encouraged the production of male babies under state-sanctioned auspices that did not incorporate marriage, and which, in the case of Rohm and the Brownshirts, included thuggish homosexuality. In this production, Anne abandoned Henry's corpse on "If I thought that. . . ." Thus Richard's courtship did not occur literally over Henry's dead body but in the web of Richard's physical and rhetorical system, of which Anne is a fellow-weaver. McKellen stripped off his general's tunic—a considerable feat considering his immobile left arm—in an ironic glance at sexuality. Later, Queen Elizabeth vigorously wiped her mouth after Richard's kiss (4.4), a necessary action, since Stanley's explanation of her agreement with Richmond (4.5) was cut. Richard's sexual adventure culminated brilliantly in his dream, where Lady Anne (Eve Matheson), coiffured and frocked like Constance Bennett, kissed Richard after her curse. He recoiled, as if kissed by a corpse. She turned to dance with Richmond to the strains of Bert Ambrose at the May Fair. Richard felt his first stab of sexual jealousy. Richmond was taking over all that Richard had "owned" and, appropriately, giving value to what Richard had scorned and debased.

Since, as Antony Hammond points out, Richard "is constantly mistreating the language in the way that modern propagandists, whether political or commercial, understand so well" (119), Eyre's "bright idea" did illuminate a major sector of the script, even as some other areas are inevitably obscured. The modernization permitted Richard to enter 2.1 with a mourning band already in place for Clarence. *He* knew that the gentle Duke was dead and could then feign rage at the insensitivity of the rest of the court. His sign of mourning was a prelude, of course, to a fascist armband. When Buckingham said "Made I him King for this?" in 4.2, he threw his own armband onto the empty throne, a divestiture that signalled further defections from Richard's party.

As with most "concept" productions, this one drew no middling responses. The question is whether a modern setting merely trades on audience familiarity and the enjoyment of "recognizing" the allusions—as many such productions do—or whether the production actually *says* something to a modern audience through the trappings of modernity. Good productions say what it is they may have to say because they are physically removed from us through devices that keep us, as Brecht would say, from identifying with the characters. That process allows for the possibility of change—as opposed to reinforcement—in those who experience something in drama beyond entertainment.

Dessen said that "British reviewers were fascinated . . . by the [production's] 'it could have happened here' insights into English fascism of the 1930s" (220). Some, looking at the cultural wasteland of Thatcherite Great Britain, said "and so it has," either ignoring what fascism is *really* like or remembering that politicians of the right in democracies work out their repressions by supporting fascists in other countries. Nightingale set a sharp ear and eye out for parallels to the England of some fifty-five years before:

> Yet is not that Big Ben booming out the time for Lord Hastings? . . . Indeed, don't those accompanying Edward IV in his wheelchair look remarkably like Queen Mary and Neville Chamberlain? Moreover, there is no mistaking the Sandhurst accent McKellen adopts. He comes stiffly across the bare, black stage in his general's uniform and talks of 'wintah' and 'myajestea' in a blend of drawl and blimpish staccato. It is one of our very own mandarins who, in a chilling coup de theatre, casts aside his khaki for a black uniform, a St. George's cross armband and a shadowy retinue of thugs. (20)

Certainly the production was aimed at an audience deeply cynical about politics and perhaps also aware of how fragile even the strongest regimes or systems really are. It is true, however, as Stanley Wells said, that "style is no guide to quality." Even superbly mounted modernizations may fail because "they have not found an appropriate metaphor for the tenor of the text" (*ShS* 43, 184). William A. Henry in *Time* suggested that the production,

> meant to evoke 20th century memories [including] the Ceauşescu and Marcos regimes . . . is entirely faithful to the politics and psychology of Shakespeare's text. No production in memory has better evoked the terrifying instability of this buccaneer world. . . . Eyre and McKellen share credit for devising a production full of startling visual imagery. McKellen casually snuffs out clumps of candles as he enumerates deadpan, the friends and relatives he means to kill. . . . Clarence hunches in custody under a single, searing overhead lamp in a scene eerily suggestive of all interrogations that turn to torture. Most

striking, the King's counsellors sit at a long table and talk in bureaucratic euphemisms about bloody murders to be done someplace out
of sight, while simultaneously the crimes are being enacted in full
view of the audience. (72)

The latter moment was described by Holland: "The executions
of Rivers, Gray and Vaughan—brutally graphic garottings—were
played out downstage in front of the board meeting, specifying
what was dooming Hastings." "Such uses of rituals as contexts
within which power-games are played out—here the ritual of the
board-room [were] simple and sustained" (SS 44 [1991]: 188).
Frank Rich was equally enthusiastic about the power the production picked up from its metaphor: "Mr. Eyre ushers the audience
into a creepy official England all too ready to collaborate with a
strongman. . . . What makes [the production] alarming are the
plausibility and urgency with which it charts totalitarianism's
easy, inky spread through a genteel world close to home" (NYT
8 August 1990, C16). Rich went further, suggesting that this production, unlike the two Lears, "is committed to ideas about the
world, as opposed to ideas simply about the theater" (C10). "Miss
Warner's stripped-to-basics King Lear is likely to strike audiences
abroad as the more esthetically advanced of the two [National
Theatre] productions, but it is Mr. Eyre's Richard III that has the
terrifying march of history on its side" (C16). That may be so,
and Rich's assertion asks for a discussion of the reason for theater
that goes beyond the premises of this book. It is the script—that
set of signals latent in the words—that has history within it. History is itself variously interpreted. The setting for the script is
itself an interpretation. The Eyre production made several of the
points that Shakespeare is making in Richard III about politics and
power and that it showed one version of the sacrifice of self (and
soul) that political success may exact. But history moves on, as
does the script. Eyre's production recedes into time.

Inevitably, of course, the production was attacked. Gerald Berkowitz said that it "offers a fascinating display of technical tricks
from Ian McKellen and little more" (SB [1991]: 10). One could say
that Richard III himself displays technique quite self-consciously
and that, until the dream at the end, offers little in the way of
"characterization beyond the purely external performance" (10).
The production, Berkowitz said, "hits us over the head with
forced and unconvincing parallels to Hitler, with blackshirt uni-
forms, armbands, and a staging of his appearance between two
clergymen from The Triumph of the Will. (Aside from the fact that

the parallel doesn't hold up—Richard is not a manipulator of the masses—its heavy-handedness patronizes the audience)" (10). Richard III was certainly not an *effective* wooer of the masses, as opposed to the supple-kneed Bolingbroke or Henry V (who, like his father, knew the uses of humility, as his return to London from Agincourt suggests), or like Elizabeth I. The parallel did press too hard, with its upward reaching rows of searchlights, imitating an inverted theatrical performance, but Rich was right to say that "McKellen's dictator is not a distanced Hitler or Mussolini: he's unambiguously an Englishman" (C16). Holland suggested that "the production singlemindedly saw in Richard's rise an analogy for a possible alternative history of Britain between the wars, a successful coup by a leader who adroitly perceived and utilized the efficacy of fascist militarism, overthrowing an atrophied aristocracy by the energy of populist thuggery" (187). The production, then, presented its audience with a version of the "parallel time" that science fiction writers use. We know, after all, that we fought and defeated Hitler. But before that was Chamberlain's "Peace in Our Time" and his chuckle as he told his audience that "Next time, Herr Hitler promised to meet me halfway"—in Paris? Before that was the refusal by Halifax and Eden to accept any contact with Moltke's anti-Hitler underground. England did not turn fascist, but it did not oppose Hitler's annexation of the Sudetenland and thus erased any chance that the German General Staff had to stage a coup before September of 1939.

One could argue a bit with Nightingale when he said "a fascist setting . . . fits oddly with a world that sets such store by curses, oaths, witchcraft, cavalry battles and other medieval matters" (20)—a group of Polish horse cavalry *did* attack a Panzer division in September of 1939. One of Hitler's propaganda posters of the late 1930s showed him as an armored knight riding righteously to war. Holland noted "the pseudo-medievalism of fascist art" (189). Himmler's SS were fascinated by and copied the secrecy of the Society of Jesus, even though the SS hated the Jesuits. Himmler, of course, rebuilt the Westphalian castle of Wewelsburg and created an Arthurian order for his twelve best *Obergruppenführer*. Indeed, Himmler saw himself as the reincarnation of the Saxon king, Heinrich I (875–936). It is true, however, that a modern setting can clash with the language in such productions: still, the parallels continue to ring. The SS marched to the song "Der Tod sie unser Kampfgenoss! Wir sind die schwarzen Scharen" ("Let death be our battle companion. We are the Black Band"). Richard says, "March on, join bravely, let us to't pell-mell / If not to heaven, then hand in hand to hell." Berkowitz agreed at least that the Eyre production "can be fun to watch" (10), even if, for him, the modern metaphor tended to drain the script of anything but a kind of flashy and momentary "relevance."

The anachronistic treatment was far more interesting and less confusing than other such productions—1910 America for *Much Ado*, the American Civil War for *Troilus and Cressida*, a twenty-first-century world for *Macbeth*, in which the Weird Sisters descended from a space ship to a heath blasted by an afterburner. It may be that for some, memories of the Hitler era remain as a powerful screen against which a Shakespearean script can be successfully projected. If so, it is not the march of history that the Eyre production captured, but a personal past that casts its long shadows over the lives of all who remember or learn about the fascist movement that culminated in Nazi Germany and which incubates constantly, world without end.*

The production for which Berkowitz called was provided by Sam Mendes and Simon Russell Beale in 1992 at The Other Place in Stratford. This one was writ small, not projected onto some vast screen of a specific past. It had, therefore, what theater must have—an intense presence in the present. It did not seem to be another Stratford effort to be different, but it was, unpretentiously and imaginatively.

One of the few points of contact between the two productions is that each was a touring production. Mendes's production should have few difficulties scaling up or down to the provincial spaces for which the production is destined, since it is a minimalist production that requires only the doorways and large windows of the set upstage of the playing area. Furthermore, the actors did a lot of doubling—as is befitting a tour without a lot of backing—and seemed to be happy, being both busy actors and versatile. Simon Dormandy, for example, played both Clarence and Ratcliffe, the former "turbidly poetic," the latter "sinister," according to Michael Coveney (*OonS* 16 August 1992, 46). Anabelle Apsion played Anne and the young Duke of York, while

*For reviews of the Eyre *Richard III* as it toured in the United States see Majorie J. Oberlander, "New York Theatre Reviews," *Shakespeare Bulletin*, Winter 1993, 10–11 and Frank Ardolino, "*Richard III*," *Marlowe Society Newsletter*, Spring 1993, 3–4. These reviews appeared after this chapter was completed. Each concentrated on the "fascist" aspect of the production.

Mike Dowling doubled as Edward IV, foolishly optimistic as Richard lurked behind his throne eying the court suspicously for any wrinkle of subversion there, and the Lord Mayor of London, a cigar-chomping politico eager to be seen as a player in aristocratic games.

Beale's Richard owed nothing to Laurence Olivier, whose suggesting eyes, sensual twist of lip, and brittle voice dominated the famous film version, which was edited around the "star" (as were Olivier's other films, each featuring a character who is, among other things, an actor and impresario). Sher's wonderful Richard was captured by Michael Coveney:

> He proceeds [towards Margaret in 1.3] with a series of slithering genuflections—the knees swivel to the left and buckle under him on the ground—furtive images and cackling commands interspersed with dangerously pious intonations. His speed is genuine and frightening and for once you really believe the court is half mesmerized and half indulgently suspicious of this extroverted cripple with the bizarre manners of a capering beetle. Stunned momentarily by Queen Margaret's . . . curses, he springs into a pew and settles, stock still, like a frog on a stone, idly flicking his tongue around his cheeks. The crutches then levitate like magnetic antennae to remove the old crone's crown. (*FT* 21 June 1984)

Lesser's pint-sized terrorist used the warm head of Hastings to show that it was Richard, not Hastings, who was the threat. Richard set word and action, piety and brutality in conflict, as he at once dictated the "official" version of events and warned the mayor about the possible fate of his own fat head. McKellen, of course, was a suave fascist who moved with all apparent legality to become a tyrant.

Beale's Richard was a stumpy little man who hovered over his cane and looked up abjectly at the other characters, almost all of whom were taller than he. This Richard was clown and satirist, an "interactive Thersites"—a role Beale played with scabrous itchiness for Mendes in 1990. His solicitude came up from a head that echoed his hump and mocked his victims. With Clarence he displayed "moist-eyed concern," said John Peter, "putting himself in the clear and relishing the things to come. This is the pathology of evil: sadistic longing disguised as tender loving care" (*ST* 16 August 1992). And that is precisely how George Anton's Lightborn had played it opposite Beale's Edward II in Gerard Murphy's powerful production of Marlowe's play in the summer of 1990. Beale flirted with the danger that Potter defines—that is the "comic role model" Richard. The blurbs that the RSC selected for its poster, however, suggest a crucial qualification: "Grotesquely funny and chilling" (Time Out), "a mesmerising and often savagely funny evening" (Daily Telegraph). The best of RSC productions—Warner's Titus, Daniels's Hamlet—provide laughter, but define the darkness against which the laughter is projected. Laughter in a nightmare, songs and flashes of merriment beside a newly dug grave and, in this instance, appreciative chuckles at a virtuouso on his way to hell. The production showed powerfully what the script suggests: Richard's victims are so busy pursuing their own shallow agendas that they accept the face Richard shows them at any given moment and recognize his role in their downfall, if at all, much too late. The script works so well for so long simply because we wait for characters to catch up to what we, the audience, already know. Since Richard is in charge of so much of the machinery of deceit and belated awareness, our experience is akin to that of watching a great artist at work, explaining what he is doing as he does it. Once Richard becomes king, much of that dynamic is gone. Richard has summoned his nemesis into the lists against him, and the fall is not as interesting as his rise had been. Richard still tries his hand at politics. The broodings of Macbeth wandering alone through his castle are more interesting—except perhaps for Richard's dream, which gave both Eyre and Mendes such an opportunity for the extension of their own imaginations into the scenes that Richard's psyche was inventing for him.

Beale's first entrance was preceded by the tapping of his cane, an ominous metronome counting down the lives of his victims. Later, his approach was signalled by the barking of countless hounds, the one entourage his sinister shadow had gathered. The clock-like tapping was taken over by Margaret, the clairvoyant whose negative view of history incorporated one of history's architects in this production—Richard. Beale poured absolute scorn into his "lute," arrived at the "reconciliation scene" on the verge of tears so that the others, in retrospect, could grasp how upset he had been to hear of the death of Clarence, his dear brother. Beale glared accusingly from behind Edward's throne, reinforcing the latter's castigation of the court for not pleading in Clarence's behalf. Richard's "features," said Paul Taylor, were "ready to become a grotesque mask of whatever spurious emotion [would] serve his turn" (I 14 August 1992). In a fit of avuncular thoughtfulness, Richard brought balloons for the arrival of York and Wales and had to keep holding one of the balloons when York failed to show. Richard "deftly clutches Hasting's head," said Michael Billington, "as if measuring it up for the block" (*G* 4 August 1992). "It is a superb, ferocious performance," Maureen Paton commented, "lacking only the weird sexual magnetism that rightly belongs to Richard" (*DE,* 12 August 1992). McKellen turned on a dark sexual charm, for example, which was even more effective for the sneering attitude his Richard had for women. Beale claimed that Richard is "not a very sexy man" (21 August 1992), but his Richard used sexuality once, tellingly, when he said "take up the sword, or take up me." It was as if Richard needed this "illusion" only once, but really *needed* it and thus could play the desiring male.

Given the intimacy of the new Other Place, a function of its smallness and of its platform, surrounded by the audience on three sides, we were his accomplices in a game whose "anarchic glee," as Nightingale called it, easily erased his bunchbacked ugliness, more so that with Richards played in larger, more proscenium spaces, and more so than with McKellen's Iago in the old Other Place in 1990.

Richard's first entrance to the throne was superb. It occurred right after the interval. Anne sat, almost comatose, on her throne, caught in a terrifying, white light. Beale fell as he scuttled forward without his cane, and refused all help until he demanded Buckingham's hand. Richard then casually told a scarcely listening Anne that she was soon to be discarded. Lesser had done the same, but with the intention of keeping Anne alert and terrified. "When [Beale] sends the little princes to the tower," said Nightingale, "he might be treating them to a Disneyland visit" (*T* 13 August 1992). Beale, as Michael Coveney put it, "negotiates his relationship with an audience at dangerously close quarters while fully investigating the psychopathology of an evil tyrant who degenerates from wise-cracking exuberance to cornered fanaticism" (*OonS* 16 August 1992). Beale's Richard commanded because his character's mind worked more quickly than the minds of the others, who tended to believe that old-fashioned "values" could be restored after their destruction in the recent wars. One of Beale's subtexts may have been that of the actor Richard must be: "like all good actors," John Peter said, this Richard "observes others rather than displays himself" (*ST* 16 August 1992). Irving Wardle noted that, although "by turns volcanically enraged, mock-innocent, feline and winsomely flirtatious, he preserves under all this the quite, rational voice on which he began: the voice of an observer, watching himself doing these things and wondering whether they really exist" (*IonS* 16 August 1992). Beale, then, showed us something of the deathcamp commandant, Rudolph Höss or Franz Stangl. Richard was just following orders, even if self-dictated.

Cherry Morris's powerful Margaret arrived on the scene chanting her prophecies just as Richard's victims remembered the words they had scorned earlier. She made a cameo appearance at Bosworth Field, interrupting Richard's *mano a mano* with Richmond and giving the latter his opening. "At one point we considered cutting Margaret," Beale said (Lewis, *ST* 2 August 1992), but she turned out to be the focus of Mendes's "retributive theory" of history and gave the production what Kirsty Milne calls "an Aeschylean" resonance (*STel* 16 August 1992). Death itself was a drawing of the executioner's hand down over the face of the victim. The spot on the face went out to the sound of the cymbal. The killer Ratcliff (Simon Dormandy, once he had himself been dispatched as Clarence), as Paul Taylor said, "simply closes their living eyes, as one would those of a corpse" (*I* 14 August 1992). These sequences were admirably *under*done, as befitted the space. Mendes intercut between Richard's and Richmond's orations, so that we got both the simultaniety of the moment when each addressed his troops and the hollowness of political rhetoric, no matter who the "good guy" may be. In a wonderful economy of time and space, Richard's dream featured his victims from this play alone (Clarence, Rivers, Vaughan, the Princes, and Anne) banqueting at a table between Richard and Richmond. This reminder of the Scottish Play found Richard seaching for evidence of the apparitions having been there and finding his own unconsumed goblet of wine. Once upon a time, critics might have discerned there a echo of failed Christian ritual. Nightingale did suggest that the production showed "that in this play history has a moral and religious logic to it" (*T* 13 August 1992). The idea for this "last supper" came up in rehearsal, Mendes said (21 August 1992) and, as in so many other places, validated the collaborative effort from which the production emerged. The table had been used tellingly earlier, for the accusation of Hastings. His head, neatly packaged in a box tied with string, was brought in. His nametag for the previous conference was placed on the package and then Richard, in an action that brought a collective shudder to the audience, drove a dagger into the package. It was most appropriate, then, that Hastings be invited back to the table by the RSVP of Richard's repressed soul to partake of some celebratory wine.

The production incorporated two problems. First, as Potter suggests in her response to the Eyre production, Richard's courtship of the crown was a lot more fun for us and for Beale than was the throne once he got there. Sic semper courtship. The problem was reduced by Mendes's quick winding up, but, as Nightingale said, Beale "fails to bring much authenticity to Richard's belated discovery of a conscience . . . where is the terror, the weight, the power?" (*T* 13 August 1992). He seemed merely excluded from the party the others were throwing for Richmond, but a social snub is not quite the same thing as a negative vision of Judgment Day, when Richard will huddle into line, prodded by a pitchfork, with the Bundys, Glaces, Specks, and the deathcamp commandants. It may be, however, that mass and institutionalized killing has become easier to comprehend as ultimate penalties have retreated to forgotten mythology. Second: why have Richard and Richmond fight in a sandbox? Yes, power politics is a child's game with deadly results. And, at least it is the final scene—as opposed to the sandbox that Peter Hall introduced for Coriolanus and Aufidius in 1987 early on (so that some of us were itching away in that vast Olivier Theatre for another two and a half hours). But poor Beale had to take his curtain calls covered in grime.

One of the great merits of Mendes's production was that it explained itself clearly in spite of the tangled web of history that leads to *Richard III* and without any cueing from modern analogies. Margaret was a unifying agent for *this* play, even as she reminded us that these events surface from the depths of an unquiet past. Milne said that "while the . . . intelligent, plain, small-scale production . . . is rich in invention . . . there is no political framework" (*STel* 16 August 1992). If so, as Wardle said, we concentrated on a Richard not "shaped for sportive tricks [but] supremely show[ing] physical self-hatred rebounding into social revenge" (*IonS* 16 August 1992). In The Other Place plays must be scaled down. That does not diminish their power but enhances it, as *Macbeth, Othello,* and now *Richard III* have proved. We the audience must complete what has been so powerfully sketched in for us within the space into which the actors invite our imaginations. "The story is unfolded," Charles Spencer said, "with such pace and clarity that you don't get bogged down in niggling detail" (*DT* 13 August 1992).

Some critics did have problems with Mendes's undifferentiated setting and eclectic costuming—the latter more confusing, I thought, in his *Troilus and Cressida* than here. Ann Fitzgerald spoke of the "mix [of] realism and symbolism . . . costumes and props . . . result[ing in] a production of some brilliant moments but patchy overall effect" (*Theatre* 15 August 1992). Billington said "this play demands a consistent world: either colourful medieval-ism as in Bill Alexander's version [with Sher], or downright mo-dernity, as in Richard Eyre's [with McKellen]" (*G* 4 August 1992). Richard Edmonds went further, saying that "other RSC produc-tions of *Richard III* in recent years . . . cast a heavy shadow over this current showing . . . played in front of a featureless grey set [where] time is a continual undifferentiated process. . . . The boots and greatcoats are unvarying." The result is a "mildly-dry lampooning of kingship" with Beale "hobbling about in glorious awfulness" (*BP* 13 August 1992). Time, in this production, was process, and a negative one at that, in the mode of the history that Henry Adams outlines, in which God could not be a *person*. It may no longer be necessary for productions to picture Rich-mond and the founding of the Tudor Dynasty as a temporal salva-tion for England. Mark Lewis Jones (Richmond) had emerged from the murkiness of Lord Grey in this production, suggesting that Henry VI's blessing was irrelevant here and that a man could come from almost anywhere and be a king if his army is strong enough. That theme has run through the prior plays, and Rich-mond's rise was perhaps the principal allusion that Mendes made to the earlier segments of the tetralogy. Both Eyre and Mendes, then, while they may not have undercut Richmond, carefully qualified the simply allegory of his victory.

Given the elaborate productions the play has received since 1984, this one was very different. Someone who did not "know the story" would have no difficulty with the story Mendes told—the "behind the scenes" that this script permits, as opposed to the gigantic political pageant that the script also allows. Like any script it will accommodate different scales—even the orations in *Julius Caesar* will work in smaller auditoriums if the orations are designed to incorporate the audience. A background that permits a performance like Beale's to emerge so vividly represents a valid decision, particularly when contrasted with the overstated sets that swallow the actors, as tends to happen in the main house up the street at Stratford.

In the next chapter, I will deal briefly with what happened to the production when it got back to London after its tour of the provinces.

11

London: February 1993

Two events dominated London theater in mid-winter, 1993. One was the queueing necessary to get a "return" for the Branagh *Hamlet.* The process did work, if one were willing to permit the triumph of time to function (and if one believed that blessed are the jetlagged for they shall see *Hamlet*). The second big story was the advent of Ciaran Hinds as Richard III, after Simon Russell Beale went the way of Quasimodo and pulled a disc while bustling around as Richard. A third event of some import was the first Shakespearean production at the Royal Court Theatre in many years—an interesting but flawed version of *King Lear.*

Hinds had done Richard eight years before at the Citizens Theatre, Glasgow, and appeared in this production after ten days of emergency rehearsal. Beale had been round-headed, round-backed, and round-eyed as he looked up at the taller denizens of late-medieval England, an amusing grotesque accompanied, if off-stage noises were any criterion, by the packs of pariah dogs predicted by his opening soliloquy. The dogs were not as funny as they escorted Hinds, nor was he as funny as Beale. Beale pretended to be an "uncle" by taking balloons to meet the princes. The affectation did not seem appropriate to Hinds's version. It was business from another interpretation that Hinds was stuck with. Hinds was taller, distinctly fascistic in leather overcoat and slicked-back hairstyle, less unctuous and more directly menacing than Beale. Hinds was capable, however, of sharing a laugh with us after his powerplay with Lady Anne.

The recasting of Richard changed the production in three interesting ways. Much of the situational comedy shifted to Stephen Boxer's excellent Buckingham, who got a big laugh as he spoke of the "general applause and cheerful shout" he attributed to the silent citizens of London. Kate Duchene's excellent Queen Elizabeth became positively heroic in standing up to an obviously stronger and clearly enraged Richard (1.3.102–9). Since Hinds's

Richard was hardly a "depraved clown" (as Benedict Nightingale had rightly called Beale's version), but physically the most powerful of the nobles, Cherry Morris heightened her performance as Margaret to combat this new and more Macbethian Richard. Morris was excellent in The Other Place's production of August 1992 as a ghost reminding characters of what their conscious agendas have repressed. Here, she became the spokesperson for Nemesis herself. This was a brilliant performance encouraged by the change in leads.

The Company had been on tour to various shires where no permanent theater existed. One result was that the fabric of the script had tightened and integrated and that the eclectic costumes that troubled some critics earlier were no problem in the Donmar Warehouse, so clear was every line, so excellent the timing of the ensemble acting.

Nightingale nicely captured the contrast between the two Richards: "Beale was as outrageous a bogeyman as I have seen, a tiny, scrubbed clown. . . . Where he scuttled, Hinds lopes. Where he squatted, Hinds looms, a massive blend of Boris Karloff in his monster mode, a tree afflicted with Dutch elm disease, and a psychopathic mortician in search of trade. Which is the better? Neither. Each uses his build and his looks to give a highly distinctive interpretation. Russell Beale's Richard is the more original, but Hinds the more menacing and inner. He raises his voice little, knowing as he obviously does that it is more sinister when he levels it down from its usual gravelly purr into a sepulchral whisper" (*T* 10 February 1993). The few negatives about this production came from Malcolm Rutherford in a largely positive review: "The costumes are dull. . . . There is not enough to differentiate the characters" (*FT* 11 February 1993), and from Jane Edwardes, again in a favorable notice: "No sense here that a whole nation is frigid with terror in the grip of a raving megalomaniac" (*TO* 17 February 1993). Director Mendes, of course, was not aiming at that larger effect, one that can be achieved in larger spaces, as Ian McKellen proved at the National and Anthony Sher in the Barbican. That we have yet a third excellent *Richard III* is remarkable. (This reviewer did not get to see Barrie Rutter's highly acclaimed Northern Broadsides production.)

This RSC *Richard III* goes on to Tokyo and Rotterdam, then back to Stratford, where Beale is expected to return. He was a splendid Richard. Hinds was also a splendid Richard, Morris a marvelous Margaret, Duchene an absolutely convincing Elizabeth, Boxer a wonder Buckingham, and Simon Dormandy rose from an effete but moving Clarence to a chilling executioner, Ratcliff. This studio production would lend itself well to television—as did Trevor Nunn's *Macbeth* and *Othello*—and one hopes that Mendes will consider that prospect before the set of this production is struck.

To call Branagh's Hamlet a "young conservative" modelled on a "bland" Prince Charles, as Frank Rich does (*NYT* 24 December 1992, C9), is to forget that it was to Charles that Branagh went for advice on playing Henry V a few years ago. Branagh's Hamlet did make for "easy listening," as Rich said (C14), but it was not muzak, rather an actor conserving his emotions for moments when their explosion can count—as when he attacked Cordelia, menaced Claudius across the space of "Gonzago," and tried to drive a cameo of King Hamlet into one of the Queen's orifices. If the historicists are correct to claim that early modern times were just discovering "interiority," then this complete New Cambridge *Hamlet* had its title character exploring that new innerness with us, "sitting at a play." Branagh indicated the Barbican audience calmly with a gesture of his hand and we stirred, recognizing ourselves and assenting to a relationship with Hamlet that did not involve total identification with Hamlet nor demand *his* constant awareness that he was in a play. It was as if stream-of-consciousness alternated with other fictional modes which denied Hamlet the rationality he shared from the zone between the action and the audience. He saved his outbursts for those he could not understand or understood all too well within the world of the play.

An observer wrote in 1989 of Branagh's Birmingham Repertory Hamlet, directed by Derek Jacobi, that "Jacobi felt that [Branagh] simply did not have the maturity, the life experience, to be all that is written into the role." This observer said of that performance that "Branagh was a lot of sound and fury, signifying not much." The current Branagh signified much more. He admired authenticity and therefore loved the unpretentious Horatio, hated the seedy, on-the-make aristocrats Rosencrantz and Guildenstern, suspected Ophelia when she pushed his hand away and rose from her bed near the wardrobe where Claudius and Polonius lurked amid the mothballs, and despised the premature rigor-mortis in which David Bradley's superbly bureaucratic Polonius had locked himself. Branagh was, according to Benedict Nightingale, "the most impressively princely Hamlet I have seen in ages" (*T* 21 December 1992).

Branagh's Hamlet was already alienated from the court of John

Shrapnel's white-suited, cocky Claudius and Jane Lapotaire's "arranged" Gertrude, white-gowned and actually fending off as she pretended to reach out with her long arms. For the "coronation scene," Branagh stood against the partially opened outer curtain, down right, mourning band in place, ignoring Claudius's opening remarks. Gertrude quaffed wine nervously. Claudius turned toward Hamlet, swinging the eyes of the court in that direction. Claudius knew that the consolidation of his own regime depended on his naming Hamlet heir. When Hamlet said "obey *you*, madam," Gertrude was delighted and relieved. Claudius's "loving and a fair reply" got a laugh, since it had not been so to us, even if Elsinore had to accept the official version.

The production's consistent contrast between what went on inside the larger and the smaller proscenium frames—one the Barbican arch, the smaller one constructed slightly upstage of the outer arch—asked us to develop and retain a "doubleness of vision." The style was what William Worthen describes as "a concentration on psychological motivation complicated by a degree of openness to the theatre audience, the post-Brechtian compromise between 'realistic' and 'theatrical' characterization" (*SQ* [1989]: 450).

Ophelia and Gertrude were each fitted to a "concept." Ophelia (Joanne Pearce) was on the brink of surrendering to Hamlet's importunity and would have yielded on the bed of her girlish room had not the King and Prime Minister been inconveniently huddled in her wardrobe. She could then have made the transition from Narnia to womanhood. Instead, after Hamlet had wrestled her to the floor and seemed about to rape her, he rose and spat upon her. She collected the scattered "remembrances," then tried to play a polonaise on her upright piano. Polonius, however, closed the lid. She would not be permitted to retreat to childhood music after her vivid victimization, or *failure*, as her father saw it. Madness became her only future, and she lost her virginity there, rolling on her back and pulling her clothes tight between her legs. That the Nunnery Scene occurred in her room meant that she had the "remembrances" handy—in an attaché case—and that she was *not* lying when she said that Polonius was "at home," the first Ophelia in recent stage history to have been telling the truth (cf. Rosenberg, *Masks of Hamlet*, 522–28).

Just after her report of Hamlet's mad visit to her room (I.3), she shivered. Polonius, in the only positive gesture he made towards her, put his overcoat around her shoulders. Later, in her madness, she wore the formal clothes in which he had been murdered, blood bright on the white shirt as a displacement of the virginity she could lose only in mime. She was a Chaplinesque clown in floppy clothes, a "fool" in that she brought uncomfortable truths to this shallow court. As she said, "Pray you, mark," Gertrude pivoted as if Ophelia were pointing to another sudden ghost. Ophelia's piano came out from under a dropcloth in a field of discarded funeral wreathes—Elsinore's dump almost exclusively a repository for the undertakers' trash. She played again, even sharing a four-handed duet with Laertes, then turned to accuse Claudius of being a "false steward." Her face was white and we knew that she was to be buried in Yorick's grave, place of the fool and the skull, or, if we did not know the play, we observed her in that bony light once her funeral train wended into view. She was pulled "bare-fac'd [from] the bier" twice, once by Laertes and once by Hamlet, a victim even in death of male posturing.

Lapotaire's Gertrude was not as successful as Pearce's Ophelia, but not as "ludicrously hammy" as Rich claimed (C9). The concept behind her characterization was simply too obvious. From her lily-white "protected zone" she moved to a lurid red that matched the gown of the Player Duchess, and from this declension to the gray of a Whistler's Mother who sat wide-eyed and oblivious amid the final tumult. She ran barefoot in to tell of Ophelia's drowning and brought lilies to Ophelia's funeral, an ironic echo of the Madonna-like status she had tried to assume. She did defend Denmark, confronting Laertes in front of a suddenly cowering Claudius, and like Lear, she repented too late. She was Niobe, the barefoot Hecuba, and the grieving Baptista, but her *ex post facto* rejection of Claudius availed her nothing. She drank the wine not in protection of Hamlet, à la Eileen Herlie of the Olivier film, but in defiance of Claudius. "Pray you, pardon me," was a sneering moment of lucidity within a madness borrowed from Lady Macbeth. Faith Brook's was a similar Gertrude, in the McKellen production of 1971. Brook became Ophelia, in compensation for her failing the younger woman. Brook's sing-song "sweets to the sweet" was a variation on Ophelia's earlier distribution of flowers. Both Gertrudes, however, called attention to *concept*, not character, but there the director and not the actor is to blame.

The full script created several virtues—including one for the Cambridge Press, in that their *Hamlet* was as sold out at the book stalls as the production was at the Barbican. A complete Horatio, elegantly delivered by Rob Edwards, allowed Horatio to take over the initial movement of the play, as Marcellus wants him to do.

Horatio became a "reflector" of Hamlet, in a Jamesian sense. To hear of that "famous ape," whose descent into oblivion has long been noted, was to watch Branagh gesture toward Gertrude. Rylance, who did not get the line in Daniels's version, would have made the gesture at us, as if to say, "You know all about that ape, of course." He would have evoked in us that amused befuddlement that was rage inside Elsinore. Brilliant as Rylance was, however, he would have had to bring more range to this full script than to the edited version and would have been hard pressed to avoid the tour de force of his American production, where he was surrounded by a cast much weaker than in the RSC version. Branagh was much less a pain-in-the-ass than Rylance and much more a prince. Branagh's Hamlet assumed a sudden maturity after seeing the Ghost and scorned "all pressures past / That youth and observation copied." Having claimed to understand himself at last, he fell into immediate confusion. His "antic disposition" was to be a cover for a self he claimed to know, but this was no Hal, biding his time. At the play scene, Branagh invaded the Players's space and came toward Claudius, forcing the latter to move and thus destroying the possibility for confession that the full script sets up through Claudius's "How smart a lash" aside. As Nightingale said, "Claudius's sudden exit seems best explained by his understandable feeling that he is being insulted by a genuine lunatic" (*T* 21 December 1992). In the Birmingham production, Branagh had helped Lucianus pour the poison, thus conflating the identities of actor and "nephew to the king." That was a psychological poisoning of Claudius. Here, the threat was more direct. Branagh was brilliant in imitating Polonius's style when the latter brought superfluous word of the Players's arrival and in parodying Osric in a quicksilver rendition of "the verity of extolment," a speech usually cut as a director desperately tries to erase running time. The full script permitted Hamlet, upstage with Horatio, to be a commentator on death as the Gravedigger worked downstage. One could be convinced that Hamlet was "changed" after his voyage, but one also saw him drawn back into Elsinore past and present as skull and corpse took on sudden specificity. Branagh was hardly bland when he threatened the cup-bearing courtier with his foil on "I'll play this bout first," or as he thrust Claudius toward the crumpled Gertrude on "Follow my mother!"

The strengths and weaknesses of this production were reflected in the staging. A graveyard sat in front of the main stage echoing the shape of the auditorium, an architectual *momento mori*. The

Ghost rose from this unweeded space to walk as the bell tolled twelve and later thrust a white arm out to participate in the swearing (I.5). Small crosses dotted this area, making it look like Stephen King's "Pet Sematary." The problem with that allusion is that only demons come back from King's burial ground. That would work were the production taking Eleanor Prosser's line on the Ghost, but here the Ghost greeted Hamlet's body at the end as if escorting his son to the Norse Table of Heros, once "soldier's music" and "rites of war" had uttered their loud voices. This production had a weak Fortinbras (Ian Hughes, who doubled as Reynaldo) and a dominating Horatio, so that the delicate negotiations under pressure that were so powerfully conducted by, for example, Robert Swann (Horatio) and Ian Charleston (Fortinbras) in the BBC version were lacking here. Fortinbras at the end is using Hamlet's "body" (singular in the NC script) for *his* purposes, so that this time "the king" will be "with the body" in the Kantorowiczian sense. Between the tawdry beginning and the hokey ending and in spite of the Christmas tree that Marcellus tells us should *not* be there (in I.1), the middle of the production was usefully set in Claudius's audition room, into which we peered as the Court, facing us, watched "Gonzago" downstage. This set permitted rapid entrances and exits—Claudius charging down the center ramp of the depicted room on "It likes us not," for example. The Prayer Scene was superb. Claudius knelt downstage in front of all the dark and empty theater seats behind him, so that it seemed that many invisible eyes stared down at him as he tried to pray. It was a reminder in a modern setting of what Alvin Kernan said about Elizabethan Theater itself: "the actual audience . . . remember[s] that they are . . . simply another group of players in a larger play, and that the physical theater in which they sit is not final reality but simply another stage on which a longer play is being enacted before an unseen audience" (*SQ* [1974]: 1). The audition room set emphasized the play's concern with theater, as had Gielgud's production of 1964, in that instance by making the entire performance a "rehearsal." If Branagh's Hamlet explored existential determinants in a new world, Shrapnel's Claudius grappled with the "Christian psychology" which his own conscience and Hamlet's mimetic depiction of guilt had presented to him. Occasionally, for set changes, the great gray curtain whirled, suggesting "occurences of fate," no doubt, but slowing the play's progress.

A dominant action in the production was the "arrested embrace." The Ghost, in a melancholy family reunion borrowed from

Daniels, tried to embrace Gertrude, but could not. Ophelia would have held Hamlet, but was spat upon instead. Claudius sought comfort from Gertrude but was rebuffed. Laertes, in his grief, almost put his arm around Gertrude, but caught himself and dropped his hands to his knees. This pattern emerged, said Dr. Murray Cox in the Program Notes, from the play's depiction of "defective ceremony [and] displaced ritual" (Program, 12). Thus did the insights of the new criticism and the old historicism emerge usefully here, to show that a world that has lost contact with larger cosmic powers, by dint of an unresolved regicide, cannot achieve interpersonal contact either. The exception was the link between Hamlet and his father, and here, Hamlet's thrust at Gertrude was not Oedipal but consciously in behalf of a father who could defend his own interests only through a surrogate.

The production paid attention to detail. "I *am* thy father's spirit," said Clifford Rose's Ghost; that is to say, "I know that the devil hath power / To assume a pleasing shape." Hamlet's "methinks I see my father" caused a stir among the messengers who have just seen him. Is the thing suddenly here again? But Claudius should pause when he says "out of this . . ." and Laertes should wait for a beat and say, "What—out of this— my lord?" so that calculation and impatience are captured in the rhythms of the dialogue.

The critical reception was largely positive. Rich found the "major chords of passion . . . luxuriantly purred in a variety of keys for surface show alone," as Branagh "protect[ed] his franchise by making sure he will do nothing to challenge or offend the audience or to diminish his princely image in the show biz firmament" (C14). Branagh, said Rich, could have been "a steely, yuppie banker of the 1980s" (C9). Nicholas de Jongh's Branagh "has the solid, invulnerable air of the chief executive" and left de Jongh "lukewarm and underwhelmed," even as de Jongh found the production itself "a feat of daring—shot through with bold imaginings, disconcerting shocks and inventions" (*ES* 21 December 1992, 7). Irving Wardle said that "Branagh has voices for every occasion, but they emerge as a rhetorical mosaic, lacking any continuous emotional undercurrent" (*IonS* 20 December 1992). But one person's "bland" Hamlet is another's "approachable" Hamlet. Charles Spencer found that Branagh "gives the finest performance of his career. . . . [H]e lets you into his character's mind with a complete absence of guile . . . and at almost every turn you feel you know exactly what he is thinking . . . and feeling. As a result many of the play's difficulties seem to dissolve" (*DT* 21 December

1992, 13). Jane Edwardes said that "there is none of the excitement of watching Alan Rickman, Mark Rylance, or Jonathan Pryce tearing themselves apart. Instead, Branagh brings clarity, moral authority and a rare dignity to the role" (*TO* 30 December 1992). Michael Billington found Branagh's "a fine Hamlet, stamped with rueful sadness. . . . Four years ago he was all reckless impulsiveness and danger: what he missed was Hamlet's inwardness" (*G* 21 December 1992). Jack Tinker went further, saying that Branagh, having "matured both emotionally and physically . . . is undoubtedly the great Hamlet of our time." Tinker suggested that "this extraordinarily powerful production . . . miraculously manages to marry inner-truth with the grand theatrical gesture" (*DM* 19 December 1992). Ian Shuttleworth found Branagh "a magnificently classical Prince Hamlet. Branagh presents the indecisions, vacillations, and tergiversations of Hamlet without selling short the bursts of dynamism, the fury and passion. He reclaims the soliloquies as the clear, comprehensible and illuminating passages they should be" (*CL* 21–28 December 1992). Paul Taylor discerned "a wonderful sense of dangerous, goading levity in the scenes of feigned madness" (*I* 21 December 1992). Christopher Grier called Branagh "truly princely in his bearing. . . . His soliloquies, conversational, sound newly-minted" (*Scotsman* 21 December 1992). Several of the critics discerned a familial emphasis in the production (de Jongh, Shuttleworth, and Tinker, for example), what Spencer called an "almost Chekhovian exploration of family life" a tonality that Billington called "a poignant Chekhovian melancholy." It may be true of *Hamlet*, as it seems to be true of *King Lear*, that what keeps the play effectively on stage is its profound exploration of familial issues. The probing of this sector in both plays goes well beyond the clichés that television has exploited for decades in its own family-based shows. It may be, however, that television helps theater in this instance by preparing us for Shakespeare's transcendence of the simplicity of the sitcom.

Rylance's antic Hamlet may have been more exciting, but Branagh's Hamlet, calmer, perhaps even verging on blandness at times, brought the words to the ear, many of them only words on a page before, and he brought them *clearly* to the ear. That alone was a great achievement and the production, in spite of its meretricious moments, was worth a trip to London.

The Royal Court *King Lear* came close to the quality of the productions of "The Year of *Lear*," 1990: the Branagh (with Richard Briers), the Hytner (with John Wood), and the Warner (with Brian

Cox). Problems in the second half of the production were balanced by an intelligent Lear (Tom Wilkinson), a menacing, Northern Irish Edmund (Adrian Dunbar), a most unusual Fool (Andy
Serkis), a splendid Kent (Philip Jackson), a strong Goneril (Lia
Williams), who had waited a long time to take over as "First Lady,"
and a slashing Regan (Saskia Reeves).

The Royal Court has not featured "traditional theatre" over the
years, but the format cannot have changed much since 1888 and
that means a proscenium facing a long auditorium. Director Max
Stafford-Clark overcame the potential problems of the building
by pacing his production rapidly, with upstage entrances coming
even as characters completed a scene downstage (as between 4.1
and 4.2, for example—Edgar leading Gloucester off even as Goneril greets Edmund as "*my* lord"). The set was a box that made
use of Royal Court's height and that could be lighted to resemble
a room in a country house, a space outside the walls of an estate,
and the inside of a huge tomb, with monuments glimmering on
the back wall and what had been a bar suddenly a sarcophagus.
A metal grate could be raised to become, for example, the place
where Gloucester was pinioned for his blinding. Sightlines were
enhanced by a modest rake (perhaps ten degrees) and the playing
was usually downstage and often toward the audience, Lear
pointing from the stage, for example, at "yon simp'ring dame"
(4.6.117). Thus the effect was partially meta-dramatic ("I know
you are there, audience, and I know that you know that I am a
character in a play") and "realistic" ("I am responding to things
that are happening to me"). Edmund's "Thou, Nature" and Goneril's "O, the difference of man and man," the latter delivered to
us from hands and knees, were particularly effective.

The "time" was the present, perhaps with a movement forward
from the moment when the florid King, seated at a table in a
formal room of a great estate, gave his lands away, and opened
up a decade for new weaponry and the effortless careers of the
yuppies. Regan dispatched Cornwall's servant with each barrel
of her husband's shotgun. During the battle a group of refugees
huddled and ducked across the stage and were mowed down by
a sweep of crossfire, a neat synecdoche for Shakespeare's indis-
criminate battle and for modern war. The moment was reminiscent of Kozintesev's great film version, based on German combat
films of the invasion of Poland, seemingly burning as if the cellu-
loid itself were curling into the fiery landscape, people dying on
the edges of pictures rushing past to record conquest. One problem with the use of "live ammunition" in theater is that the reek of

cordite overcomes cough suppressants. The swordfight between Edgar and Edmund occurred without its sequence of medieval challenges and was "something that officers do for exercise" or a reversion to the older formats that the duelling code prescribes. Edgar came close to losing when he paused before a disarmed and helpless Edmund. The production did not, then, attempt to imitate what Trewin called "a cry from the dawn in Britain that is borne away upon the gale" (205), nor could it avoid "the stage's fragmentation of what can seem unified in a reader's platonizing imagination" (Barrow, *UC*, 147). Theater exists to disrupt such platonizing "readings." The production values were closer to Warner's spare eclecticism than to other recent versions of *King Lear*, and that is a good sign.

Wilkinson's Lear was reminiscent of Wood's, who "broke the role down into a multitude of tiny performance units," as Irving Wardle said "sometimes changing emotional tack half a dozen times within as many lines, but never losing his central idea of the character as a man of passionate nature but short attention span, continually dragged back to face an unendurable reality" (*TC* 102). As Wilkinson said, "crawl towards death" in the deposition scene, Regan gave a murmur, as if to say "Oh no!", suggesting that Lear was not above encouraging sympathetic responses and that, of course, one point of his abdication was to manipulate his beneficiaries into subsequent guilt, should they fail to be sufficiently grateful. Thus a small moment motivated a large sequence of the action. Wilkinson was splendid as he paused to consider that Cornwall might indeed be unwell (2.4.102–9), and when he recognized that it was *his* "flesh begot / Those pelican daughters" (3.4.73–74). One of the things that was driving him mad was his recognition that *he* was part of nature, that Cordelia had been right to challenge what Jeffrey Stern calls "the dream-sustaining rhetoric of Goneril and Regan" at the beginning (*SQ* [1990]: 302).

Wilkinson got a laugh when he said, "But I'll not chide thee" (2.4.223), and that meant that his curse of Goneril ("a boil / A plague-sore," etc.) had been heard by the audience—a lot of curses have been uttered already—and that his pause was splendidly timed. Lear signaled a stage in his growth when both Goneril and Regan moved to comfort him as "water drops" threatened to "stain his man's cheeks" (2.4.275–76). Lear waved them violently away.

Jackson's Kent changed from a Major General to Lear's servant with utter conviction and delivered his condemnation of Oswald and his satire of courtly speech in 2.2 superbly. He was subject to a great indignity as he sat helpless in the stocks as Fraser James's black and nasty Oswald pissed on him. The moment was powerful, as Andrew Gurr describes it: "how little respect for age authority now has under this new regime. Lear and Gloucester together contrive to have him freed, but Kent's similarity to them in age provides a visual warning on stage of what is to come for them too. He has lost his status, and can easily be victimized" (19).

Edmund had been on duty in Northern Ireland as an Army officer and perhaps had been conceived there, during one of Gloucester's diplomatic missions. He represented a threat within the world of the play *and* for the immediate audience, as had Raul Julia's Edmund for Joseph Papp's New York production in the 1970s. Lia Williams's Goneril moved from society hostess, elegant in a low-cut black velvet gown (and angry because her guest of honor, the King Emeritus, insisted on the informality of a smoking jacket), to a woman fatally in pursuit of this dashing junior officer. She charted her role to parallel a world that had lost any sense of sanction or continuity.

Goneril's initial efforts at a normative suburban "lifestyle" were challenged by Serkis's transvestite Fool, also in a black, if less elegant dress. Serkis was the voice of "otherness," of the intentionally marginalized, whose "transgressive acts" mocked "woman's domestic containment," as Jean Howard says of women who went to the theater (*SQ* [1988]: 440), and, of course, Goneril could not abide this "all-licens'd Fool" (1.4.198). This Fool was "Lear's shadow" (1.4.251)—all that he has suppressed from his persona, and therefore a "woman." If, as Robert Kimbrough says of Rosalind in *As You Like It*, "as a man, she is freed from societal conventions and can speak her mind" (110; his emphasis), this Fool, also free of stereotypes, could speak his mind. Serkis's mockery kept reminding Lear of his error and thus held Goneril within the space of a mistake that pulled her from her future, much as Edmund's bastardy deprived him of what he felt he deserved. The conflict between the two sisters was set up when they exited past Edmund, who was entering for his soliloquy. Each turned to look at him, a borrowing from Jonathan Miller, whom Stafford-Clark consulted for this production (Program, 8). Miller's Goneril (Gillian Barge) and Regan (Penelope Wilton) swiveled their eyes past Edmund as they exited in the BBC version. We felt the emerging triangle in the instant.

That tug-of-war, in which a vivid, jutting-faced Regan engaged with increasing desperation—having been so calm earlier, as Goneril insisted that "We must do something" (1.1.307)—and within which Edmund carefully considered the merits of each of his suitors, was one of the few good things about the second half of the production, which began with Edgar's entrance at the beginning of act four. Admittedly, the conflated script is episodic in this area, with Edgar-Gloucester, then Goneril-Edmund-Albany, then Cordelia's return (3.3 was cut), then Regan-Oswald, and finally, after Gloucester's non-fall, the return of Lear. It is one of the least unified of the late-middle areas in Shakespeare's scripts where he gives his lead actor a breather, as in the scene in England in *Macbeth*, and the Ophelia's madness/Laertes's return scenes in *Hamlet*. Lear was not helped by having to deliver much of what should be his entrance while marching back and forth behind a door, upstage center. His "attention [is drawn by] Gloster's recognition of the voice" (4.6.95), as Marvin Rosenberg says (*Masks of King Lear*, 270), but the business was distracting, and "Goneril with a white beard" (4.6.96) did not get the laugh we need at that moment. The production's rhythm finally picked up again when Lear comforted a weeping Gloucester (4.6.174), a moving moment which reminded us of Lear's wiping the Fool's face on "Nay, get thee in" (3.4.27). But we got far too much of Edgar, whose cruel revenge against his father was taken at its allegorical face value. Surely his role can be cut down and still make whatever comparison or contrast it creates with the main plot. The reconciliation (4.7) was inhibited by a Cordelia who had been denied her asides in 1.1 and thus had to be seen as having *planned* her rejection of Lear's gift. Certainly she did not enjoy being part of an opening auction sale and had to be prodded from her chair by Goneril. If anything, Goneril and Regan seemed more sympathetic early on than did Cordelia—*they* had to deal with their father, *she* got to go to France.

The Fool survived his going to bed at noon (3.6.83) to deliver another part of Merlin's riddle, to take on the Gentleman's role in 4.6, where "twain" (4.6.204) meant Goneril and Regan, and to be captured by Edmund's soldiers. He was hanged above a broken wall upstage right and reminded one, not positively, of the chunks of meat and bodies hanging over David Hare's awful production at the National in 1987. After the rapid tensions so well developed in the first half of the play, which ran for an hour and forty-five minutes, it seemed as if Michael Bogdanov had taken over for the final hour to show us how bad the script really is.

A strength of this finale, however, was Jason Watkins's frail Albany, insisting quietly on the values that the new generation had trampled. The Royal Court remains a "human and generous" space, as Richard Eyre says, where Shakespeare sounds superb when spoken by good actors (Program, 7). The play continues to ask the questions that Ann Thompson lists: "Is there a god who permits suffering, a god who uses suffering in a positive way as some kind of test of human worth, a god who sadistically delights in suffering, or no god at all?" (36). For reasons that may be in the inherited script or that might have resulted from the editing of *this* script, where we were overpowered by Edgar's "answers," this production ceased its interrogation just as it had us intensely interested in what the question was.

Postscript

CARY MAZER suggests that a modern "assumption is that there is a connection between language and emotion, that dramatic language can be employed as a vehicle for the actor's expressive energies" (*SB* 18). The danger, however, is that "of assuming that the actor's 'truth' in the latter half of the twentieth century is identical or even equivalent to the actor's truth in 1600; and that what actors understand to be emotions are indentical from one period to the next; and that the means of expressing these emotions are universal and eternal" (18). Mazer makes some compelling distinctions:

> Since the art of acting involves both the experience of emotions and their expression through the physical body, the theory and practice of acting in any period are often articulated and codified in the period's scientific theories about the mind, the passions and the body. And so Elizabethan acting is related to Galenic theories about bodily fluids, eighteenth-century acting to Cartesian theories about the body as a machine, and late nineteenth-century acting to theories about the conscious and unconscious mind. (19)

Mazer quotes Hamlet's response to the Player's Hecuba Speech:

> Is it not monstrous that this player here,
> But in a fiction, in a dream of passion,
> Could force his soul so to his own conceit
> That from her working all his visage wann'd,
> Tears in his eyes, distraction in his aspect,
> A broken voice, and his whole function suiting
> With forms to his own conceit?

The process that Hamlet describes "makes sense," Mazer says, "only if we understand what actors and scientists from 1600 meant when they talked of 'forcing' the 'soul' to the 'conceit' and of one's 'function' suiting 'forms' to it" (19).

That exploration, of course, awaits several volumes, but Mazer concludes that even if we "cannot assume that [emotions as defined in the 1600s] were thought to come from the same sources" as ours, "the potential for connecting emotions—even in our definitions—with their verbal expression is still there; and it is even more important for us to recover that connection to day, when we are not used to finding expression for our emotions through heightened speech" (20). The point is to avoid falsifying the script as it is delivered to us from the past while at the same time expressing emotions that communicate to an audience in the 1990s. Mazer warns against "two invalid assumption . . . when we have found a way for an actor to create an emotional life in and through Shakespeare's language, we must not assume that we have found Shakespeare's own way" and "we must not assume that the way we have found will continue to have any validity when our own paradigms of acting have shifted to the next" (20). Mazer defines the dynamic within which the system called "Shakespeare" can be found, even as that source of energy continues to be the major source of fuel for the dynamic.

The author hoped that Mazer had developed his theories on the assumptions underlying Elizabethan action, when the author wrote him in November 1992:

> What *is* Elizabethan acting style, as expressed in Hamlet's response to the Player? Polonius seems to feel that the Player has gone too far, and Hamlet, who has been scathing to Polonius, seems to agree. BBC Player (Emrys James) seemed to have become personally involved in grief. Has Player gone beyond holding the mirror up *to* nature and become the thing itself? Hamlet's advice to Players certainly argues "naturalism," even if that would be an "academic" approach if delivered by Hamlet, the university student, and even if the Players may resent his "amateur" advice. They know their trade and can be shown as indulging Hamlet only because he is their patron. James in BBC was furious with Hamlet when the latter interrupted "Gonzago." And how does one play "Gonzago" "naturalistically"? Shakespeare must have known that it couldn't be done and shouldn't be attempted since the inner play contrasts so markedly with the outer script (cf. Harry Levin on the contrastings styles) and is itself shattered by the imploding energy of that outer script—Hamlet interrupting as the script shows, or Claudius breaking down as a lot of edited productions try to show (the Olivier film, for example). Does Hamlet see Player as a rebuke to Hamlet's authenticity, as opposed to "actions that a man might play"? Hamlet's earlier response to Gertrude contains many of the signals he assigns to the Player. But the Player weeps for Hecuba! If Hamlet and Player are linked—and not favorably for Hamlet ("monstrous")—then Hamlet must engage in the same over-doing ("drown the stage with tears" etc.) that he will tell the Players to avoid. The

speech you quote represents one of Hamlet's negative responses to himself, thus a spur to anger. It also represents—and here we get beyond what an actor can convey and *to* what a spectator must somehow grasp—an ignoring of the equation between Pyrrhus and Hamlet, where the act Hamlet sees himself as called upon to perform is terrible and "hellish," its perpetrator "damn'd." *Hamlet* is then, among many other things, an exploration of what it is "to act." Acting is engaging in a fiction *and* encountering reality. Do we act from stereotypic premises—"the revenger"—or out of a sense of who we believe ourselves to be or not to be? How do we find out who the *authentic* actor is? We must act "naturalistically," but no "technique" can discover one's nature and permit one to act from that nature. The actor, however, does that in responding to Hecuba. He can inseminate himself with real passion even within "a dream of passion," while Hamlet can only "unpack [his] heart with words." If Gertrude is an inadequate "objective correlative" for Hamlet's response, as Eliot argues (assuming that nothing *but* his mother's infidelity has come between Hamlet and happy days at university), Hamlet finds Hecuba an inadequate fiction for the Player's reaction. Hamlet has "that within" yet can "do nothing." He cannot act. He can only "act."

Cary Mazer's response answers a number of questions, including what difference any of this does make to a modern audience and how a director and an actor find that "modern equivalent for emotion" that his article discussed. In this instance, the actor was playing Ferdinand, who harbors an incestuous desire for his sister, the Duchess of Malfi:

> In answer to your central question, I really don't have a clue about what an Elizabethan acting style is. But you're absolutely right that *Hamlet* is centrally about the differences between what it means to "act," in the many senses of the word. And Hamlet's response to the Player is central to this. . . . My interest nowadays is not so much interpretations—i.e., what things are/were supposed to "mean"—but how to balance my own interests in contemporary theatrical possibilities with the presence of so many new-historicist colleagues in my department. Yes, I know that in that informal *SB* article I say that we shouldn't assume that the Elizabethans' assumptions about acting are our own. But let me shift gears about this: a contemporary audience can't know/won't care about historical/cultural mindsets. How do we identify what might be going on in the script in terms of historical/ Elizabethan assumptions about acting/feeling/doing/being, and then translate it into contemporary definitions of all of these terms so that it is meaningful to a contemporary audience member watching the play in performance?
>
> Let me give you a *Duchess of Malfi* example. My historicist colleagues

and graduate students (including a grad student working as my dramaturg) would say that there was no sense of interiority and self when the play was written, and that the play shows the fault-lines of the culture when these notions were first emerging in primitive form, with the shift from aristocratic power and dynastic marriage (cf. Ferdinand and the Cardinal) to marriage based on love and households and the rising bourgeoisie (Antonio). Well and good, but I'm not going to stage an historical footnote. On the other hand, I'm working with contemporary student actors, who want to know who their characters are and what makes them the way they are. Now, I want to work with contemporary actors's methods and vocabulary, so that the characters will be legible and comprehensible to the audience; but I don't want to start off a rehearsal process by discussing with the actor playing Ferdinand what his (Ferdinand's) toilet training was like, and whether his weirdness with his sister is or isn't incest. After all, I think my colleagues are essentially *right* about the interiority stuff; I just don't think you can play it. So, instead, I work with the actors on a) the action of each scene, in the most Stanislavskian sense of the word: what does the character want, what is *happening* in the scene in terms of conflict, energies, etc. *without* discussing *why* the characters are the way they are yet; and b) I identify, thematically and theatrically, the relevant systems of meaning that reflect the characters' dilemmas, i.e. Ferdinand's voyeurism; images of twinning, mirrors, purity of blood, etc. We discover (in the case of Ferdinand) that he has almost no sense of boundaries between himself and his sister, that he's afraid, not of wanting to sleep with her, but that her desires (for someone outside of their twin-ness) and her sexual activity somehow violates the integrity of his own ill-defined and misplaced sense of his "self." The result of this is that we tap the energies of the play (ambiguities about the status of the "self") unlocked by historical conceptualizing, and we make *that* the issue that a modern actor can play, and that a modern audience can perceive: i.e., that this is a character who has a tenuous grip on his sense of self, and his terror about this drives him to sororicide and madness.

A modern audience probably does not care about the process whereby as Mazer says "you put the play's initial, historically based values in dialogue with contemporary definitions of these same values." The process becomes, like so much modern criticism, an exploration of the interfacing between early modern concepts and our own definitions, using the latter to reveal the former to the imagination, psyche, and mind of an audience today. Mazer's approach makes some use, then, of the findings of the new historicists which otherwise, as he says, won't play. One could say that Shakespeare's plays and those of some of his contemporaries,

Webster and Middleton, are an exploration of what it means to *have* interiority. Intelligent production shares that process with us, as the all-powerful Prospero does when, observing the weeping Gonzalo, he discovers that he, too, has within him the equivalent of the sea from which he had escaped—human tears.

Appendix

Note: Items in the production information below have not been indexed unless they appear in the text.

1987

Antony and Cleopatra: National Theatre, Olivier Theatre, beginning 9 April 1987. Directed by Peter Hall. Designed by Alison Chitty. Cleopatra: Judi Dench. Antony: Anthony Hopkins. Octavius: Tim Pigott-Smith. Charmian: Miranda Foster. Octavia: Sally Dexter. Enobarbus: Michael Bryant. Lepidis/Clown: John Bluthal. Philo: Mike Hayward. Eros: Jeremy Flynn. Ventidius/Procleius: Brian Spink. Dolabella/Scarus: Andrew C. Wadsworth. Soothsayer/Seleucus: Desmond Adams. Thidias: Michael Carter. Agrippa: Basil Henson. Pompey: David Schofield. Mardian: Iain Ormsby-Knox. Iras: Helen Fitzgerald. Menas: Michael Carter.

King Lear: National Theatre, Olivier Theatre, beginning 11 December 1986. Directed by David Hare. Sets by Hayden Griffin. Costumes by Christine Stromberg. Fights by Terry King. Kent: Philip Locke. Gloucester: Michael Bryant. Edmund: Douglas Hodge. Lear: Anthony Hopkins. Goneril: Anna Massey. Regan: Suzanne Bertish. Cordelia: Miranda Foster. Albany: Ken Drury. Cornwall: Fred Pearson. Burgundy: Guy Williams. Edgar: Bill Nighy. Oswald: Basil Henson. Fool: Roshan Seth. France: Philip Brook.

Titus Andronicus: Royal Shakespeare Company, Swan Theatre, Stratford-on-Avon, beginning April 1987. Directed by Deborah Warner. Designed by Isabella Bywater. Titus: Brian Cox. Lucius: Derek Hutchingson. Tamora: Estelle Kohler. Demetrius: Piers Ibbotson. Chiron: Richard McCabe. Aaron: Peter Polycarpou. Marcus: Donald Sumpter. Lavinia: Sonia Ritter. Saturninus: Jim Hooper. Bassianus: Mike Dowling. Quintus/Valentine: Ian Bailey. Martius/Caius: Linus Roach. Young Lucius: Jeremy Gilley. Sepronius/Alarbus: Stephen Elliot. Mutius/Publius: Sean Pertwee.

Julius Caesar: Royal Shakespeare Company, Main Stage, Stratford-on-Avon, beginning April 1987. Directed by Terry Hands. Sets by Farrah. Costumes by Alexander Reed. Fights by Ian McKay. Antony: Nicholas

Farrell. Caesar: David Waller or Joseph O'Conor. Brutus: Roger Allam. Portia: Janet Amsbury. Calpurnia: Susan Colverd. Casca: Geoffrey Freshwater. Cassius: Sean Baker. Decius/Titinius: William Chubb. Ligarius: Ian Barritt. Cinna: Gordon Case. Lepidus: Dennis Clinton. Cicero: Richard Conway, Octavius: Gregory Doran. Messala: Mike Dowling. Pindarus/Trebonius: Stephen Elliott. Metellus/Strato: Derek Hutchinson. Lucius/Young Cato: Piers Ibbotson. Soothsayer: Griffith Jones. Cinna the Poet: Hakeem Kae-Kazim.

Twelfth Night: Royal Shakespeare Company, Main Stage, Stratford-on-Avon, beginning 2 July 1987. Directed by Bill Alexander. Sets by Kit Surrey. Costumes by Deirdre Clancy. Fights by Malcolm Ranson. Malvolio: Anthony Sher. Andrew: David Bradley. Toby: Roger Allam. Feste: Bruce Alexander. Maria: Pippa Guard. Orsino: Donald Sumpter. Olivia: Deborah Findlay. Viola: Harriet Walker. Sebastian: Paul Spence. Fabian: Jim Hooper. Curio: Jeremy Gilley. Antonio: Paul Webster. Priest: Arnold Yarrow. Captain: Richard Conway.

The Merchant of Venice: Royal Shakespeare Company, Main Stage, Stratford-on-Avon, beginning 23 April 1987. Directed by Bill Alexander. Sets by Kit Surrey. Costumes by Andreane Neofitu. Shylock: Anthony Sher. Portia: Deborah Findlay. Nerissa: Pippa Guard. Jessica: Deborah Goodman. Lorenzo: Paul Spence. Morocco: Hakeem Kae-Kazim. Bassanio: Nicholas Farrell. Antonio: John Carlisle. Solanio: Gregory Doran. Gratiano: Geoffrey Freshwater. Launcelot: Phil Daniels. Arragon: Richard Conway. Salerio: Michael Cadman. Tubal: Bill McGuirk. Old Gobbo: Arnold Yarrow.

1989

The Plantagenets: Royal Shakespeare Company, Main Stage, Stratford-on-Avon, 1988, and Barbican Theatre, London, 1989. Directed by Adrian Noble. Adapted by Charles Wood from the *Henry VI–Richard III* tetralogy. Sets by Bob Crowley. Fights by Malcolm Ranson. [This list is based on the Barbican production]. Richard Plantagenet: David Calder. Edward IV: Ken Bones. Clarence/Vernon: David Morrissey. Richard of Gloucester: Anton Lesser. Rutland/Murderer/Norfolk: Jason Watkins. Duchess of York: Marjorie Yates. Rivers/Hume: Edward Harbour. Hastings: Edward Peel. Buckingham/Cade/Suffolk: Oliver Cotton. Brakenbury/Clifford/Bevis/Father who has killed his son: Roger Watkins. Henry VI: Ralph Fiennes. Queen Margaret: Penny Downie. Somerset: Tom Fahy. Exeter: Nicholas Smith. Young Clifford/Young Talbot/Simcox/Lovel: Mark Hadfield. Mrs. Simcox: Cissy Collins. Bassett/Smith/Sinklo: Trevor Gordon. H. Stafford/Richmond/Dauphin: Simon Dormandy. W. Stafford/Catesby: Jack James. Oxford/Clerk/Ratcliffe: Richard Bremmer.

Iden/Bedford/Mayor of Saint Albans/Lewis XI/Tyrrel: Raymond Bowers. Dick the Butcher/Talbot/Keeper/Stanley: Robert Demeger. Michael: Anthony Dixon. Smith: Trevor Gordon. Holland/Son who has killed his father/Grey: Kevin Doyle. Dorset: Kenn Sabberton. Michael: Christian Dixon. Warwick: David Lyon. Anne: Geraldine Alexander. Queen Elizabeth: Joanne Pearce. Duke Humphrey: David Waller. Duchess of Gloucester: Cherry Morris. Winchester: Antony Brown. Salisbury/Mortimer/Tressel: Jeffrey Segal. Bastard of Orleans/Roger Bolingbroke: Patrick Robinson. Burgundy/Mayor of London: Darryl Forbes-Dawson. Joan: Julia Ford. Margery Jourdain: Denis Armon. Lady Bona: Candida Gubbins. Prince Edward: Duncan Beiny/James Holland. Richard, Duke of York/Young Stanley: Joseph Arton/James Goodwin. Ghost of Prince Edward: Lyndon Davies. Young Richmond: Paul Cuttle/Neil Smith.

A Midsummer Night's Dream: Royal Shakespeare Company, Main Stage, Stratford-on-Avon, 11 April to 24 August 1989, later on tour and at the Barbican, London. Directed by John Caird. Designed by Sue Blane. Hippolyta/Titania: Clare Higgins. Theseus/Oberon: John Carlisle. Puck: Richard McCabe. Bottom: David Troughton. Moonshine: Dhobi Oparei. Snug: Jimmy Gardner. Quince: Paul Webster. Egeus: Russell Enoch. Hermia: Amanda Bellamy. Helena: Sarah Crowden. Demetrius: Paul Lacoux. Lysander: Stephen Simms. Flute: Graham Turner. Snout: David Shaw-Parker. Peaseblossom: Charlotte Bridgewater and Fiona Gibson. Moth: Curtis Mason and Mark Seavers. Mustardseed: Chloe Trotman and Jodie Ball. Cobweb: Richard Gregory and Zachary Gregory. Boy: Mandip Jheeta.

A Midsummer Night's Dream: New Shakespeare Company, Regent's Park, London, Summer 1989. Directed by Guy Slater. Designed by Simon Higlett. Hippolyta: Brigitte Kahn. Theseus: David Henry. Titania: Sally Dexter. Oberon: Saeed Jaffrey. Philostrate: Stefan Bednarczyk. Puck: Trevor Laird. Bottom: Christopher Benjamin. Snug: Jason Hart. Quince: Christopher Ettridge. Egeus: William Haden. Demetrius: Teddy Kempner. Lysander: Sam Miller. Hermia: Vicky Licorish. Helena: Tricia Morrish. Flute: Robert Styles. Snout: Jo Jones. First Fairy: Kim Barry. Moth: Annette Fraser. Cobweb: David Jarvis. Peaseblossom: Kathryn Salt.

Cymbeline: Royal Shakespeare Company, Main Stage, Stratford-on-Avon, 29 June to 31 August 1989. Directed by Bill Alexander. Designed by Timothy O'Brien. Iachimo: John Carlisle. Pisano: Rob Heyland. Cymbeline: Bernard Horsfall. Posthumus: David O'Hara. Arviragus: Vincent Regan. Guiderius: Stephen Simms. Cloten: David Troughton. Queen: Linda Spurrier. Belarius: Paul Webster. Imogen: Naomi Wirthner. First Lord: Ben Miles. Second Lord: Andrew Bridgmont. Philario: Mark Brignall. Frenchman: Francis Johnson. Lucius: Michael Loughnan. Roman Captain: Roger Tebb.

Twelfth Night: The Hull Truck Company, Donmar Warehouse, London, Summer 1989. Directed by John Godber. Designed by Robert Cheesmond. Music by Richard Stone and Steve Pinnock. Olivia: Andrina Carroll. Orsino: Andrew Dunn. Malvolio: William Inkley. Toby: Nick Kemp. Feste: Paul Rider. Andrew: Martin Ronan. Viola: Meriel Scholfield. Antonio: Richard Stone. Fabian: Steve Weston. Sebastian: Tom Whitehouse. Maria: Deborah Winckles.

The Merchant of Venice: The Phoenix Theatre, London, beginning 1 June 1989 and later in New York City at the 46th Street Theater. Directed by Peter Hall. Designed by Chris Dyer. [This list based on the London production.] Shylock: Dustin Hoffman. Portia: Geraldine James. Antonio: Leigh Lawson. Lorenzo: Richard Garnett. Jessica: Francesca Buller. Bassanio: Nathaniel Parker. Gratiano: Michael Siberry. Morocco: Jeffery Kissoon. Solanio: Ian Lavender. Tubal/Judge: Leon Lissek. Nerissa: Abigail McKern. Arragon: Michael Carter. Duke: Basil Henson. Salerio: Robert Arnold.

Hamlet: Royal Shakespeare Company, Main Stage, Stratford-on-Avon, 26 April to 2 September 1989, and subsequently at the Barbican, London. Directed by Ron Daniels. Designed by Antony McDonald. Music by Claire van Kampen. Hamlet: Mark Rylance. Claudius: Patrick Wright. Gertrude: Clare Higgins. Horatio: Jack Ellis. Polonius: Patrick Godfrey. Ghost/First Player: Russell Enoch. First Clown: Jimmy Gardner. Laertes: John Ramm. Ophelia: Rebecca Saire. Marcellus: Neil Richardson. Francisco: John Oxborrow. Reynaldo: Andrew Havill. Voltemand: Mark Brignall. Cornelius: Peter Carr. Rosencrantz: Andrew Bridgmont. Guildenstern: Patrick Brennan. Second Player: Katherine Stark. Third Player: Roger Tebb. Fortinbras: Jared Harris. Osric: Paul Lacoux.

The Summer of *King Lear*

King Lear: Royal Shakespeare Company, Main Stage, Stratford-on-Avon, 28 June 1990 to 25 January 1991. Directed by Nicholas Hytner. Designed by David Fielding. Lear: John Wood. Goneril: Estelle Kohler. Regan: Sally Dexter. Cordelia: Alex Kingston. Kent: David Troughton. Gloucester: Norman Rodway. Fool: Linda Scott Kerr. Edmund: Ralph Fiennes. Albany: Paul Webster. Oswald: Paterson Joseph. Edgar: Linus Roach. Cornwall: Richard Ridings. Burgundy: Michael Gardiner. France: Clarence Smith.

King Lear: National Theatre, Lyttleton Theatre, London, 10 July to 25 August 1990, in repertory. Directed by Deborah Warner. Sets by Hildegard Bechtler. Fights by John Waller. Lear: Brian Cox. Goneril: Susan Engle. Regan: Clare Higgins. Cordelia: Eve Matheson. Kent: Ian McKellen. Gloucester: Peter Jeffrey. Fool: David Bradley. Edmund: Hakeem

Kae-Kazim. Albany: Richard Bremmer. Oswald: Nicholas Blane. Edgar: Derek Hutchinson. Cornwall: Richard O'Callaghan. Burgundy: Mark Strong. France: David Collings.

King Lear: International Theatre Festival, Blackstone Theatre, Chicago, 1990, on tour with the same company's *A Midsummer Night's Dream.* Directed by Kenneth Branagh. Designed by Jenny Tiramani. Fights by Nicholas Hall. Lear: Richard Briers. Goneril: Sibohan Redmond. Regan: Francine Morgan. Cordelia: Ethna Roddy. Kent: Jimmy Yuill. Gloucester: Edward Jewesbury. Fool: Emma Thompson. Edmund: Simon Roberts. Albany: Karl James. Oswald: James Larkin. Edgar: Kenneth Branagh. Cornwall: Gerard Horan. France: Max Gold.

Winter of the Scottish Play

Die Tragödie des Macbeth: In German, Dorothea Tieck's translation. Mermaid Theatre, London, 30–31 January and 1 February 1992. Directed by Katharina Thalbach. Designed by Ezio Toffoluth. Rock music by George Kranz. Duncan/Macduff/Murderer: Guntbert Warns. Malcolm/Murderer: Horst Stenzel. Macbeth: Markus Wollenklee. Banquo/Seyton: Heinz Werner Kraehkamp. Lennox: Tobias Beyer. Ross: Walter Pfeil. Lady Macbeth: Maria Hartmann. Fleance/Witch: Wenka von Mikulicz-Radecki. Siward/Doctor/Bleeding Captain/Murderer: Peter Lohmeyer. Young Siward/Witch: Nadja Reichardt. Porter/Lady Macduff/Hecate: Katherina Thalbach. Son of Macduff/Gentlewoman/Witch: Adisat Semenitsch.

Macbeth: Buttonhole Theatre Company, New End Theatre, Hampstead, London, 4 February to 1 March 1992. Directed by Christopher Geelan. Set by Sarah Milton. Costumes by Andy Collyer. Fights by Tim Large. Weird Sisters: Sonia Beck, Emma Healy, Antonia Loyd. Duncan/Siward: Bernard Lawrence. Malcolm: Steven Elder. Macbeth: Ian Reddington. Banquo: George Sweeney. Ross: Christopher Gilling. Lady Macbeth: Sally Mortemore. Donalbain/Seyton: Michael Wright. Macduff: Richard Sockett. Angus/Murderer: Clive Kendall. Porter/Murderer: Gerald Heys. Lady Macduff: Belinda Cawdron. Young Macduff: Danny Nestor/Ben Winston. Lennox: Dickon Tyrell.

Macbeth: English Shakespeare Company. Spring/Summer Tour. Warwick Arts Centre, Coventry, February 1992. Directed by Michael Bogdanov. Designed by Claire Lyth. Fights by Malcolm Ransom. Weird Sisters: Vivian Munn, Allie Byrne, Tracey Mitchell. Duncan/Old Man/Doctor: Derek Smith. Malcolm: Michael Mueller. Donalbain/Young Siward: Vivian Munn. Lennox: Timothy Davies. Captain/Murderer: John Berlyne. Ross/Porter/Lord: James Hayes. Angus/Murderer: Sean Gilder. Macbeth: Michael Pennington. Banquo/Siward: Colin Farrell. Lady Macbeth:

Jenny Quayle. Macduff: Edward Little. Seyton: Gerald Doyle. Lady Macduff: Allie Byrne. Gentlewoman: Tracey Mitchell.

Richard III: **Large and Small**

Richard III: National Theatre, Lyttleton Theatre, London, 9 July to 25
August 1990, and then on tour. Directed by Richard Eyre. Designed by
Bob Crowley. Fights by John Waller. Buckingham: Brian Cox. Margaret:
Susan Engle. Elizabeth: Clare Higgins. Catesby: Derek Hutchinson.
Clarence: Peter Jeffrey. Duchess of York: Joyce Redman. Tyrrel: Hakeem
Kae-Kazim. Anne: Eve Matheson. Richard: Ian McKellen. Mayor/Ghost
of Henry VI: Sam Beaszley. Keeper: Nicholas Blane. Hastings/Herbert:
David Bradley. Brakenbury: Richard Bremmer. Stanley: David Collings.
Richmond/Grey: Colin Hurley. Lovel/First Murderer: Mark Strong. Sec-
ond Murderer: Phil McKee. Dorset: Stephen Marchant. Ratcliffe: Rich-
ard O'Callaghan. Edward IV/Oxford: Bruce Purchase. Prince of Wales:
Theo Cronin. York: Matthew Hearne. Ely: Richard Simpson. Rivers: Peter Sullivan.

Richard III: The Royal Shakespeare Company, The Other Place, Stratford-
on-Avon, beginning 5 August 1992 and subsequently on tour. Directed
by Sam Mendes. Designed by Tim Hatley. Fights by Terry King. Buck-
ingham: Stephen Boxer. Margaret: Cherry Morris. Elizabeth/Prince of
Wales: Kate Duchene. Catesby: Daniel Ryan. Clarence/Ratcliffe: Simon
Dormandy. Tyrrel/Rivers: Michael Packer. Anne/Duke of York: Annabelle
Apison. Richard: Simon Russell Beale. Mayor/Edward IV: Mike Dowling.
Hastings/Second Murderer/Urswick: Christopher Hunter. Brakenbury/
Stanley: Sam Graham. Richmond/Grey: Mark Lewis Jones. First Mur-
derer/Ely/Dorset: Mark Benton. Duchess of York: Ellie Haddington.

Richard III: The Royal Shakespeare Company, The Donmar Warehouse,
London, early 1993, on tour, with Ciaran Hinds replacing Simon Russell
Beale as Richard, due to the latter's back injury.

Measure for Measure

Measure for Measure: Stratford, Canada, 8 August to 14 November 1992,
in repertory. Directed by Michael Langham. Designed by Desmond
Heeley. Music by Stanley Silverman. Duke: Brian Bedford. Escalus: Leon
Pownall. Angelo: Colm Feore. Lucio: Nicholas Pennell. Gentlemen:
Wayne Best and Tim MacDonald. Mistress Overdone: Kate Reid. Pom-
pey: Bernard Hopkins. Claudio: Antoni Cimolino. Juliet: Carolyn Hay.
Provost: Lorne Kennedy. Friar Thomas: Mervyn Blake. Isabella: Eliza-
beth Marvel. Nun: Mary Hitch Blendick. Elbow: Brian Tree. Froth: Tom

Wood. Mariana: Michelle Fisk. Abhorson: Peter Donaldson. Barnadine: Diego Matamoros. Friar Peter: Richard Fitzpatrick.

The Good, the Horrid, and the In-Between

Richard II: Mark Taper Forum, Los Angeles, 12 April to June 1992. Directed by Robert Egan. Set by Vael Pardess. Costumes by Robert Blackman. Fights by Randy Kovitz. Dramaturgy by Diana Maddox. Northumberland: Carlos Carrasco. Aumerle: Michael Gerveris. Green/Salisbury: Ryan Cutrona. Murderer/Bushy/Scroop: Tom Fitzpatrick. Richard II: Kelsey Grammer. Queen: Melora Hardin. Gaunt/Exton: Barry Shabaka Henley. Bolingbroke: Robert Jason. Gloucester/Ross/Groom: Eugene Lee. Willoughby: Philip Moon. Duchess of Gloucester/Duchess of York: Natsuko Ohama. Henry Percy: Luis Antonio Ramos. Duke of York: Armin Shimmerman. Mowbray/Carlisle: John Vickery.

Hamlet: The Shakespeare Theatre, Washington, D.C., 17 November 1992 to 10 January 1993. Directed by Michael Kahn. Set by Derek McLane. Costumes by Catherine Zuber. Fights by David Leong. Hamlet: Tom Hulce, with Gary Sloan taking the role for seven performances. Claudius: Jack Ryland. Gertrude: Franchelle Stewart Dorn. Ghost/Osric: Daniel Southern. Polonius: Ted van Griethuysen. Laertes: Jay Goede. Ophelia: Francesca Buller. Reynaldo: Eric Hoffman. Horatio: Hank Stratton. Marcellus: Bernard K. Addison. Bernardo: Craig Wallace. Francisco: Stevie Ray Dallimore. Rosencrantz: Paul Mullins. Guildenstern/Second Clown: J.C. Cutler. Player King: Emery Battis. Player Queen: Jason Novak. Lucianus: Michael Donlan. First Clown: Eric Hoffman. Voltemand/Priest: Robert G. Murch.

A Midsummer Night's Dream: The Olivier, National Theatre, London, 9 July 1992 through Summer. Directed by Robert Lepage. Designed by Michael Levine. Theseus: Allan Mitchell. Hippolyta: Lolita Chakrabarti. Lysander: Rupert Graves. Demetrius: Simon Coates. Hermia: Indra Ove. Helena: Rudi Davies. Egeus: Trevor Thomas. Philostrate: Paul Meston. Oberon: Jeffery Kisson. Titania: Sally Dexter. Puck: Angela Laurier. Quince: Steven Beard. Bottom: Timothy Spall. Flute: Adrian Scarborough. Snout: Brian Pettifer. Snug: John Cobb. Starveling: Mark Hadfield.

1992

All's Well That Ends Well: Royal Shakespeare Company, Swan Theatre, Stratford-on-Avon, beginning 1 July 1992. Directed by Peter Hall. Set by John Gunter. King of France: Richard Johnson. Countess: Barbara Jefford. Helena: Sophie Thompson. Bertram: Toby Stephens. Parolles: Michael Siberry. Diana: Rebecca Saire. Lavache: Anthony O'Donnell. Lafew: Alfred Burke. Widow: Andree Evans.

As You Like It: Royal Shakespeare Company, Main Stage, Stratford-on-Avon, beginning 14 April 1992, and going on to the Barbican, London in 1993. Directed by David Thacker. Designed by Johan Engles. Fights by Terry King. Oliver: Adrian Lukis. Jaques de Boys: Alan Cox. Orlando: Peter de Jersey. Adam: Alfred Burke. Dennis: Jack Waters. Duke Frederick: Andrew Jarvis. Celia: Phyllida Hancock. Rosalind: Samantha Bond. Touchstone: Anthony O'Donnell. Le Beau: Nick Kemp. Charles/William: Nick Holder. Duke Senior: Jeffery Dench. Amiens: David Burt. Jaques: Michael Siberry. Corin: John Bott. Silvius: Andrew Cryer. Audrey: Susan-Jane Tanner. Martext: James Walker. Phebe: Emma Gregory.

As You Like It: The New Shakespeare Company, Regent's Park, London, Summer 1992. Directed by Maria Aitken. Designed by Bruno Santini. Fights by Peter Woodward. Oliver: Ken Bones. Jaques de Boys: Rhys Ifans. Orlando: Oliver Parker. Adam: Richard Butler. Dennis: Paul Hawkyard. Duke Frederick/Duke Senior: David Sumner. Celia: Sarah-Jane Holm. Rosalind: Cathryn Harrison. Touchstone: John Kane. Le Beau: Paul Aves. Charles: Edward Max. William/Hymen: Gavin Payne. Amiens: Daniel Gillingwater. Jaques: Bette Bourne. Corin: George Pensotti. Silvius: Nigel Hastings. Audrey: Samantha Spiro. Martext: Alister Cameron. Phebe: Anna Patrick.

The Taming of the Shrew: Royal Shakespeare Company, Main Stage, Stratford-on-Avon, beginning 26 March 1992. Directed by Bill Alexander. Designed by Tim Goodchild. Christopher Sly: Maxwell Hutcheon. Landlord/Pedant: James Walker. Landlady: Stephanie Jacob. Lucentio: John McAndrew. Tranio: Richard McCabe. Baptista: Trevor Martin. Katherine: Amanda Harris. Bianca: Rebecca Saire. Gremio: Paul Webster. Hortensio: Graham Turner. Biondello: Andrew Cryer. Petruchio: Anton Lesser. Grumio: Geoffrey Freshwater. Vincentio/Tailor: Ciaran McIntyre. Rupert Llewellyn: Jack Waters. Simon Llewellyn: Dominic Mafham. Hugo Daley-Young: Dorian MacDonald. Sarah Ormsby: Catherine Mears. Ruth Banks-Ellis: Emily Watson. Peter Sinclair: Barnaby Kay.

The Winter's Tale: Royal Shakespeare Company, Main Stage, Stratford-on-Avon, beginning 25 June 1992. Directed by Adrian Noble. Designed by Anthony Ward. Music by Shaun Davey. Archidamus: John Bott. Camillo: Benjamin Whitrow. Polixenes: Paul Jesson. Leontes: John Nettles: Hermione: Samantha Bond. Mamillius: Marc Elliott/Stephan Weclawek. Antigonus: Andrew Jarvis. Paulina: Gemma Jones. Cleomenes: Pearce Quigley. Dion: James Walker. Shepherd: Jeffery Dench. Young Shepherd:

Graham Turner. Autolycus: Richard McCabe. Florizel: Alan Cox. Perdita: Phyllida Hancock. Dorcas: Jenna Russell. Mopsa: Stephanie Jacob.

Early 1993

Hamlet: Royal Shakespeare Company, Barbican Theatre, London, from 12 December 1992. Directed by Adrian Noble. Designed by Bob Crowley. Fights by Malcolm Ranson. Bernardo/Priest: Anthony Douse. Francisco/Lucianus: David Birrell. Marcellus/Player: Tim Hudson. Horatio: Rob Edwards. Ghost: Clifford Rose. Claudius: John Shrapnel. Gertrude: Jane Lapotaire. Hamlet: Kenneth Branagh. Polonius: David Bradley. Laertes: Richard Bonneville. Ophelia: Joanne Pearce. Reynaldo/Fortinbras: Ian Hughes. Guildenstern: Angus Wright. Rosencrantz: Michael Gould. Player King: Jonathan Newth. Player Queen: Sian Radinger. First Clown: Richard Moore. Second Clown: Howard Crossley. Osric: Guy Henry.

King Lear: Royal Court Theatre, London. From 14 January 1993. Directed by Max Stafford-Clark. Designed by Peter Hartwell. Fights by Terry King. Lear: Tom Wilkinson. Burgundy: Rupert Wickham. Cornwall: Peter-Hugo Daly. Albany: Jason Watkins. Kent: Philip Jackson. Gloucester: Hugh Ross. Edgar: Iain Glen. Edmund: Adrian Dunbar. Oswald: Fraser James. Fool: Andy Serkis. Goneril: Lia Williams. Regan: Saskia Reeves. Cordelia: Cara Kelly. France: Nigel Lindsay.

Works Cited

Alexander, Bill. "Director's Note." *The Taming of the Shrew*, 20. Stratford-on-Avon, RSC: 1992.

Alter, Iska, and William B. Long. "Royal National Theatre: *King Lear*." *Shakespeare Bulletin* 9:1 (Winter 1991): 23.

Anon. Letter to author. "Branagh's Birmingham Hamlet."

Anon. "Living Hell on Stage." *Burton Mail*, 5 April 1992.

Anon. "Review of *Measure for Measure*" (Stratford, Canada). *Thunder Bay Chronicle*, 20 September 1992.

Anon. "Muddled Madness." *Time*, 7 December 1992, 83.

Arditti, Michael. "Crass Absurdity." *Evening Standard*, 31 January 1992.

Associated Press. "Language Wars in Quebec." *Maine Sunday Telegram*, 30 August 1992, 7-A.

Bale, Doug. "*Measure for Measure* is a Spellbinding Triumph." *London Free Press* (Ontario), 19 August 1992.

Barnet, Sylvan. "*Othello* on Stage and Screen." *Othello*. New York: Signet, 1987.

Barroll, Leeds. "A New History for Shakespeare and His Time." *Shakespeare Quarterly* 39 (1988): 441–64.

Barrow, Craig. "Alabama Shakespeare Festival: 1992." *Upstart Crow* 12 (1992): 146–51.

Bawcutt, N. W., ed. *Measure for Measure*. Oxford: Oxford University Press, 1991.

Bayley, Clare. "All the world's a bed." *What's On*, 15 July 1992, 56.

Beckerman, Bernard. *Theatrical Presentation: Performer, Audience and Act*. New York: Routledge, 1990.

Berger, Thomas. "Double Casting Shakespeare's Plays: A Select Bibliography." *Shakespeare Bulletin* 7:6 (November/December 1989): 30–31.

Berkowitz, Gerald M. "Shakespeare in London, January-July, 1987." *Shakespeare Quarterly* 38:4 (Winter 1987): 495–500.

———. "The London and Stratford Seasons, 1991." *Shakespeare Bulletin* 9:1 (Fall 1991): 8–11.

Berry, Ralph. "The Reviewer as Historian." *Shakespeare Quarterly* 36:5 (1985): 594–97.

———. *On Directing Shakespeare*. London: Hamish Hamilton, 1989.

———. "Hamlet and the Audience: The Dynamics of a Relationship." In *Shakespeare and the Sense of Performance*, edited by Marvin and Ruth Thompson, 24–28. Newark: University of Delaware Press, 1989.

Bevington, David. *Action is Eloquence: Shakespeare's Language of Gesture*. Cambridge: Harvard University Press, 1984.

———. "Singing in the Rain." *Shakespeare Quarterly* 41:4 (Winter 1990): 499–502.

Billen, Andrew. "Time to say goodbye to Mr. Ugly: Interview with Simon Russell Beale." *The Observer on Sunday,* 9 August 1992, 43.

Billington, Michael. "A Merchant of Irony." *Guardian,* 11 June 1989, 26.

———. Remarks. Theatre in England. August 1989.

———. "The Sanity of Madness." *Guardian,* 13 July 1990, 36.

———. "*Lear* at the National." *Guardian,* 28 July 1990.

———. "The Sexual Cauldron." *Guardian,* 1 February 1992.

———. "The Shock of *The Shrew.*" *Guardian,* 3 April 1992, 36.

———. "*As You Like It.*" *Guardian,* 24 April 1992.

———. "Godfather's Myth, Child's Dark Fantasy." *Guardian,* 3 July 1992.

———. "Nightmare's Muddy Waters." *Guardian,* 11 July 1992.

———. "First Night." *Guardian,* 21 December 1992.

———. "*Richard III.*" *Guardian,* 4 August 1992.

———, ed. *Director's Shakespeare: Approaches to Twelfth Night.* London: Nick Hern, 1990.

Booth, Stephen. "Speculations on Doubling in Shakespeare's Plays." In *Shakespeare: The Theatrical Dimension,* edited by Philip C. McGuire and David A. Samuelson. New York: AMS Press, 1979.

Borot, Luc. "*Hamlet.*" *Cahiers Elisabethains* 36 (October 1989): 102–3.

Borot, Luc, F. Laroque, and J. M. Maguin. "*Titus Andronicus.*" *Cahiers Elisabethains* 32 (October 1987): 98–99.

Bradley, A. C. *Shakespearean Tragedy* London: Macmillan, 1904.

———. *Oxford Lectures on Poetry.* Oxford: Oxford University Press, 1909.

Brennan, Marion. "Shrewd Bard's Lengthy Taming." *Kidderminster Express & Star,* 2 April 1992.

Brook, Peter. *The Empty Space.* London: Penguin, 1968.

———. *The Shifting Point.* New York: Harper & Row, 1987.

Brooke, Nicholas, editor. *Macbeth.* Oxford: Oxford University Press, 1990.

Brown, Stewart. "Final Stratford Entry Does Measure Up." *Hamilton Daily,* 17 August 1992.

Carstensen, Candy. "Stage Review." *Beverly Hills Courier,* 24 April 1992, 35.

Chapman, Geoff. "Bard Casts Sharp Eye on Today's Mores." *Toronto Star,* 16 August 1992, C-1.

Chomsky, Noam. "The Reality of 'Education.'" *New York Review of Books,* 27 June 1986, 1 & 14.

Christopher, James. "Mixed Double." *Critic's Choice,* 29 April–6 May 1992.

Clayton, Thomas. "'Balancing the Script': (R)evoking the Script in Performance and Criticism." *Shakespeare and the Sense of Performance,* pp. 228–49.

Collins, Michael "'You Can Never Bring in a Wall': Some Thoughts on Teaching Shakespeare." *Shakespeare Bulletin* 7:2: 25–26.

Cook, Dorothy, and Wayne Cook. "*Hamlet.*" *Shakespeare Bulletin* 10:1 (Winter 1992): 38–40.

Cook, Judith. *Shakespeare's Players.* London: Harrap, 1983.

Coursen , H. R. *Christian Ritual and the World of Shakespeare's Tragedies.* Lewisburg, Pa.: Bucknell University Press, 1976.

——. "Why *Measure for Measure?*" *Literature/Film Quarterly* 12:1 (1984): 65–69.

——. *A Jungian Approach to Shakespeare.* Lanham, Md.: University Press of America, 1986.

——. *Shakespearean Performance as Interpretation.* Newark: University of Delaware Press, 1992.

——. *Watching Shakespeare on Television.* Madison, N.J.: Fairleigh Dickinson University Press, 1993.

Coveney, Michael. "Landmark of a Play." *Observer,* 15 July 1990, 35.

——. "*The Taming of the Shrew.*" *Observer,* 5 April 1992.

——. "*As You Like It.*" *Observer,* 26 April 1992.

——. "*All's Well* that comes up freshly minted." *Observer,* 5 July 1992.

——. "A Midsummer night's mud wresting." *Observer,* 12 July 1992, 54.

——. "Steel, grace and frenzy." *Observer on Sunday,* 16 August 1992, 46.

Cox, Brian. Remarks. Theatre in England. August, 1990.

Crowl, Sam. *Shakespeare Observed.* Athens: Ohio University Press, 1992.

Dash, Irene. "*The Merchant of Venice.*" *Shakespeare Bulletin,* 8:2 (1990): 10–11.

Davies, Michael. "What a Week for a Theatre Feast." *Evening Mail,* 3 July 1992.

Davison, Peter. *Hamlet: Text & Performance.* London: Macmillan, 1983.

Dawson, Anthony. *Watching Shakespeare.* London: Macmillan, 1988.

de Jongh, Nicholas. "A dream-struck magical *Shrew.*" *Evening Standard,* 2 April 1992.

——. "*As You Like It.*" *Evening Standard.* 23 April 1992.

——. "A modern feast for the imagination in dream country." *Evening Standard,* 2 July 1992.

——. "Bewitched in bed with a Dream transformed." *Evening Standard,* 10 July 1992, 7.

——. "Branagh Underwhelms." *Evening Standard,* 21 December 1992.

Deese, Helen. "*Richard II.*" *Shakespeare Bulletin* (Spring 1993): 38–9.

Dessen, Alan. *Elizabethan Stage Conventions and the Viewer's Eye.* Chapel Hill: University of North Carolina Press, 1977.

——. "Shakespeare's Scripts and Modern Directors." *Shakespeare Survey* 36 (1983): 57–64.

——. *Elizabethan Stage Conventions and Modern Interpreters.* Cambridge: Cambridge University Press, 1984.

——. "The Supernatural on Television." *Shakespeare on Film Newsletter* (1986): 1 and 8.

——. "Exploring the Script: Shakespearean Payoffs in 1987." *Shakespeare Quarterly* 39:2 (Summer 1988): 217–25.

——. "Adjusting Shakespeare in 1989." *Shakespeare Quarterly* 41:3 (Fall 1990): 352–64.

——. "Resources and Images: Shakespeare in 1990." *Shakespeare Quarterly* 42:2 (Summer 1991): 214–224.

——. "Taming the Script: *Henry VI, Shrew,* and *All's Well* in Ashland and Stratford." Forthcoming.

DeVine, Lawrence. "A *Measure* of Charm." *Detroit Free Press,* 17 August 1992, 3E.

Dodsworth, Martin. "Gesturing at Escape." *Times Literary Supplement*, 16–22 June 1989, 666.

———. "*King Lear*." *Times Literary Supplement*, 10–16 August 1990, 848.

———. "Grace Notes." *Times Literary Supplement*, 10 July 1992, 18.

Donahue, Patricia. "*A Midsummer Night's Dream* and *King Lear*." *Shakespeare Bulletin* 8:2 (Spring 1990): 24–25.

Donaldson, Peter. "Summer Programs." Cambridge: M.I.T. Press, 1992.

Drake, Sylvie. "*Midsummer* and *Lear* Presented by Branagh's Renaissance Theatre Co." *Los Angeles Times*, 22 January 1990, F1 and F10.

———. "*Richard II:* No Great Shakes." *Los Angeles Times*, 24 April, 1992, F1 and F18.

Drinkwater, John. *Shakespeare*. 1932; New York: Collier, 1962.

Duguid, Lindsay. "*As You Like It*." *Times Literary Supplement*, 8 May 1992.

Duke, Marion. "Pennell Steals the Show in *Measure for Measure*." *Listowe Banner*, 26 August 1992, 12.

Dunbar, Mary Judith. "*A Winter's Tale*." Paper presented to the International Shakespeare Association, Stratford, England, 1992.

Dungate, Rod. "*Hamlet*." *Plays & Players*, June 1989, 33.

Edmonds, Richard. "Over the top is just enough for imaginative *Tale*." *Birmingham Post*, 3 July 1992.

———. "Beale's grandiose awfulness." *Birmington Post*, 13 August 1992.

Edwards, Jane. "*Taming of the Shrew*." *Time Out*, 8 April 1992.

———. "*All's Well that Ends Well*." *Time Out*, 8 July 1992.

———. "*Hamlet*." *Time Out*, 30 December 1992.

———. "*Richard III*." *Time Out*, 17 February 1993.

Erstein, Hap. "Crowning Performance of *Hamlet*." *The Washington Times*, 24 November 1992, E3 and E5.

Everett, Barbara. "On a Sumptuous Scale." *Times Literary Supplement*, 24 April 1987, 439.

Feld, Bruce. "*Richard II*," *Drama-Logue*, 30 April–6 May 1992.

Fisher, James. "*Antony and Cleopatra*." *Shakespeare Bulletin* 5:6 & 6:1 (November 1987/February 1988): 37.

Fisher, Paul. "*Dream* at Regent's Park." *Guardian*, 1 June 1989, 24.

Fitzgerald, Ann. "*All's Well that Ends Well*." *Theatre*, 2 July 1992.

———. "*The Winter's Tale*." *Theatre*, 2 July 1992.

———. "*Richard III*." *Theatre*, 15 August 1992.

Foakes, R. H. "*King Lear* and the Displacement of *Hamlet*." *Huntington Library Quarterly* 50 (1987): 263–78.

Freud, Clement. "Midnight Cowboy as Loan Ranger." *The Times*, 1 June 1989, 14A.

Frey, Charles. "Shakespeare and the Next Generation." Quoted in Martha Tuck Rozett, "First Readers as Moralists," *Shakespeare Quarterly* 41:2 (Summer 1990): 221.

Fuzier, J., and J.-M. Maguin. "*The Merchant of Venice*." *Cahiers Elisabęthains* 32 (October 1987): 105–6.

Gardner, Lynn. "Theatre." *Mail on Sunday*, 5 July 1992.

George, Andrew. *"Shrew." Financial Times*, 3 April 1992.

Gilbert, Miriam. "Tranio Tames the *Shrew*." Abstract of paper delivered at the Shakespeare Association of America, April 1993.

Gilbey, Liz. "A New Look at 'The Shrew:' An Interview with Bill Alexander." *Plays International*, April 1992, 10–11.

Goldberg, Jonathan. "Shakespearean Inscriptions: The Voicing of Power." In *Shakespeare and the Question of Theory*, edited by Patricia Parker and Geoffrey Hartman. London: Metheun, 1985.

———. "*Macbeth* and Its Sources." In *Shakespeare Reproduced*, edited by Jean Howard and Marion O'Connor. New York: Metheun, 1987.

Goldman, Michael. *Acting and Action in Shakespeare*. Princeton: Princeton University Press, 1985.

Goldstraw, Aidan. "A Mild Offering—Like It Or Not." *Kidderminster Express & Star*, 23 April 1992.

Goy-Blanquet, Dominique. "Apolitical Aspects." *Times Literary Supplement*, 17 April 1987, 414.

———. "Strange Eventful Histories." *Times Literary Supplement*, 4–10 November 1988, 1229.

———. "Unruly Elements." *Times Literary Supplement*, 21–27 April 1989, 424.

———. "The Plantagenets." *Cahiers Elisabethains* 35 (April 1989): 95–98.

Grant, Steve. "A Dream." *Time Out*, 15 July 1992.

Granville-Barker, Harley. *Prefaces to Shakespeare*. Volume 2. Princeton: Princeton University Press, 1946.

Greenblatt, Stephen. *Shakespearean Negotiations*. Berkeley: University of California Press: 1988.

Grier, Christopher. "Brilliant Branagh in Exceptional *Hamlet*." *The Scotsman*, 21 December 1992.

Grimley, Terry. "Vivid beauty of Bard shines through." *Birmingham Post*, 2 July 1992, II/10.

Gross, John. *"Hamlet." Sunday Telegraph*, 30 April 1989, 19.

———. *"As You Like It." Sunday Telegraph*, 26 April 1992.

Gurr, Andrew. *Studying Shakespeare: An Introduction*. London: Edward Arnold, 1988.

Gustafson, Dwight. Letter to author. 9 December 1992.

Halio, Jay. *Understanding Shakespeare's Plays in Performance*. Manchester: Manchester University Press, 1988.

———. "Three Days, Three *King Lears*," *Shakespeare Bulletin* 9 (1991): 19–21.

Hammond, Anthony. *King Richard III*. London: Metheun, 1981.

Hapgood, Robert. "Review of *Acting and Action in Shakespeare*." *Shakespeare Quarterly* 38 (1987): 531–33.

Hassel, R. Chris. "Context and Charisma: The Sher-Alexander *Richard III* and its Reviewers." *Shakespeare Quarterly* 36:5 (1985): 630–43.

Hatten, Tom. KNX Radio, California. 24 April 1992, 9:53 a.m.

Hawkes, Terry. Comments. International Shakespeare Association, Stratford, England, 1992.

Hayes, Elliott. "Program Note." *Measure for Measure*, 11–12. Stratford, Canada, 1992.

Hayman, Edward. "*Measure for Measure* Is Brimming with Humor." *Detroit News*, 18 August 1992.

Heeley, Desmond. Interviewed by Pat Quigley. *Stratford for Students* (Autumn 1992): 8–10.

Henry, William A., III. "A Trio of Triumphs in London." *Time*, 3 July 1989, 73.

————. "Made Glorious Summer." *Time*, 22 June 1992, 72.

Herman, Jan. "Too Many Stars." *Quarto*, 2 February 1992, 4.

Hewison, Robert. "*The Taming of the Shrew.*" *Sunday Times*, 5 April 1992.

————. "*Winter's Tale.*" *Sunday Times*, 5 July 1992.

————. "Such stuff as dreams . . ." *Sunday Times*, 12 July 1992, VII-6.

Hiley, Jim. "Lear Carrier." *The Listener*, 1 January 1987, 29.

————. "Short on Psychology." *The Listener*, 16 April 1987, 46–47.

————. "Refined Sensuality." *The Listener*, 23 April 1987, 35.

————. "Drill Hall Drama." *The Listener*, 14 May 1987, 39 and 41.

————. "Group Practice." *The Listener*, 16 July 1987, 30.

————. "Leaf Encounters." *The Listener*, 3 November 1988, 38–39.

————. "Battle and Hum." *The Listener*, 13 April 1989, 32.

————. "Tangled Webber." *The Listener*, 27 April 1989, 30–31.

————. "Hollywood Shuffle." *The Listener*, 15 June 1989, 34.

Hilsman, Hoyt. "Legit Reviews." *Daily Variety*, 24 April 1992.

Hirschhorn, Clive. "Great tune, pity about the songs." *Sunday Express*, 12 July 1992.

Hodgdon, Barbara. "In Search of the Performance Present." In *Shakespeare: The Theatrical Dimension*, edited by Philip C. McGuire and David A. Samuelson. New York: AMS Press, 1979.

————. "Parallel Practices or the *Un*-necessary difference." *Kenyon Review* 7 (1985): 57–65.

————. "Performing Dream Work." Shakespeare Association of America, Atlanta, 3 April 1993.

Holderness, Graham. "*Macbeth*: Tragedy or History?" Program Notes. English Shakespeare Company, 1992.

Holland, Peter. "Shakespearean Performances in England, 1989–90." *Shakespeare Survey* 44 (1991): 157–90.

————. "Shakespeare Performances in England, 1990–91." *Shakespeare Survey* 45 (1992): 115–44.

————. "The Eyes Have It," *Times Literary Supplement* (7 May 1993): 3–4.

Hornby, Richard. "Understanding Acting." *Journal of Aesthetic Education* 17:3 (Fall 1983).

————. "Shakespeare in New York." *Hudson Review* (Summer 1988): 339–44.

————. "The London Theatre." *Hudson Review* (Winter 1988): 637–45.

————. "Interracial Casting." *Hudson Review* (Autumn 1989): 459–66.

————. "The Blind Leading the Blind." *Hudson Review* (Autumn 1990): 467–74.

————. "The London Theatre." *Hudson Review* (Winter 1990): 629–36.

———. "Theatre." *Hudson Review* 43:4 (Winter 1991): 412–27.

Howard, Jean. *Shakespeare's Art of Orchestration.* Urbana: University of Illinois Press, 1984.

———. "Crossdressing, the Theatre, and Gender Struggle in Early Modern England." *Shakespeare Quarterly* 39 (1988): 418–40.

Hunter, G. K., ed. *King Lear.* London: Penguin, 1968.

Hurren, Kenneth. "The Taming of the Shrew." *Mail on Sunday,* 5 April 1992.

———. "As You Like It." *Mail on Sunday,* 26 April 1992.

———. "A bad dream in the mud." *Mail on Sunday,* 12 July 1992.

Jacobson, Lynn. "Lepage's Playground." *American Theatre,* November 1991, 17–22.

James, Caryn. "Too Oft, Fault Lies In the Stars." *New York Times,* 6 January 1991, H13 and H19.

Jenkins, Harold, ed. *Hamlet.* London: Routledge, 1989.

Jones, Emrys. "On Assuming the Trappings of Power." *Times Literary Supplement,* 21 October 1983, 1159.

Jones, Welton. "Ethnic coloring of *Richard II* a little off." *San Diego Union-Tribune,* 24 April 1992, E-9.

Kemp, Peter. "Review of *Hamlet.*" *Independent,* 28 April 1989, 24.

Kernan, Alvin. "This Goodly Frame the Stage: The Interior Theater of the Imagination in English Renaissance Drama." *Shakespeare Quarterly* 25:1 (Winter 1974): 1–12.

Keyishian, Harry and Marjorie. "Shakespeare Abroad: *Hamlet.*" *Shakespeare Bulletin* 8:1 (Winter 1990): 32.

Kimbrough, Robert. *Shakespeare and the Art of Humankindness.* Atlantic Highlands, N.J.: Humanities Press, 1990.

King, T. J. *Casting Shakespeare's Plays: London Actors and Their Roles.* Cambridge: Cambridge University Press, 1992.

Kingston, Jeremy. "Truth, Fakery and Madness." *The Times,* 8 July 1987, 18.

———. "Juggernaut Runs Out of Steam." *The Times,* 3 April 1989, 15.

———. "Charmless Dream Redeemed." *The Times,* 10 August 1990, 18.

Kliman, Bernice. "The Hall/Hoffman *Merchant.*" *Shakespeare Bulletin* 8:2 (Spring 1990): 11–13.

Kreiswirth, Sandra. "*Richard II* takes modern look at political power." *Daily Breeze,* 26 April 1992, D-5.

Lacey, Liam. "Ages-old Hypocrisy Still Rings True." *Globe & Mail* (Ontario), 17 August 1992.

Langham, Michael. Interviewed by Pat Quigley. *Stratford for Students* (Autumn 1992): 6–7.

Lapworth, Paul. "Gentlemen and Players." *Stratford Herald,* 10 April 1992.

———. "A Marvelous *Tale.*" *Stratford Herald,* 27 June 1992.

Laroque, François. "Twelfth Night." *Cahiers Elisabethains* 32 (October 1987): 106–9.

Lewis, Peter. "Crowning of a Clown Prince: Interview with Simon Russell Beale." *Sunday Times,* 2 August 1992, Arts, 6–7.

Little, Arthur L., Jr. "*Richard II* and the Essence of Rebellion: A Multicultural Inquiry." *Performing Arts* (Los Angeles, 1992): 8–9.

Litvak, Joseph. "What Is Deconstruction?" Lecture. Bowdoin College, 4 March 1985.

Loehnis, Dominic. "Hall's not so well." *Sunday Telegraph*, 5 July 1992.

Logan, Robert A. "*A Midsummer Night's Dream* and *King Lear.*" *Marlowe Society of America Newsletter* 10:2 (Fall 1990): 5–7.

Maguin, Francois. "*Hamlet.*" *Cahiers Elisabethains* 26 (October 1984): 123–25.

Maguin, Jean-Marie. "*King Lear.*" *Cahiers Elisabethains* 38 (October 1990): 86–87.

Marc, David. "Understanding Television." *Atlantic*, August 1984, 33–44.

Mason, M. S. "Kaleidoscope of World Drama." *Christian Science Monitor*, 26 June 1992.

Massey, Daniel. Quoted in *Players of Shakespeare*, edited by Russell Jackson and Robert Smallwood. Cambridge: Cambridge University Press, 1988.

Mathewson, George. "*Measure for Measure* Addresses Matters of Concern." *Sarnia Observer* (Ontario), 17 August 1992.

Mazer, Cary. "Shakespeare, the Reviewer, and the Theatre Historian." *Shakespeare Quarterly* 36:5 (1985): 648–61.

———. "The People's Light and Theatre Company's *Hamlet.*" *Shakespeare Bulletin* 6:2 (1988): 14.

———. "The (Historical) Actor and the Text." *Shakespeare Bulletin* 10:1 (Winter 1992): 18–20.

———. Letter to author, 31 December 1992.

McElroy, Bernard. "Odd Couple: *Hamlet* and *Rosancrantz and Guildenstern* at the New Jersey Shakespeare Festival." *Shakespeare Quarterly* 40:1 (Spring 1989): 94–96.

McGarry, Peter. "Shakespeare Company's *Macbeth.*" *Coventry Evening Telegraph*, 20 February 1992.

———. "An impressive vision of a confused tale." *Coventry Evening Telegraph*, 1 July 1992.

———. "Folklore tale of hits and misses." *Coventry Evening Telegraph*, 2 July 1992.

McGill, Stewart. "A Sulky Toad: Interview with Simon Russell Beal." *What's On*, 14 August 1992, 13.

McGuire, Philip C. *Speechless Dialect.* Berkeley: University of California Press, 1985.

McKerrow, R. B. "The Elizabethan Printer and Dramatic Manuscripts." *The Library* 4: 12 (1931): 255–75.

Micheli, Linda McJ. "Reading the Script: Some Aims and Assumptions of Performance-oriented Criticism." *Shakespeare Bulletin* 8:2 (Spring 1990): 31–33.

Miller, Daryl H. "*Richard*, a rare play in rare form." *Daily News: LA Life*, 24 April 1992, 23.

Milne, Kirsty. "*The Taming of the Shrew.*" *Sunday Telegraph*, 5 April 1992.

———. "Tragedy on a tide of balloons." *Sunday Telegraph*, 5 July 1992.

———. "Cockroach without a cause." *Sunday Telegraph*, 16 August 1992.

Morley, Sheridan. "Hottest Plays of the Summer." *International Herald Tribune*, 1 August 1990, 11.

———. "In 'Mother Tongue,' Language to Bash by." *Intenational Herald Tribune*, 12 August 1992, 14.

Morris, Tom. "*King Lear.*" *Times Literary Supplement,* 24–30 August 1990, 896.

Mullaney, Steven. "Review of *Shakespearean Negotiations.*" *Shakespeare Quarterly* 40 (1989): 495–500.

Murray, David. "*As You Like It.*" *Financial Times,* 24 April 1992.

Nathan, David. "*The Taming of the Shrew.*" *Jewish Chronicle,* 10 April 1992.

———. "*All's Well that Ends Well.*" *Jewish Chronicle,* 10 July 1992.

Neill, Michael. "Unproper Beds: Race, Adultery, and the Hideous in *Othello.*" *Shakespeare Quarterly* 40 (1989): 383–412.

Newman, Karen. "'And Wash the Ethiop White'." In *Shakespeare Reproduced,* edited by Jean Howard and Marion O'Connor. New York: Metheun, 1987.

Nicholls, Graham. *Measure for Measure: Text & Performance.* London: MacMillan, 1986.

Nightingale, Benedict. "A Fine Summer for Raging in the Storm." *Times Saturday Review,* 23 June 1990.

———. "A Very Modern Nightmare." *The Times,* 26 June 1990, 20.

———. "Suburban Savagery within a Sanitized City." *The Times,* 7 July 1990, 25.

———. "Clowning in All Seriousness." *The Times,* 27 July 1990, 20.

———. "*The Taming of the Shrew.*" *The Times,* 3 April 1992.

———. "Subdued Light on Love's Follies." *The Times,* 24 April 1992.

———. "Risks Rewarded by Enchantment." *The Times,* 7 July 1992.

———. "Hall Thrives on Moral Ambiguity." *The Times,* 10 July 1992.

———. "Dreaming in the Goo." *The Times,* 11 July 1992, Arts, 4.

———. "Rise & Fall of a Depraved Clown." *The Times,* 13 August 1992.

———. "Princely and Noble in Lunacy." *The Times,* 21 December 1992.

———. "*Richard III* at the Warehouse." *The Times,* 10 February 1993.

Noble, Adrian, ed. *The Plantagenets.* London: Faber and Faber, 1988.

O'Brien, Robert. "*Twelfth Night.*" *Plays & Players,* August 1989, 30–31.

O'Connor, Thomas. "Grammer Shines in Updated *Richard II.*" *Orange County Register,* 24 April 1992.

O'Keeffe, Brendan. "*The Taming of the Shrew.*" *What's On,* 8 April 1992.

Osborne, Charles. "Madness Reigns in a Paper Hat." *Daily Telegraph,* 30 July 1990, 17.

Paton, Maureen. "Disastrous revenge of hen-pecked Husband." *Daily Express,* 2 April 1992.

———. "A surly swine in love." *Daily Express,* 6 July 1992.

———. "Slinging mud at a dream of a fairy story." *Daily Express,* 10 July, 1992.

———. "Waspish Beale is the king of villains." *Daily Express,* 12 August 1992.

Pearce, Jill. "*Antony and Cleopatra.*" *Cahiers Elisabethains* 32 (October 1987): 104–5.

———. "*Richard III.*" *Cahiers Elisabethains* 38 (October 1990): 96–98.

———. "*King Lear.*" *Cahiers Elisabethains* 38 (October 1990): 98–99.

Pennington, Michael. Quoted in *Players of Shakespeare* I, edited by Philip Brockbank, 115–28. Cambridge: Cambridge University Press, 1985.

Peter, John. "The RSC *Hamlet.*" *Sunday Times,* 30 April 1989, C-8.

———. "Hoffman's Shylock." *Sunday Times,* 4 June 1989, C-9.

———. *"As You Like It."* *Sunday Times,* 26 April 1992.

———. "A touch of true evil." *Sunday Times,* 16 August 1992.

Pinkston, William. Letter to author. 10 December 1992.

Pitcher, John. "Edges of Darkness." *Times Literary Supplement,* 15 May 1987, 518.

Pollack, Joe. "Chicago Cachet." *St. Louis Post-Dispatch,* 14 June 1992, Arts & Entertainment, 3 and 6.

Porter, Peter. "Clear-cut Comedy." *Times Literary Supplement,* 10 July 1992, 18.

Portman, Jamie. "Bard's Blast at Harassment Timeless." *Windsor Star* (Ontario), 17 August 1992.

Potter, Lois. "Realism Versus Nightmare: Problems of Staging *The Duchess of Malfi.*" In *The Triple Bond: Plays, Mainly Shakespearean, in Performance,* edited by Joseph Price, 170–89. University Park: Pennsylvania State University Press, 1975.

———. "Into the Abyss." *Times Literary Supplement,* 5–11 May 1989, 487.

———. "A Country of the Mind." *Times Literary Supplement,* 3–9 August 1990, 825.

Price, Joseph, ed. *The Triple Bond: Plays, Mainly Shakespearean, in Performance.* University Park: Pennsylvania State University Press, 1975.

Proctor, Roy. "Hulce's Hamlet is Endearing, But in need of Stature." *Richmond Times-Dispatch,* 24 November 1992.

Prosser, Eleanor. *Hamlet and Revenge.* Stanford, Calif.: Stanford University Press, 1967.

Provenzano, Tom. "The Toast of the Taper as Richard II." *Drama-Logue* (Hollywood, Calif.), 7–13 May 1992.

Ratcliffe, Michael. *"Merchant* without content." *Observer,* 4 June 1989, 44.

Rabkin, Norman. *Shakespeare and the Problem of Meaning.* Chicago: University of Chicago Press, 1981.

Reade, Simon. *"The Taming of the Shrew."* *City Limits,* 16 April 1992.

Reaume, Brad. "Play's a Measure of Fine Acting." *Canadian Champion,* 9 September 1992.

Reid, Robert. "Well-measured Success." *Kitchner-Waterloo Record,* 15 August 1992.

Reiner, Jay. *"Richard II."* *Hollywood Reporter,* 24 April, 1992.

Reynolds, Oliver. "Kiss of Life." *Times Literary Supplement,* 10 April 1992, 18.

Reynolds, Peter, *Shakespeare: Text into Performance.* London: Penguin, 1991.

Rich, Frank. "View of London's Shakespeare." *New York Times,* 21 June 1989, 15.

———. "Of Dueling Lears and a Fascist Richard III." *New York Times,* 8 August 1990, C11 and C16.

———. "Branagh's Hamlet as a Young Conservative." *New York Times,* 24 December 1992, C9 and C14.

Richards, David. "Three Faces of Richard III." *New York Times,* 7 October 1990, H5 and H30.

Robinson, Gill. *"The Taming of the Shrew."* *Stratford Observer,* 10 April 1992.

Rogoff, Gordon. "Playing With Ire." *Village Voice,* 23 January 1990, 97.

Rose, Linda. "Linda Live." KWNK Radio, California. 30 April 1992.

Rosenberg, Marvin. "Subtext in Shakespeare." In *Shakespeare and the Sense of Performance*, pp. 79–90.

———. *The Masks of King Lear*. Newark: University of Delaware Press, 1972.

———. *The Masks of Hamlet*. Newark: University of Delaware Press, 1992.

Rothstein, Mervyn. "For Actress in *The Merchant* Hatred of Portia Turns to Love." *New York Times*, 2 January 1990, C13 and C17.

Royal Court Theatre. Program for *King Lear*. London, 1993.

Royal Shakespeare Company. Program for *Hamlet*. London, 1992.

Ruby, Michelle. "*Measure for Measure* Timely Play." *Simcoe Reformer*, 4 September 1992.

Russell, Thomas. "The Renaissance Theatre Company in Los Angeles, 1990." *Shakespeare Quarterly* 41:4 (Winter 1990): 502–07.

Rutherford, Malcolm. "A Brechtian *Macbeth*." *Financial Times Weekend*, 1–2 February 1992.

———. "*All's Well that Ends Well*." *Financial Times*, 2 July 1992.

———. "A Winter's Tale." *Financial Times*, 3 July 1992.

———. "Night of errours." *Financial Times*, 10 July 1992.

———. "*Richard III*." *Financial Times*. 11 February 1993.

S., P. J. "*The Merchant of Venice*." *Cahiers Elisabethains* 36 (October 1989): 92–5.

———. "*A Midsummer Night's Dream*." *Cahiers Elisabethains* 36 (October 1989): 108–11.

———. "*Measure for Measure*." *Cahiers Elisabethains* 38 (October 1990): 79–81.

———. "*The Merchant of Venice*." *Cahiers Elisabethains* 40 (October 1991): 92–95.

———. "*A Midsummer Night's Dream*." *Cahiers Elisabethains* 37 (October 1989): 109–11.

Shaughnessy, Robert. "Theatre." *Critical Survey*, 1989, 100.

Sherbo, Arthur, ed. *Johnson on Shakespeare*. New Haven: Yale University Press, 1966.

Shrimpton, Nicholas. "Shakespeare Performances, 1981–2." *Shakespeare Survey* 36 (1983): 149–55.

Shuttleworth, Ian. "*As You Like It*." *City Limits*, 30 April 1992.

———. "RSC at Stratford." *City Limits*, 9 July 1992.

———. "Dream." *City Limits*, 16–23 July 1992.

———. "Hamlet." *City Limits*, 21–28 December 1992.

Silverman, Stanley. Interviewed by Pat Quigley. *Stratford for Students* (Autumn 1992): 8–9.

Slater, Douglas. "This giant of a *Shrew*." *Daily Mail*, 7 April 1992.

———. "Nettles grasps the great demon." *Daily Mail*, 7 July 1992.

Smallwood, Robert. "Shakespeare at Stratford-upon-Avon, 1988." *Shakespeare Quarterly* 40:1 (Spring 1989): 83–94.

———. "Shakespeare at Stratford-upon-Avon, 1989 (Part I)." *Shakespeare Quarterly* 41:1 (Spring 1990): 101–13.

———. "Shakespeare at Stratford-upon-Avon, 1989 (Part II)." *Shakespeare Quarterly* 41:4 (Winter 1990): 491–99.

———. "Shakespeare at Stratford-upon-Avon, 1990." *Shakespeare Quarterly* 42:3 (Fall 1991): 345–59.

Smith, Bruce R. "Recent Studies in Elizabethan and Jacobean Drama." *Studies in English Literature* 33: 2 (Spring 1993).

Smith, Matthew. "Stratford Production Measures Up." *Ingersoll Times*, 19 August 1992.

Speaight, Robert. "Shakespeare in Britain." *Shakespeare Quarterly* 21:4 (Autumn 1970): 439–47.

Spencer, Charles. *"The Taming of the Shrew."* *Daily Telegraph*, 3 April 1992.

———. *"As You Like It."* *Daily Telegraph*, 24 April 1992.

———. "A not-so-well *All's Well*." *Daily Telegraph*, 2 July 1992.

———. "Breath of fresh air." *Daily Telegraph*, 3 July 1992.

———. "Beyond slapstick into midsummer magic." *Daily Telegraph*, 13 July 1992.

———. "Poison and laughter." *Daily Telegraph*, 13 August 1992, 13.

———. "A Hamlet of hidden mysteries." *Daily Telegraph*, 21 December, 1992.

Sprinchorn, Evert. "An Intermediate Stage Level in Elizabethan Theatre." *Theatre Notebook* 48:2 (1992): 73–94.

States, Bert O. *Great Reckonings in Little Rooms: On the Phemonenology of Theater.* Berkeley: University of California Press, 1985.

Staunton, Denis. "Bound Upon a Wheel of Fire." *The European*, 29 July 1990, 2–10.

Steele, Kenneth B. "The Stratford, Ontario, Festival 1992: A Canadian's Overview." *"Shakespeare Bulletin* 10:4 (Fall 1992): 13–17.

Stern, Jeffrey. *"King Lear:* The Transference of the Kingdom." *Shakespeare Quarterly* 41 (1990): 299–308.

Styan, J. L. *Drama, Stage and Audience.* Cambridge: Cambridge University Press, 1975.

———. "Psychology in the Study of Drama: The Negative and the Positive." *College Literature* 5:2 (Spring 1978): 77–93.

———. "Stage Space and the Shakespeare Experience." *Shakespeare and the Sense of Performance*, pp. 195–209.

Suczek, Alex. "Shakespeare's Study of Corruption Still Measures Up." *Grosse Pointe News*, 3 September 1992.

Tannen, Deborah. *You Just Don't Understand.* New York: Ballantine Books, 1990.

Taylor, Gary. *Reinventing Shakespeare.* London: Hogarth, 1990.

Taylor, Neil. *"The Taming of the Shrew."* *Plays International*, June 1992, 23.

Taylor, Paul. "Shakespeare Blitzkrieg." *Independent*, 1 February 1992.

———. "The toffs and the toughs." *Independent*, 3 April 1992.

———. *"As You Like It."* *Independent*, 24 April 1992.

———. "Marriage of two minds." *Independent*, 2 July 1992.

———. "Noble's novelty shop." *Independent*, 3 July 1992.

———. "Mud, mud, inglorious mud." *Independent*, 10 July 1992.

———. "King of comedy." *Independent*, 14 August 1992.

———. "Long sad tale of a great Dane." *Independent*, 21 December 1992.

Thalbach, Katharina. Remarks at the Goethe Institute, London, 3 February 1992.

Thompson, Ann. *King Lear.* Atlantic Highlands, N.J.: Humanities Press, 1988.

Thompson, Marvin, and Ruth Thompson, eds. *Shakespeare and the Sense of Performance.* Newark: University of Delaware Press, 1989.

Thornber, Robin. "Bogdanov's *Macbeth.*" *The Guardian,* 27 February 1992.

Thornton, Salley. "Yesterday's Play Brings Home Today's Issues." *Brighton-Pittsford Post,* 19 August 1992.

Tinker, Jack. "*As You Like It.*" *Daily Mail,* 23 April 1992.

———. "Wallowing in a not so glorious mudbath." *Daily Mail,* 10 July 1992, 10.

———. "Masterful Branagh claims crown as great Hamlet of our time." *Daily Mail,* 19 December 1992.

Trewin, J. C. *Going to Shakespeare.* London: Allen & Unwin, 1978.

———. *Five & Eighty Hamlets.* London: Hutchinson, 1987.

Unger, Arthur. "Derek Jacobi: A Special Kind of Hamlet." *Christian Science Monitor,* 7 November 1980, 19.

Vollenklee, Marcus. Remarks at the Goethe Institute, London, 3 February 1992.

Virey, Pierre. "*King Lear.*" *Cahiers Elisabethains* 32 (October 1987): 80–83.

Wall, Stephen. "A Sense of Restriction." *Times Literary Supplement,* 10–16 August 1990, 848.

Waller, Gary. "Review." *Shakespeare Quarterly* 43:1 (Spring 1992): 103.

Wardle, Irving. "Electrifying Detail and Tragic Exhilaration." *The Times,* 11 April 1987, 14.

———. "National Family at War." *The Times,* 24 October 1988, 21.

———. "*The Merchant of Venice.*" *The Times,* 2 June 1989.

———. "Court without Cobwebs." *The Times,* 25 November 1989, 41.

———. "Three First Persons Singular." *Independent on Sunday,* 2 February 1992.

———. "*The Taming of the Shrew.*" *Independent on Sunday,* 5 April 1992.

———. "*As You Like It.*" *Independent on Sunday,* 26 April 1992.

———. "Subterranean homesick blues." *Independent on Sunday,* 5 July 1992.

———. "A Strange Case of Swamp Fever." *Independent on Sunday,* 12 July 1992.

———. "Terrifying Richard III." *Independent on Sunday,* 16 August 1992.

———. "Theatre." *Independent on Sunday,* 20 December 1992.

———. *Theatre Criticism.* London: Routledge, 1992.

Warren, Roger. "Shakespeare in England: 1983." *Shakespeare Quarterly* 34:4 (Winter 1983): 457.

———. "Shakespeare in England, 1986–87." *Shakespeare Quarterly* 38:4 (1987): 359–65.

Watermeier, Daniel J. "*Measure for Measure.*" *Shakespeare Bulletin* 10:4 (Fall 1992): 20–21.

Webster, Margaret. *Shakespeare Without Tears.* New York: McGraw-Hill, 1942.

Weil, Herbert S., Jr. "On Expectation and Surprise: Shakespeare's Construction of Character." *Shakespeare Survey* 34 (1981): 39–50.

Weimann, Robert. "Bifold Authority in Shakespeare's Theatre." *Shakespeare Quarterly* 39:4 (Winter 1988): 401–417.

Weiss, Alfred. "The Edinburgh International Festival, 1990." *Shakespeare Quarterly* 42:4 (Winter 1991): 462–71.

Weiss, Hedy. "Troupe's Two Shows Are No Great Shakes." *Chicago Sun-Times*, 1 June 1992, 23 and 26.

Wells, Stanley. "Goes Out, Followed by a Furry Animal." *Times Literary Supplement*, 20 February 1981, 197.

——. "Acting Out Illyria." *Times Literary Supplement*, 17 July 1987, 770.

——. "Shakespeare Performances in London and Stratford-upon-Avon, 1986–7." *Shakespeare Survey* 41 (1989): 159–81.

——. "Shakespeare Production in England in 1989." *Shakespeare Survey* 43 (1991): 183–203.

Welsford, Enid. "The Fool in *King Lear.*" Quoted in Frank Kermode. *Four Centuries of Shakespearian Criticism.* New York: Avon, 1965.

West, Robert. *Shakespeare and the Outer Mystery.* Lexington: University Press of Kentucky, 1968.

Wiggins, Martin. "Shakespeare's Life, Times, and Stage." *Shakespeare Survey* 45 (1993): 175–92.

Willems, Michele. "Verbal-Visual, Verbal-Pictorial, or Textual-Televisual? Reflections on the BBC Shakespeare Series." *Shakespeare Survey* 39 (1986): 91–102.

Williams, Gary Jay. "On Theatre Criticism." *Shakespeare Quarterly* 35:5 (1985): 598–601.

Williams, Raymond. *Television: Technology and Cultural Form.* London: Fontana/Collins, 1974.

Williams, Susanne. "A Real Romp." *Burton Mail*, 24 April 1992.

Williamson, Jane. "The Duke and Isabella on the Modern Stage." In *The Triple Bond*, edited by Joseph Price, 149–69. University Park: Pennsylvania State University Press, 1975.

Williamson, Richard. "Nettles lacks a bit of sting." *Sun Mercury*, 5 July 1992.

Willson, Robert, Jr. "Why Teach Shakespeare? A Reconsideration." *Shakespeare Quarterly* 41:4 (Summer 1990): 206–10.

Woddis, Carole, *"All's Well that Ends Well."* *What's On*, 8 July 1992.

Wolf, Matt. "Lepage in Britain." *Theatrum* (Sept./Oct. 1992): 14.

Wolf, Stephen. "Lost in Multicultural Space." *Downtown News*, 27 April 1992, 15 and 17.

Worthen, William. "Deeper Meanings and Theatrical Technique: The Rhetoric of Performance Criticism." *Shakespeare Quarterly* 40 (1989): 441–55.

——. Review of *Shakespeare and the Sense of Performance. Shakespeare Studies* 21 (1993): 300–317.

Woudhuysen, H. R. "Savage Laughter." *Times Literary Supplement*, 22 May 1987, 551.

Wright, George T. "An Almost Oral Art: Shakespeare's Language on Stage and Page." *Shakespeare Quarterly* 43:2 (Summer 1992): 159–69.

Wright, Louis. "Introduction to *Othello.*" The Folger *Othello.* New York: Washington Square Press, 1957.

Zitner, Sheldon. "Wooden O's in Plastic Boxes." *University of Toronto Quarterly* 51 (Fall 1981): 1–12.

Index

Actor's Equity, 185
Adams, Henry, 186, 246
Aeschylus, 244
Alchemist, 197
Alexander, Bill, 26, 83, 85, 86, 95, 96, 97, 99, 100, 103, 104, 220, 221, 222, 223, 224, 225, 226, 246
Allam, Roger, 81, 82
All for Love, 73
All's Well That Ends Well, 26, 212–17
Alter, Iska, 153
Ambrose, Bert, 236
American Repertory Theatre (Massachusetts), 107, 203, 204
Anton, George, 241
Antony and Cleopatra, 19, 22, 49, 67-74, 78
Antoon, A. J., 22, 233
Apsion, Anabelle, 240
Arditti, Michael, 161, 162
Ardolino, Frank, 240n
Arena Theater (D.C.), 20, 95, 97, 185
Aristotle, 27, 149, 161
Armin, Robert, 229
Arnold, Matthew, 49
Artaud, Antonin, 33, 160
As You Like It, 28, 142, 178, 184, 192–94, 217–20, 258
Atkins, Eileen, 84
Augustine, 165, 233

Bale, Doug, 179
Baley, Clare, 196
Bara, Theda, 145
Barbican Theatre, 88, 161, 248, 251
Barge, Gillian, 258
Barnet, Sylvan, 39
Barroll, J. Leeds, 37
Barrow, Craig, 257
Barton, John, 23, 35, 39, 48, 91, 109, 186, 187, 188, 190
Battis, Emery, 205

Bawcutt, N. W., 178
Beale, Simon Russell, 211, 232, 240, 241, 242, 243, 244, 246, 247, 248
Beckerman, Bernard, 27, 32, 175
Beckett, Samuel, 39
Bedford, Brian, 179, 180
Bennett, Constance, 236
Bennett, Jill, 207
Bennett, Rodney, 36, 109
Bennett, William, 75
Berger, Thomas, 208
Bergman, Ingmar, 105n
Bergman, Ingrid, 179
Bergson, Henri, 25
Berkowitz, Gerald, 70–71, 73, 74–75, 97, 150, 238–39, 240
Berry, Ralph, 27, 173, 174, 177, 182, 203
Betterton, Thomas, 24
Bevington, David, 135, 137, 142
Big Ben, 237
Billington, Michael, 101, 103, 109, 111, 146, 147, 149, 156, 159, 160, 199, 216, 220, 221, 224, 228–29, 243, 246, 255
Birmingham Repertory Company (G.B.), 249, 252
Bissonnette, Lise, 201
Blackstone Theater (Chicago), 135, 136
Blake, William, 27
Blane, Sue, 94
B'nai B'rith, 104
Bob Jones University, 184, 192
Bogart, Humphrey, 179
Bogdanov, Michael, 18, 36, 156, 167–72, 173, 259
Bond, Samantha, 218, 219, 220, 226, 227
Booth, Edwin, 34
Booth, Stephen, 208
Borot, Luc, 79, 105n

Boxer, Stephen, 247, 248
Boy Scouts, 235
Bradley, A. C., 37, 76, 151, 161, 188
Bradley, David, 84, 145–46, 234, 249
Branagh, Kenneth, 28, 49, 135, 136, 142, 143, 148, 149, 185, 249–50, 252, 254, 255
Brecht, Bertolt, 39, 75, 156, 161, 170, 191, 250
Breeslaw, Bernard, 98
Brennan, Marion, 225
Briers, Richard, 98, 136, 140–41, 143, 255
Brook, Peter, 17, 18, 27, 40, 75, 76, 77, 94, 145, 147, 148, 161, 162, 199, 231
Brook, Faith, 251
Brooke, Nicholas, 158
Brooke, Rupert, 200
Brooklyn Academy of Music, 234
Brown, J. R., 27
Brown, Stewart, 182
Brown Shirts, 236
Bryant, Michael, 73
Buller, Francesca, 205
Bulman, James, 27
Bundy, Ted, 245
Burford, Ann, 75
Burghley, William Cecil, 205
Burton, Richard, 34, 202, 207
Buttonhole Theatre (London), 156, 163, 171
Byles, Joan Montgomery, 230

Caird, John, 92, 94
Carlisle, John, 86, 95
Carstensen, Candy, 190
Casablanca, 179
"Castle of the Spider's Web," 157
Cats, 92
CBS, 34
Ceauşescu, Nicolae, 230, 237
Chamberlain, Neville, 237, 239
Chamberlin, Lee, 185
Chambers, David, 20, 185
Chaplin, Charles, 251
Chapman, Paul, 89
Charles, Prince of Wales, 211, 231, 249
Charleston, Ian, 253
Cheers, 189
Chekhov, Anton, 30, 48, 84, 255

Chekhov, Michael, 180
Chicago Bears, 195
Chippendale, 147
Chitty, Allison, 67, 73
Chomsky, Noam, 42–43, 161
Christopher, James, 218, 219
Church, Madeline, 153
Church, Tony, 153
"Cinderella," 230
Civil War (American), 240
Clayton, Thomas, 27, 136, 183
Clinton, Bill, 189
Coe, Peter, 47
Coleridge, Samuel Taylor, 178
Colley, Kenneth, 177
Collings, David, 234
Collins, Michael J., 153, 154, 177–78, 226
Commission for the Protection of the French Language (Quebec), 201
Cook, Dorothy, 107
Cook, Judith, 177
Cook, Wayne, 107
Coriolanus, 245
Cotton, Oliver, 89
Coveney, Michael, 147, 196–97, 199, 216, 219, 225, 228, 229, 240, 241, 243
Cox, Alan, 227
Cox, Brian, 79, 80, 143–44, 149–53, 255–56
Cox, Murray, 254
Cromwell, Oliver, 99
Cronyn, Hume, 21
Crowl, Sam, 43–44
Cuilei, Liviu, 197
Curry, Julian, 176
Cymbeline, 20, 95–97, 185

Dachau, 181
Daniels, Ron, 88, 104, 105, 106, 107, 203, 204, 205, 242, 252, 254
Dante, 168, 182
Dash, Irene, 99, 102
Davies, Michael, 216, 229
Dawson, Anthony, 27
Death of a Salesman, 26, 103
De Fougerolles, Ludmilla, 201
De Jersey, Peter, 218
De Jongh, Nicholas, 197, 199, 214, 215, 219, 224–25, 229, 254, 255
Dench, Jeffrey, 43

Dench, Judy, 67–71, 155
Desert Storm, 169
Dessen, Alan, 21, 22, 27, 34, 41, 69n, 70, 71, 72, 74, 78, 79, 89, 90, 96–97, 106, 108, 109, 143, 144, 146, 148, 152, 165, 212, 213, 222, 233, 235, 237
DeVine, Lawrence, 182
Dexter, Sally, 94, 146, 198
"Disabled," 234
Disneyland, 243
Dodber, John, 97
Dodsworth, Martin, 99–100, 102–3, 148, 149, 215, 217
Dominion Theatre (London), 135
Donahue, Patricia, 138, 140, 141
Donaldson, Peter, 46
Donmar Warehouse (London), 80, 97, 235
Dormandy, Simon, 240, 244, 248–49
Dorn, Franchelle Stewart, 206, 207
Dowling, Mike, 241
Downie, Penny, 89
Dr. Faustus, 80
Drake, Sylvie, 141–42, 190–91
Drinkwater, John, 174
Dryden, John, 24, 73
Dublin, 159
Dubrovnik, 84
Duchene, Kate, 247, 248
Duchess of Malfi, 263–64
Duguid, Lindsay, 220
Duke, Marion, 181
Dunbar, Adrian, 256
Dunbar, Mary Judith, 31
Dungate, Ron, 105, 111

Eden, Anthony, 239
Edmonds, Richard, 229, 230, 246
Edward, Duke of Windsor, 233
Edward II, 241
Edward IV, 88, 89
Edwardes, Jane, 215, 216, 217, 222, 248, 255
Edwards, Rob, 251
Egan, Robert, 184, 187, 188, 189, 190, 191, 202
Eisenhower, Dwight, 39
Elder, Steven, 167
Eliot, T. S., 191
Elizabeth I, 239

"Elizabethan World Picture," 25, 146, 160
Elliott, Michael, 20
Elmer's Glue, 76
Engel, Susan, 145
Engles, Johan, 219
English Shakespeare Company, 156
Enoch, Russell, 106
Erstein, Hap, 206
Everett, Barbara, 69n, 70, 73–74
"Eyewitness Video," (NBC), 33
Eyre, Richard, 232, 236, 237, 238, 240, 240n, 242, 245, 246, 260

Faithfull, Marianne, 206
Falklands, 169
Farrell, Nicholas, 82, 86
Father Knows Best, 177
Feld, Bruce, 190
Feore, Colm, 180
Fielding, David, 147
Fiennes, Ralph, 91, 146
Findlay, Deborah, 86, 100
Fisher, James, 71
Fisher, Paul, 95
Fitzgerald, Ann, 216, 229, 245–46
Fitzgerald, F. Scott, 84
Fitzpatrick, Tim, 188
"Flash Gordon," 219
Foakes, R. H., 134
Folger Theater (D.C.), 202, 208
Follows, Megan, 202
Foster, Julia, 89
Foucault, Michael, 37
Freeman, Morgan, 202
Freud, Clement, 101
Freud, Sigmund, 146, 196, 225
Frey, Charles, 24
Frye, Northrop, 26, 30
Fuzier, J., 85

Galen, 261
Galileo, 75
Gardner, Lyn, 215
Garvie, Elizabeth, 31
Geckle, George, 200
Geelan, Chris, 164
George, Andrew, 224
George Inn (London), 197
Ghosts, 185
Gibson, Mel, 202
Gielgud, John, 21, 207, 253

Gilbert, Miriam, 221
Glace, John Wayne, 245
Goddard, Harold, 43
Godfrey, Patrick, 106, 203
Goldberg, Jonathan, 43
Golden Fleece, 99
Goldman, Michael, 27, 50, 203
Goldstraw, Aidan, 219
Goy-Blanquet, Dominique, 82–83, 91, 92
Grammer, Kelsey, 189, 190, 191, 202
Grant, Steve, 196
Granville-Barker, Harley, 18, 72
Gratzia, Margaret de, 47
Gray, Charles, 31
Great Gatsby, 98
Greenblatt, Stephen, 37–38, 46
Gresham's Law, 197
Grier, Christopher, 255
Grimley, Terry, 214, 216–17
Gross, John, 111, 219
Gurr, Andrew, 258

Hakluyt, Richard, 38
Halifax, Edward, 239
Halio, Jay, 20, 27, 41, 137, 139, 140, 142–43, 147, 150, 153
Hall, Peter, 18, 20, 32, 33, 34, 67–68, 69, 70, 72, 73–74, 78, 88, 99, 100, 101, 103, 196, 202, 212, 215, 216, 245
Hamlet, 19, 21, 24, 28, 34, 35, 36, 37, 45–46, 48, 70, 87, 88, 104–12, 134, 198, 201–8, 223, 230–31, 242, 247, 249–55, 259, 261, 262, 263
Hamlet (BBC), 107, 109, 262
Hamlet (Q1), 197
Hammond, Anthony, 236
Hancock, Phyllida, 220, 227
Hands, Terry, 23, 43, 81, 82, 89, 91, 189
Hardy, Thomas, 148
Hare, David, 74–77, 138, 259
Harkins, Tom, 189
Harris, Amanda, 225
Harris, Jarred, 105
Harrison, Cathryn, 218
Hassan, Ihab, 43–44
Hassell, R. Chris, 232
Hawkes, Terry, 211
Hayes, Elliott, 180
Hazlitt, William, 24, 103

Heathrow, 86
Heeley, Desmond, 175–76, 181
Hegel, Georg W. F., 161
Heinrich I (Saxony), 239
Heller, Joseph, 195
Henreid, Paul, 179
Henry, David, 94
Henry, William A., 101, 237–38
Henry IV, 36, 49, 70, 91
Henry IV, Part Two, 213
Henry V, 23, 42–45, 49, 81, 95, 185, 189, 239, 249
Henry VI, 88
Henry VI: Part One, 109
Henry VI: Part Two, 34, 89–90, 92, 246
Hepburn, Katherine, 68
Herlie, Eileen, 207, 251
Herman, Jan, 202, 204
Hewison, Robert, 197–98, 216, 223, 229, 230
Heys, Gerard, 166
Higgins, Claire, 94, 106, 145, 207
Higlet, Simon, 86
Hiley, Jim, 69n, 71, 73, 77, 82, 84–85, 86, 90, 92, 99, 100, 103
Hill, Anita, 180
Hilsman, Hoyt, 189–90
Himmler, Heinrich, 76, 239
Hinds, Ciaran, 247, 248
Hirschhorn, Clive, 197
Hitler, Adolf, 46, 186, 232, 233, 234, 235, 240
Hitler Youth, 235
Hoban, James, 228n
Hodgdon, Barbara, 40–41, 45, 50, 200
Hoffman, Dustin, 26, 34, 88, 99, 101–4, 108, 202
Hoffman, Eric, 205
Hogarth, William, 142
Holbein, Hans, 83
Holderness, Graham, 156, 167, 168
Holland, Peter, 80, 144–45, 146–47, 149–50, 151–52, 172, 205, 234, 235, 239
Holmes, Justice Oliver W., 88
Hopkins, Anthony, 39, 70, 71, 73, 76, 77
Hornby, Richard, 77, 103–4, 176, 179, 185
Hoskins, Bob, 39
Hoss, Rudolph, 244

Howard, Alan, 81, 91, 189
Howard, Jean, 258
Howell, Jane, 34, 79, 89
Hughes, Ian, 253
Hulce, Tom, 184, 201, 202, 203, 205, 206, 208
Hull Truck Company, 97
Humpty Dumpty, 76
Hunter, G. K., 141
Hurren, Kenneth, 199, 218, 223, 225
Hytner, Nicholas, 143, 144, 146, 147, 148, 153, 154, 255

Ibsen, Henrik, 30, 105n, 185
Ickley, William, 97
Interpretation of Dreams, 176
Ionesco, Eugene, 161

Jackson, Philip, 256, 257–58
Jackson, Russell, 177
Jacobi, Derek, 107, 109, 110–11, 189, 203, 249
Jacobson, Lynn, 201
Jaeger, Tom, 209
James, Emrys, 91, 262
James, Fraser, 258
James, Feraldine, 100, 101, 102, 104
James, Henry, 252
James, Karyn, 202
James, Peter Fancis, 20, 185
"James Bond," 219
James I of England, 168
Jason, Robert, 189
Jefford, Barbara, 207, 213
Jesson, Paul, 227
Jesuits, 239
Jewesbury, Edward, 137
Jew of Malta, 80
Johnson, Celia, 207
Johnson, Jack, 94
Johnson, Lyndon, 94
Johnson, Richard, 71–72, 213–14
Johnson, Samuel, 43, 165, 214
Jones, Emrys, 41
Jones, Gemma, 227
Jones, Griffith, 155
Jones, James Earl, 34, 47, 185, 190
Jones, Mark Lewis, 246
Jones, Welton, 190
J.P., 67, 69n
Julia, Raul, 185, 258
Julius Caesar, 18, 73, 78, 81–83, 246

Jung, C. G., 140, 198, 200

Kae-Kazim, Hakeem, 80, 100
Kahn, Bridgitte, 94
Kahn, Michael, 201, 202, 203, 204, 205, 206, 208
Kane, John, 218
Kantorowitz, Ernst, 46, 253
Kapital, 156
Karloff, Boris, 248
Kean, Edmund, 103
Kemp, Peter, 111
Kemp, Will, 229
Kendall, Clive, 166
Kennedy Center (D.C.), 234
Kennedy, Dennis, 28n
Kermode, Frank, 140
Kernan, Alvin, 253
Keyishian, Harry, 105, 105n
Keyishian, Marjorie, 105, 105n
Kilmer, Joyce, 200
Kimbrough, Robert, 258
King, Stephen, 167, 253
King, Thomas, 208
King Lear, 21, 24, 35, 37, 74–77, 84, 95, 134–54, 161, 168, 185, 232, 238, 247, 255–60
King Lear (BBC), 258
King John, 80, 216
King's Men, 21
Kingston, Alex, 143, 145
Kingston, Jeremy, 83, 90, 141, 142
Kisson, Jeffrey, 100
Kliman, Bernice W., 102
Kline, Kevin, 34, 202, 204
Knights, L. C., 37
Knox, Patrick, 197
Kohler, Estelle, 39, 78–79, 80, 146
Kott, Jan, 161
Kozintsev, Grigori, 201, 256
Kreiswirth, Sandra, 191
Kübler-Ross, Elisabeth, 167
Kurosawa, Akira, 157
Kyle, Barry, 217

Lacey, Liam, 182
Lahr, Bert, 212
Laing, R. D., 109
Laird, Trevor, 94–95
Langham, Michael, 175, 176, 179, 182
Lapotaire, Jane, 250, 251
Lapworth, Paul, 225, 229, 230

Laroque, F., 79
Laurier, Angela, 196
Lawrence, Bernard, 163
Leary, Timothy, 95
LeBow, Will, 98–99
Leonard, John, 172
Lepage, Robert, 18, 33, 169, 194, 195, 196, 198
Lepage's Glue, 197
Lessner, Anton, 221, 225, 226, 241
Levin, Bernard, 199
Levin, Harry, 262
Lewis, Peter, 244
Lionel trains, 217
Lissek, Leon, 101
Little, Arthur L., 184, 185–86
Litvak, Joseph, 44
Loehnis, Dominic, 215, 216
Logan, Robert, 140, 141
Long, William, 153
Love's Labour's Lost, 37, 84, 87, 175, 217
Lusitania, 105

Macbeth, 18, 21, 24, 25, 28, 33, 36, 76, 155–72, 173, 198, 218, 235, 240, 244, 245, 248, 249, 259
Macbeth (BBC), 160
Macbeth (Classic Theatre TV Production), 167
Magi, 99
Maguin, J.-M., 79, 85, 105, 150
Marc, David, 30
Marcos, Ferdinand, 237
Mark Taper Forum (L.A.), 135, 136, 184, 186, 187, 188, 189, 190, 202
Marlowe, Christopher, 241
Marvel, Elizabeth, 179–80
Marx, Karl, 43, 49, 156
Mason, M. S., 172
Massey, David, 177
Matheson, Eve, 143, 236
Mathewson, George, 181
May Fair, 236
Mazer, Cary, 23, 27, 45, 261–62, 263–64
McCabe, Bill, 94, 220, 221, 227, 229, 230
McCarroll, Earl, 81, 82
McConnell, Steve, 35–36, 98
McCowen, Alec, 98
McDonogh Players, 19

McElroy, Bernard, 106
McEnery, Peter, 89, 91
McGarry, Peter, 171, 215, 230
McGillis, Kelly, 202
McGinity, Terrence, 177
McGuire, Philip, 27, 39, 40, 179
McKellen, Ian, 21, 34, 155, 229, 232, 234, 235, 236, 237, 238, 241, 243, 246, 248, 251
McKenna, Virginia, 207
McKerrow, R. B., 45
McManus, Mark, 82
Measure for Measure, 26, 28, 30, 39, 40, 48, 79, 173–83, 189
Measure for Measure (BBC), 177
Medieval Players (G.B.), 197
Meese, Edmund, 75
Mendes, Sam, 211, 232, 240, 241, 242, 244, 245, 248, 249
Mendonca, Carla, 177
Merchant of Venice, 21, 26, 34, 41, 80, 81, 85–86, 88, 99–104, 178, 216
Merchant of Venice (BBC), 98
Mermaid Theatre (London), 156
Merrimac Theater (Massachusetts), 35, 98–99
Merry Wives of Windsor, 83, 95
Middlemarch, 21
Middleton, Thomas, 265
Midsummer Night's Dream, 19, 28, 74, 86–87, 88, 92–95, 135, 140, 184, 194–201
Miller, Daryl H., 191
Miller, Jonathan, 31, 36, 39, 41, 102, 134–35, 176, 185, 258
Milne, Kirsty, 223, 227, 230, 244, 245
Mirren, Helen, 89, 91
Mitchell, Warren, 98
Moltke, Baron von, 239
Momento Mori, 252
Monmouth Theater (Maine), 81, 82, 208–9, 226
Morley, Sheridan, 146, 151, 195–96, 233
Morris, Cherry, 244, 248
Morris, Tom, 135, 139, 140–41, 142
Mortemore, Sally, 164
Mosley, Oswald, 233
Much Ado About Nothing, 22, 221, 233, 240
Murder in the Cathedral, 191

Mullaney, Steven, 46–47
Munch, Edvard, 139
Murphy, Gerard, 241
Murray, David, 219
Mussolini, Benito, 232, 239

Narnia, 250
Nathan, David, 214, 225
Nebuchadnezzar, 76
Nelligan, Kate, 177
Nettles, John, 226, 229–30
New Jersey Shakespeare Festival, 39
New Criticism, 38
New End Theatre, 156, 163
New York (football) Giants, 195
New Yorker, 180
Newman, Karen, 38
Nichols, Graham, 179
Nightingale, Benedict, 134, 135, 142, 144, 145, 149, 151, 177, 197, 212–13, 215, 217, 222, 227, 230, 235–36, 237, 239, 243, 249, 252
"Night of the Long Knives," 82
Nixon, Richard, 94
Noble, Adrian, 28, 88, 89, 90, 91, 134, 173, 179, 217, 226, 227–28, 229
Norse Table of Heros, 253
Northern Broadsides Company (G.B.), 248, 249
Nunn, Trevor, 34, 72, 73, 155, 161, 248
Nuremburg Party Conference (1934), 82, 232

Oberlander, Marjorie J., 240n
O'Brien, Robert, 98
O'Connor, Thomas, 191
O'Conor, Joseph, 81, 176
O'Donnell, Anthony, 217
Oedipus, 161
O'Hara, David, 95–96
O'Keeffe, Brendan, 223, 225
Old Vic, 84
Olivier Theatre, 67, 70, 74, 77, 82, 102, 245
Olivier, Laurence, 41, 98, 107, 185, 203, 241, 251, 262
One Flew Over the Cuckoo's Nest, 109
O'Neill, Eugene, 30
Open Air Theatre (Regent's Park), 86, 94–95, 142, 198, 218
Orwell, George, 200

Osborne, Charles, 145, 151
Othello, 22, 24, 31, 34, 38, 39, 47, 88, 185, 230, 235, 245, 249
Other Place (G.B.), 34, 80, 88, 95, 96, 173, 176, 232, 235, 240, 243, 245
"Our Gal Sunday," 202
"Our Town," 227
Owen, Wilfred, 234
Oxford Theatre (G.B.), 177

Packard, Tina, 184, 208, 209
Panay, 195
Papp, Joseph, 184, 185, 258
Parfitt, Judy, 207
Parker, Nathaniel, 100
Pasco, Richard, 190
Paton, Maureen, 199, 214, 223–24, 226, 243
Peacham, Henry, 80
Pearce, Jill, 67, 69n, 144, 151
Pearce, Joanne, 250, 251
Pennington, Michael, 109, 170–71, 174, 206, 229
Peter, John, 101, 103, 111–12, 218, 241, 243
Pet Sematary, 253
Pfeiffer, Michelle, 202
Phillips, Robin, 182
Phoenix Theatre, 34, 99, 216
Pickup, Ronald, 82
Pierce, Samuel, 75
Piggot-Smith, Tim, 69, 226
Pinkston, William, 192, 194
Pirandello, Luigi, 221
Pitcher, John, 100
P.J.S., 93, 94, 103
Plantaganents, 88, 90–92
Plummer, Christopher, 34, 47
Plutarch, 73
Poe, Edgar Allan, 165
Polanski, Roman, 159, 160
Pollack, Joe, 172
Porter, Eric, 167
Porter, Peter, 229
Potter, Lois, 21–22, 105n, 108, 110, 234–35, 241–42, 245
Presley, Elvis, 107
Price, Joseph, 22
"Pride and Prejudice" (BBC), 31
Procter, Roy, 202
Prospect Theatre (G.B.), 98
Prosser, David, 175, 180

Prosser, Eleanor, 253
Provensano, Tom, 189
Pryce, Jonathan, 168, 255

Quasimodo, 247
Quayle, Anthony, 36
Quayle, Jenny, 170, 171, 174
Queen Mary, 237

Rabkin, Norman, 43
Ratcliffe, Michael, 102, 103
Reade, Simon, 224
Reagan, Ronald, 46, 76, 186
Reaum, Brad, 181
Reddington, Ian, 164
Redgrave, Corin, 69
Redmond, Siobhan, 138
Reeves, Saskia, 256
Reid, Robert, 181
Reiner, Jay, 191
Rembrandt, 214
Renaissance Players (U.S.), 228
  (footnote)
Return of the Jedi, 219
Reynolds, Oliver, 224, 226
Reynolds, Peter, 27
Rich, Frank, 49, 103, 134, 143, 149,
  152, 235, 238, 249, 251, 254
Richard II, 18, 21, 23, 28, 31, 40, 48,
  82, 168, 184, 185–91, 202
Richard II (BBC), 189
Richard III, 28, 88, 90, 91, 92, 173,
  211, 232–46, 240n, 247–49
Richardson, Ian, 186, 190
Richardson, Tony, 203, 206
Rickman, Alan, 255
Rider, Paul, 97
"Rime of the Ancient Mariner," 178
Rimini, Francesca, 182
Roberts, Simon, 139
Robertson, Pat, 235
"Robin Hood," 219
Robinson, Gill, 220
Rockwell, Norman, 22
Roddy, Ethna, 137
Rodeheaver Auditorium (S.C.), 192
Rogoff, Gordon, 111
Rohm, Ernst, 236
Romeo and Juliet, 35, 40, 172, 212
Ronan, Martin, 97
Rose, Clifford, 254
Rose, Linda, 191

Rosenberg, Marvin, 27, 177, 250, 259
Round House Theatre (G.B.), 203,
  206
Rowe, Nicholas, 35
Royal Court Theatre (London), 28,
  247, 255, 256, 260
Royal Shakespeare Company, 23, 35,
  82, 83, 89, 92, 94, 95, 101, 104, 108,
  109, 111, 143, 144, 145, 147, 152,
  203, 204, 211, 212, 217, 228, 228n,
  246, 252
Russell, Thomas, 136, 137–38,
  139–40, 141
Rutherford, Malcolm, 161, 198,
  214–15, 228, 248
Rutter, Barrie, 248
Rutter, Carol, 177
Ryan, Robert, 68
Rylance, Mark, 88, 106, 107, 108,
  109–10, 111, 203, 204, 205, 252, 255
Ryland, Jack, 206

Saire, Rebecca, 213, 220
Sandhurst, 237
Sartre, Jean Paul, 39
Schiller Theatre (Berlin), 156, 163, 171
Schoenberg, Arnold, 182
Scholfield, Meriel, 97
Scott, Linda Kerr, 147
Serkis, Andy, 256
"Seven Brides for Seven Brothers,"
  219
Shakespeare and Company (Massa-
  chusetts), 208
Shakespeare Theatre (D.C.), 48, 184,
  208
Shaughnessy, Robert, 174
Sher, Anthony, 26, 84–85, 97, 98, 99,
  101, 103, 104, 232, 241, 246, 248
Shrapnel, John, 249–50, 253
Shrimpton, Nicholas, 36, 179
Shuttleworth, Ian, 196, 216, 219, 255
Siberry, Michael, 212, 213
Silverman, Stanley, 183
Slater, Douglas, 224, 229
Slater, Guy, 94
Sloan, Gary, 184, 201, 202, 203, 204,
  206
Smallwood, Robert, 88–89, 91, 92–93,
  94, 96, 105n, 106–7, 108, 109, 110,
  143, 146, 147, 150–51, 177
Smith, Bruce, 18

Smith, Caroline, 86, 87
Smith, Matthew, 181–82
Smith, Peter D., 176
Solomon, 200
Sophocles, 161
Sorvino, Paul, 185
Southern, Daniel, 205
Spanish-American War, 22
Speaight, Robert, 72, 107
Speck, Richard, 245
Spenser, Charles, 197, 214, 215–16, 218, 222–23, 225, 228, 245, 254–55
Spiro, Samantha, 218
Spriggs, Elizabeth, 207
Sprinchorn, Evert, 35
SS, 239
Stafford-Clark, Max, 256, 258
Stangl, Franz, 244
Stanislavsky, Konstantin S., 264
States, Bert O., 25
Staunton, Dennis, 143–44, 146, 150, 151
Steele, Kenneth B., 180
Stern, Jeffrey, 257
Stevens, James, 228n
Stevens, Toby, 212, 213
Stevenson, Juliet, 177, 180
Stewart, Patrick, 73, 101, 107
"Strangers in the Night," 164
Stratford Festival (Ontario), 28, 173, 176, 182, 202
Stratford Theater (Connecticut), 68
Styan, John, 27, 46, 173, 174, 176–77
Sudetenland, 239
Sumpter, Donald, 78, 84
Suszek, Alex, 175, 182
Suzman, Janet, 68, 71
Swann, Robert, 253
Swan Theatre (G.B.), 67, 77–78, 79, 80, 173, 212, 214, 216
Swander, Homer, 69, 153
Swift, Jonathan, 161
"Sympathetic magic," 86

Talbot, Ian, 98
Tamberlaine, 80
Taming of the Shrew, 21, 36, 95, 169, 172, 220–26
Tannen, Deborah, 189
Taylor, Elizabeth, 202
Taylor, Gary, 49, 178
Taylor, Neil, 225

Taylor, Paul, 158, 160, 161, 198–99, 212, 216, 218, 220, 221, 224, 229, 230, 242, 244, 255
Tempest, 22, 94, 178, 194, 265
Thalbach, Katharina, 33, 156, 157, 160–63, 167, 168, 170
Thacker, David, 217, 218
Thatcher, Margaret, 76, 237
Thompson, Ann, 40, 42, 260
Thompson, Emma, 139–40, 141
Thompson, Marvin, 45, 173, 203
Thompson, Ruth, 45, 173, 203
Thompson, Sophie, 213, 214, 215
Thornber, Robin, 171
Throne of Blood, 157
Tieck, Dorothea, 156
Tinker, Jack, 219, 255
Titanic, 75
Titus Andronicus, 67, 77–81, 84, 185, 242
"Trees," 200
Trewin, J. C., 213, 257
Triumph of the Will, 232, 238
Troilus and Cressida, 240, 241
Troughton, David, 96
Twelfth Night, 18, 21, 25, 26, 34, 35–36, 81, 83–85, 97–99, 178, 184, 202, 208–10
Twelfth Night (BBC), 83, 98

Ungar, Arthur, 111

Van Griethuysen, Ted, 205
Van Meter, John, 19
Vickery, John, 188
Virey, Peter, 77
Vollenklee, Marcus, 157
Volpone, 220

Wagner, Richard, 89
Waldo Theater (U.S.), 209
Walker, James, 35
Wall, Stephen, 144, 147–48, 150, 153, 154
Waller, Gary, 30
Wanamaker, Sam, 197
Wardle, Irving, 17, 22, 24, 27, 40, 67, 69n, 70, 73, 77, 79–80, 90, 91, 100, 101–2, 107, 112, 152, 161, 169, 171, 198, 215, 216, 219, 223, 225, 226, 229, 243, 245, 254, 257

Warfield, Wallis, 233
Warner, Deborah, 18, 21, 67, 77, 79,
  140, 143, 144, 145, 146, 156, 148,
  149, 153, 162, 178–79, 211, 216,
  231, 232, 242, 255
Warren, Roger, 69n, 71, 76, 77, 178,
  179
"Wars of the Roses," 91
Warwick University Theatre, 36, 169,
  173
Washington, Denzel, 202
Watergate, 40, 48, 186
Waterloo, 233
Watermeier, Daniel, 180, 181, 182
Watkins, Jason, 260
Watt, James, 75
We Bombed in New Haven, 195
Webster, John, 265
Webster, Margaret, 183
Webster, Paul, 95
Weimann, Robert, 211, 212
Weiss, Alfred, 135, 140, 141, 142
Weiss, Hedy, 171–72
Wells, Stanley, 27, 31, 67, 70, 71, 73,
  77, 78, 79, 80, 81, 82, 83, 84, 85, 86,
  93, 96, 99, 102, 103, 111, 228, 237
Welsford, Enid, 140
West, Roy, 135
Wewelsburg, 239
Whistler, James McNeill, 251
White House, 39
Whitfield, Michael J., 181
Whittington, Harrell, 194

Wiggins, Martin, 37, 47
Wight, Peter, 106, 203
Wight, William, 226
Wilkinson, Tom, 256, 257
Willems, Michele, 31, 34, 36
Williams, Cheryl, 39
Williams, Gary Jay, 18
Williams, Lia, 256, 258
Williams, Raymond, 29, 32
Williams, Susanne, 218–19
Williamson, Jane, 179
Williamson, Nicol, 203
Willamson, Richard, 229
Willson, Robert, 24
Wilson, J. Dover, 49
Wilton, Penelope, 176, 258
Winesburg, Ohio, 180
Winter's Tale, 20, 31, 32, 50, 226–30
Wirthner, Naomi, 95
Woddis, Carole, 215
Wolf, Stephen, 189
Woman Killed With Kindness, 197
Wood, John, 143, 144, 149–52, 255,
  257
World War I, 227, 233
World War II, 227
Worthern, William, 27, 45–46, 250
Woudhuysen, H. R., 79, 80
Wright, George T., 25
Wright, Louis, 38

Yachnin, Paul, 47

Zitner, Sheldon, 31–32, 75–76